Fuels, Furnaces, Refractories and Pyrometry
Second Edition

Fuels, Furnaces, Refractories and Pyrometry

Second Edition

A.V.K. Suryanarayana

Formerly Head, Metallurgy Section
Government Polytechnic,
Vijayawada (A.P.). &
Head, Metallurgical Section
V.I.S.S.J. Polytechnic,
Bhadravathi (Karnataka).

BSP **BS Publications**
4-4-309, Giriraj Lane, Sultan Bazar,
Hyderabad - 500 095 - A.P.
Phone : 040 - 23445688, 23445605

Published by :

BSP BS Publications
4-4-309, Giriraj Lane, Sultan Bazar,
Hyderabad - 500 095 - A.P.
Phone : 040 - 23445688, 23445605
Fax : 91+40-23445611
e-mail : contactus@bspublications.net

Printed at

Adithya Art Printers
Hyderabad

Price : Rs. 225.00

ISBN : 978-81-7800-154-8 (PB)

Dedicated to

My wife,

Smt. Annapurna

Preface to Second Edition

In the Second Edition, the units are converted to S.I.units from CGS or FPF systems. Nuclear and Solar materials are added in Non-Conventional Energy. I hope the readers will appreciate for this effort.

I thank the readers and teaching community for providing me valuable suggestions for the improvement of the book. My heartful thanks are due to Dr.Narayana Naik of Aerospace Department and Prof.Kasturi Rangan of Cryogenics Department of I.I.Sc., Bangalore for their help in the process of adding some important material to this volume. Constructive suggestions are always welcome.

- Author

Preface to First Edition

Fuel is the second essential thing in a man's life in the order Food, Fuel, Clothing and Shelter according to Thoraeu. A furnace and its refractory linings are a must to utilise the fuel. Of course, when the fuel is burnt and some process / processes are performed in the furnace, it becomes a consequential necessity to measure the temperature in the furnace, to have a proper control over the operations. This book is titled Fuels, Furnaces, Refractories and Pyrometry to encompass the aforesaid fuel utilisation to a satisfactory level.

Present day technology is vibrant and changing rapidly. But, the essential characteristics remain the same; when a fuel is burnt, the aim will always be to completely burn it and derive maximum heat out of it. How it is done is a matter of technological development but the fundamental concept of economically extracting the maximum heat out of the fuel remains the same.

An effort is made to give the students a deep insight into the utilisation of fuels, with some fundamentals, essential to have a grasp of the subject. I hope the readers will receive the book open-heartedly. All suggestions for improvement of quality of the book are welcome.

- Author

Contents

UNIT - II
FURNACES

UNIT - III
REFRACTORIES

UNIT - IV
PYROMETRY

1 Fuels

Fuel is a material which gives out energy on combustion. Many fuels are available of which the main classification can be based upon their state :

1. Solid fuels,
2. Liquid fuels,
3. Gaseous fuels.

Besides the above, the atomic power is also becoming a vital source of energy supply. So, it can be added to the above list to make it four.

Solid fuels

The most important solid fuel is coal. Fallen trees and the other plant remains are attacked by the oxygen of the air. The chief constituent of trees, cellulose, is thus converted into water and various gases, so that it soon rots away and no traces of the remains would be present. But, if the trees and other vegetable matter are submerged under water (due to natural calamities), the plant remains are decomposed, only by the action of bacteria. The decomposition products accumulate until the bacteria itself can exist no longer. Due to certain geological influences causing the land level, relative to the sea, rise or fall, the accumulations of decayed plant material get covered layer by layer, by sediment and rocks. Under the influence of heat and pressure, other changes which are more profound are brought about. Pressures, not only due to the weight of the overlying rocks but also from the lateral earth movements, cause the folding and compression of the seams. Chemical action also results, which includes the elimination of water and the oxides of carbon. All these actions are varied, and also their influences, resulting in the ultimate coal substance consisting of varying degrees of volatile matter. Thus, a large varieties of coals are formed.

The variations in the coals have resulted due to the following reasons :

(i) variations in the original vegetable matter,

(ii) extent of bacterial decay,

(iii) extent of removal of the volatile matter by the pressure and heat.

Continuous coal fields are known in which the character of the coal changes steadily as one proceeds across the coal field. Thus, even in one seam, a range of coals may be present. It is established, that it is the segregation of different parts of similar vegetation that has led to the marked differences in their compositions.

The coals resulting from geological action on vegetable material of differing degrees of bacterial decay will have widely different properties and characteristics.

The heat and pressure experienced by the decaying vegetable matter during coalification, control the properties of the coal to a remarkable degree. It is proved that the deepest coal seams possess relatively less moisture and volatile matter. This is because of the fact that they experience higher pressures from the overlying strata of rocks.

Coals are generally classified into four groups;

(i) Peat

(ii) Lignite

(iii) Bitumenite

(iv) Anthracite

These are in this order of 'age' of coalification; Anthracite being the oldest.

1. *Wood*

This is an important domestic fuel. It is normally used in the air-dried condition and contains about 15% moisture. In general, wood consists of majorly cellulose (43%). The advantages of wood as an industrial fuel are its low ash content (0.3-0.6%) and its capacity to yield a clean and long flame.

Much of the furniture industry's wastage is used as a fuel in the industrial boilers and households. Wood can also be successfully gasified.

2. *Peat*

Peat is a 'recent' growth consisting of partly decomposed vegetable matter, under temperate marshy conditions. The deposits are of a large variety. The moisture content may be as high as 90%. This poses a great disadvantage because of the problems involved in drying. Thus, in spite of being a low ash fuel, peat remains only as a local and domestic fuel.

3. *Lignite and Brown Coal*

Lignite can conveniently be regarded as intermediate in composition and character between peat and other coals. Lignites have 30-50% moisture. The lower moisture content lignites are known as brown coals.

4. *Bituminous Coal*

The term is applied to high and medium volatile matter coals (20-45%). Their coking characteristics are given in Table 1.1

Table 1.1

Composition (on moisture and mineral matter free basis)	Medium Volatile	Very strongly caking	High Volatile		Weakly caking
			Strongly caking	Medium caking	
%C	88.5 - 91.00	85.0 - 89.0	84 - 87	83 - 86.5	82.5 - 86
% H_2	4.5 - 5.3	5.1 - 5.6	–	5.2 - 5.7	–
% V.M.	19.5 - 32.0	32.0	–	–	–
Colorific value 1Cal/gm=1k.Cal/kg	8,670 - 8,830	8,440	8,330	8,220	8,110
Inherent	0.5 - 2.0	0.5 - 2.5	1.0 - 4.0	1.5 - 5.5	2.0 - 10.0

Most of the industrial coals fall into the bituminous variety. Nearly all the coals exhibit a banded structure. These are classified into dull and bright bands. Stopes classified the bands into four types– vitrain, clarain, durain and fussain. Vitrain and clarain together constitute the bright bands of the coal and durain, the dull and harder variety.

The caking characteristics are imparted to the coal due to the presence of the bright constituents. Durain and fussain are of non-coking nature. Fussain is the dull, friable, silky-looking material found in thin layers in the coal.

Low volatile carbonaceous coals are older bituminous coals. They are intermediate between the bituminous and anthracite varieties. They consist of 10.00 - 20.00% volatile matter and carbon upto 93%.

Anthracite

Anthracite can be defined as the coal containing more than 92.00% carbon and volatile matter not more than 9.1%. Many anthracites occur in folded and highly compressed strata and hence it becomes difficult to detect the banded structure.

2 Coal

Classification of coals

Many schemes for classifying the coals based on proximate or ultimate analysis are formulated. The idea behind any classification is to enable the fuel technologist and the fuel user to assess or predict the properties of a coal, the uses to which it could be put and its behavior during the use.

Gruner and Brame had classified the coals as per their proximate analysis and the types. This classification is no more used.

Rank of coal

The biological and geological processes by which wood and other vegetable matter have been converted into lignite and coals are charted. The chart starts from wood and ends up with anthracite. This is a simple straight line classification. Such a straight line classification is very difficult for, many coals cannot fit into it. The wood lignite coal series has a practical value and the position of the coal within it, is referred to as the 'rank of the coal'. This is defined as the degree of metamorphosis or coalification that the original woody or other vegetable matter has undergone. Coals that have been produced as a result of having undergone the least change are known as the low rank coals – the extreme examples being the lignites or brown coals.

While proceeding from low rank to the high rank coals, the volatile matter and hydrogen contents decrease whereas the carbon content and the calorific values rise. The caking power rises to a maximum after which it falls off again until anthracite is reached.

Seyler's classification

Seyler's classification is aimed at predicting the nature and properties of coal solely from the analytical data, on the, dry-ash-free, basis. The positions of all the coals are plotted in a diagram using the percentages of

(a) total carbon, and

(b) hydrogen,

as the main parameters.

In this, all the coals are found to occupy positions within a fairly well defined curved band. It is also found that all coals with a specified volatile matter content occupied positions along a straight line. Thus, a series of nearly parallel 'ISOVOLS' can be constructed across the diagram (Fig. 2.1).

Similarly, coals having any specified calorific value occupied positions along a straight line and thus a series of roughly parallel 'ISOCALS' can also be constructed across the diagram. The 'ISOVOLS' and 'ISOCALS' are roughly at right angles to each other and inclined to the carbon and hydrogen zero lines or axes.

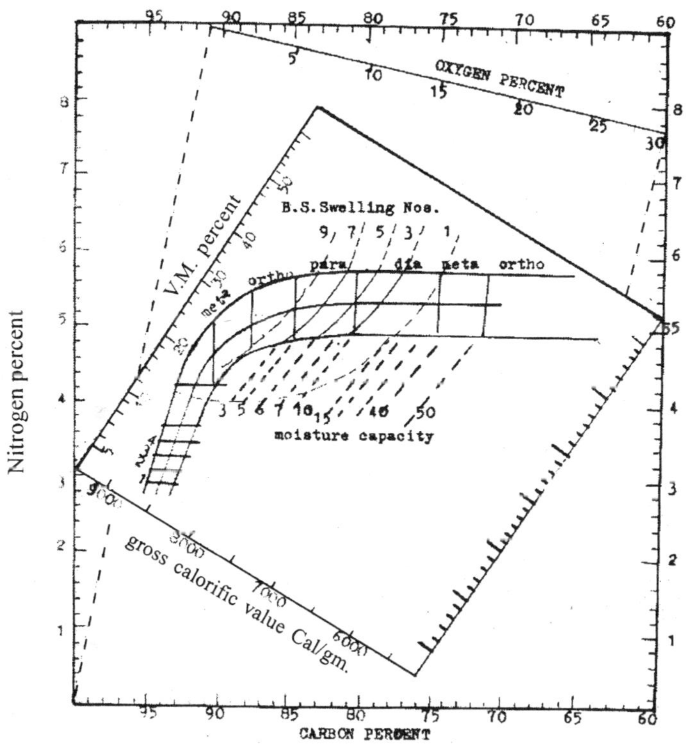

Fig. 2.1 Seyler's classfication of coal.

The E.C.E International Coal Classification

The Economic Commission for Europe had worked out a system for classifying coals. It is a two dimensional scheme. The horizontal parameter is based upon volatile matter upto 33% (on a dry-ash-free basis). This parameter divides the coals into classes from 0-9. Each class is divided into groups and sub-groups. The groups are determined according to the caking properties of the coals (by either Free-Swelling index or Raga index), the sub-groups being determined by caking properties (either dilatometer test or Gray-King Assay).

Analysis of coal

Proximate analysis

The procedure for the determination of the percentages of moisture, volatile matter, fixed carbon and ash in a coal sample is called the proximate analysis. The actual practice is to determine the moisture, volatile matter and ash and subtract their sum total from 100, to obtain the fixed carbon. Thus, 'fixed carbon' is actually a hypothetical concept, derived purely arithmetically. This does not imply the existence of uncombined carbon in coal nor does it bear any direct relationship to the total carbon in the coal, carbon is not a precise constituent of coal.

Moisture

All coals contain free or surface moisture, i.e. water. This might have gone to the coal due to the percolation through the strata and workings of the mine from the surface. This may also be present due to adopting a wet cleaning process or exposure to rain.

The loosely adhering surface moisture can be dried off on exposure to the air. The coal is then known as 'air-dried'.

In the laboratory, the determination is carried out on a coal sample ground to Is 212 μm or equivalent. The drying is performed at a temperature 105 ± 2 °C to a constant weight. The sample used is a 1gm sample (air-dried).

Volatile matter

One gram sample, dried before hand, is heated in a silica crucible at 925 °C for 7 minutes. Then it is cooled in a desiccator and weighed. The loss of weight is expressed as a percentage.

Ash content

Dried coal (1 gram) is completely burned in controlled conditions. The ash is defined as the fully oxidised residue of the mineral matter. This may comprise the loss of water, of hydration of clays, or of carbon dioxide or oxidation of iron sulphide.

The incombustible matter of the coal is largely made up of the mineral matter. The residue of this, on complete combustion is the ash.

Ultimate analysis

Ultimate analysis of the coal is defined as the exact chemical determination of the chemical elements present in it. The elements generally determined are :

(i) Carbon, (ii) Hydrogen, (iii) Nitrogen and (iv) Sulphur.

Carbon and hydrogen

A weighed quantity, generally 1 gram of the coal, is burned in Oxygen at 800 °C. The products of combustion are passed over heated copper oxide so that they are fully oxidised to carbondioxide and water. The oxides of sulphur are removed by passing over heated lead chromate and the chlorine present is absorbed by a silver-guage spiral. The gases are then passed through two weighed vessels containing suitable absorbents, KOH and concentrated H_2SO_4 for CO_2 and H_2O respectively. The increase in the weights of the vessels will give the quantities of ingredients absorbed.

An alternative method involves the burning a coal sample at 1350 °C. The loss of weight gives the total of carbon and hydrogen.

Nitrogen

Nitrogen in the coal is determined by the Kjeldahl method. A 0.1 gram coal sample is decomposed by boiling sulphuric acid containing a catalyst. The nitrogen is converted into ammonia. The ammonia forms ammonium sulphate with the acid. Subsequently ammonia is liberated by the addition of an alkali and steam-distilled into a known amount of standard acid. The excess acid is titrated and the equivalent amount of ammonia is calculated and therefrom, nitrogen.

Sulphur

The sulphur in the coal is determined by heating a 1 gram sample with Eschka mixture (one part anhydrous sodium carbonate and two parts of magnesium oxide by weight). The heating is continued until all the carbonaceous matter is burnt out. Sulphur is retained by the Eschka mixture, from which it is later removed as a soluble sulphate. From this solution the sulphate is obtained as a precipitate of barium sulphate; dried and weighed.

Alternately, a 0.5 gram of coal is burned at 1350 °C and the products of combustion are passed through hydrogen peroxide which is converted into sulphuric acid due to the action of SO_2. The amount of sulphuric acid is estimated by titration and therefrom, the amount of sulphur.

Calorific Value

This is a very important property of a fuel for, it expresses the amount of heat generated by the complete combustion of a unit weight of the fuel.

A standard special apparatus is used and the procedure adopted is also standardised. An accurate weight of the fuel (1 gram of the fuel) is burned in an atmosphere of compressed oxygen in a calorimetric bomb, immersed in water. The temperature rise of the water is very accurately measured. The heat generated, is thus calculated, knowing the weight of the water. The result is defined as the 'gross calorific value at constant volume'.

When the coal is burnt in a furnace for industrial purposes, no element of 'pressure' is in the case of the above experimental determination is involved. The operative calorific value is the calorific value at constant pressure. The difference between the two is of the order of 1 in 1000 for bitumenous coals and 0.5 part in 1000 for anthracite. Since the accuracy of a laboratory determination itself is of the order of 2 parts in 1000, the difference between the calorific values at constant volume and at constant pressure is ignored.

The calorific value of coal can also be empirically calculated, knowing the ultimate analysis of the coal, as per the formula,

$$\text{C.V.(Gross)} = \frac{1}{100}\left[8080\text{C} + \left(\frac{\text{H} - (0 + \text{N} - 1)}{8}34{,}500\right) - 2220\text{S}\right]4.187\ \text{K.J/kg}$$

Caking properties of coal

The behavior of a coal when it is heated has a marked effect on its performance and use for different purposes. Only those coals which yield a hard dense coke when heated out of contact with air are useful in producing metallurgical coke. Coals of poorer caking property are needed if a free-burning reactive coke is needed. For many domestic and industrial applications however, feebly caking or non-caking coals are often desirable. Therefore, it is important when selecting coals for certain purposes or judging the relative merits of different coals for use in the same appliance, that we have a measure of its caking properties. There are a number of laboratory tests and each give some measure of the caking properties.

British standard crucible swelling test

One gram of coal, ground to pass IS 212 μm mash is heated in a standard crucible for not less than $2\frac{1}{2}$ minutes upto a temperature of 820 °C. The method and rate of heating are standardised. The profile of the coke residue is matched against standard cokes. The coals are classified into groups, designated by numbers $\frac{1}{2}$ to 9 in increments of 0.5. The number thus obtained is known as the 'Swelling number'.

Gray-King Coke type assay

Coke is produced with a 20 gram coal sample, ground to pass 72 mesh B.S. sieve by carbonising under standard conditions to a final temperature of 600 °C. The coke obtained is defined by its size and appearance if the coal is non-swelling. If the coal is swelling, the coke is defined by the number of parts of electrode carbon powder in 20 parts of mixture that produces a standard coke which is hard and of the same volume as the original 20 gram sample of the coal in the assay tube. There are 17 coke types, designated by letters. Coals of type 'A' are non-caking and 'G' give a hard strong coke but do not swell. For coals more swelling than those of type G, subscripts are added i.e., G_1 to G_{10} (Fig. 2.2).

Sufficiently large reserves of coal are estimated in our country. Large (83,000 million tonnes) deposits occur predominantly in Bihar, Bengal, Madhya Pradesh and Assam. All these are of the hard bituminous type. In addition, about 100 million tons of lignite is estimated to occur in Tamil Nadu and Orissa. The Table 2.1 gives the approximate resources of coal,

Table 2.1 Indian Coal Reserves (1972) (in million tones).

1.	Prime Coking	5651
2.	Medium Coking	9433
3.	Weakly Coking	5070
4.	Non-coking including tertiary coals and lignites.	62896
		83050

Courtesy C.F.T.R.I. Dhanbad

The coal deposits are geologically classified as belonging to the Damuda series of the lower Gondwana family. These are divided into (a) the Barakar measures and (b) the Ranigunj measures.

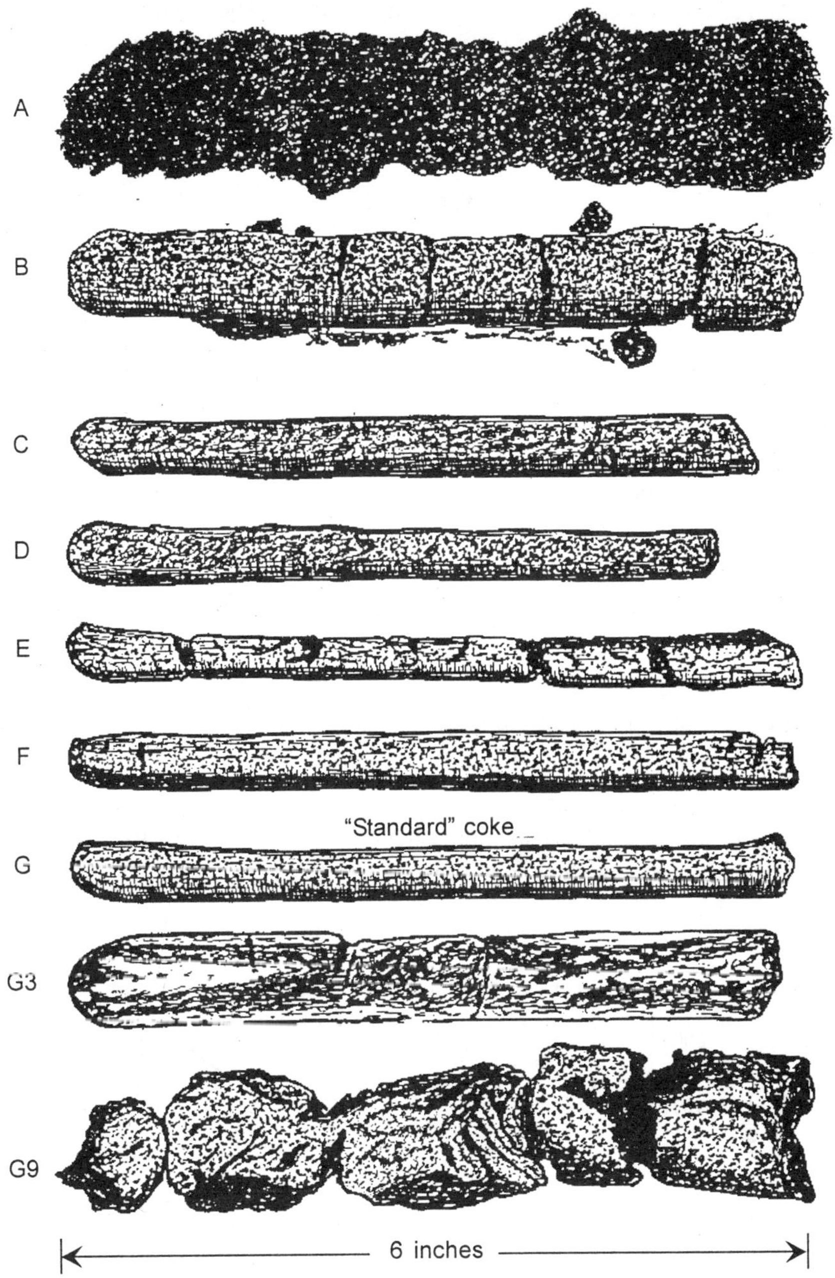

Fig. 2.2 Types of solid residue from Gray-King low-temperature assay.

The coal-seams in Ranigunj are separated by heamatite shales.

Generally, Indian coals are weakly coking to coking in nature. The ash (mineral matter) is found to be distributed as fine particles, making it difficult for treatment by washing. The coals of excellent coking quality, suffer from the drawback of high ash content. Fortunately, all Indian coals are low in sulphur, except those of Assam. Coal analyses are given in Table 2.2.

Table 2.2

Property	Ranigunj coals		Jharia coals	Kanakapura coals
	Upper	Lower		
Carbon %	78 - 84	85 - 89	89 - 92	81 - 84
Hydrogen %	4 - 6	4.5 - 5.5	4.5 - 6.0	-
Volatile matter %	30	30	0 - 33.0	33 - 39
Ash %	10 - 17	15 - s21	20 - 22	-
Calorific value (KJ/kg)	3400 0 - 36000	36000 - 37000	36000 - 36500	32500
Coking	Weakly coking	Coking	Weakly coking	Weakly coking & non-coking

Further, large deposits of coking coals are also found near Bokaro (Bihar). Non-coking deposits of voluminous nature are also found near Kothagudem in Andhra Pradesh. Both the Andhra Pradesh coals and Tamil Nadu lignites are being largely utilised for power generation.

With the steep rise in the international crude prices, the Govt. of India is making strenous efforts to exploit the domestic coal reserves to the maximum extent and discouraging the use of oil-firing in industry and power generation. Consequently coal output in our country is increasing every year (See Fig. 2.3).

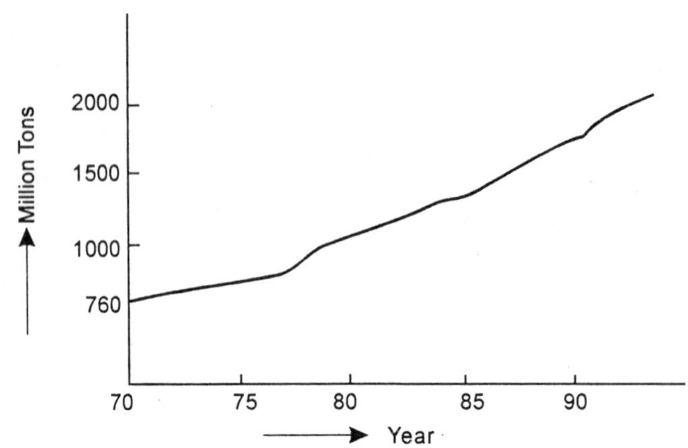

Fig. 2.3 Coal output in India.

The efforts of increasing thermal power and nuclear power production are manifest in Fig. 2.4 which shows that the basic policy of our Government is to save foreign exchange.

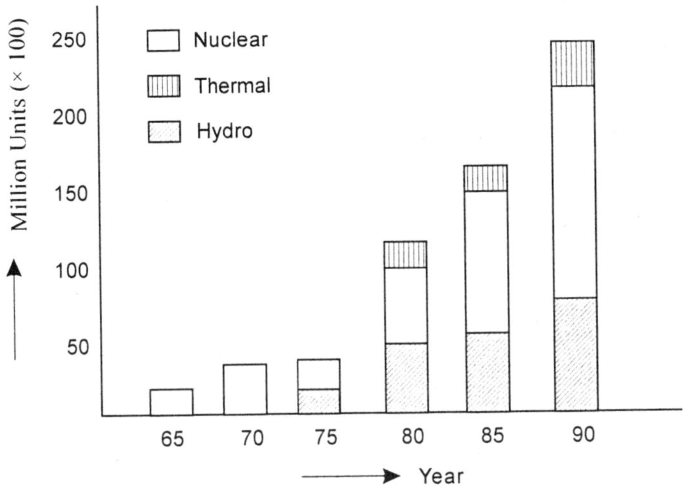

Fig. 2.4 Power generation in India.

3 Combustion of Solid Fuels

Combustion of solid fuels

Perfect combustion is attained when a fuel is burned with the exact quantity of air required – no more or no less. This is a theoretical aspect and in practice, complete combustion is not ensured unless a substantial excess of air is provided.

The fuel and air should be brought into contact with each other under the right conditions, namely,

(a) an adequate portion of the air at the right places throughout the fue,

(b) adequate time and turbulance must be arranged at a temperature sufficiently high to ensure that the chemical reactions involved are completed within the space available.

Air supply

To bring the air into contact with the fuel and then to remove the products of combustion, there must be a flow of gases throughout the system. Part of the air entering the furnace is needed and consumed in the combustion of the fuel and the unwanted excess is simply heated up. The products of combustion as well as the heated air pass through the remainder of the system. Heat exchange occurs between the products of combustion in the furnace bed, walls and roof and the charge. The gases give up their heat; the furnace charge gets heated up.

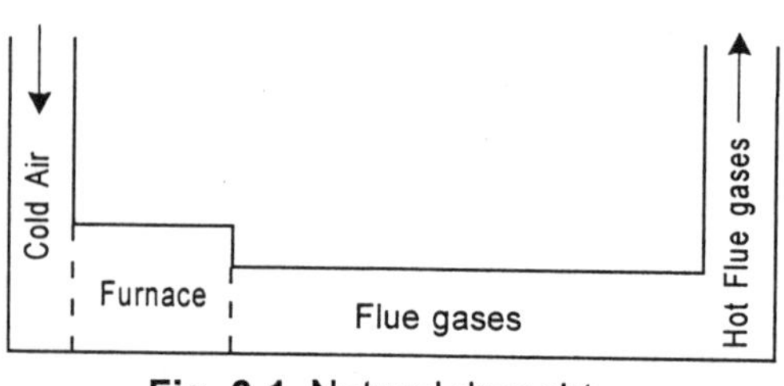

Fig. 3.1 Natural draught.

If the air entering the furnace is insufficient, all the fuel is not burnt. Thus, a serious wastage of the fuel results. Incomplete combustion may be due to :

(a) insufficient air,

(b) failure to make complete use of the air admitted and

(c) irregularities in the fuel bed.

The remedy is usually, a combination of measures – proper arrangements for draught.

Admission of air into the furnace and its subsequent movement throughout the system are brought about in the following ways :

(i) air may be drawn by the natural draught created by a chimney (see Fig. 3.1).

(ii) air may be drawn by a fan at the chimney base induced draught,

(iii) air may be forced in under pressure, by a fan, the pressure serving to propel the gases onwards through the fuel bed and the chimney draught being used to remove the gases-forced draught,

(iv) air may be forced in through the action of a steam jet in a venturi, the chimney draught being used to remove the gases,

(v) Air may be forced in by a fan, the products of combustion being removed by a second fan or by chimney action in such a way as to leave zero pressure in the combustion space above the fuel bed. This is, by far, the most flexible arrangement. The system is known as balanced draught.

Though zero pressure is referred to, in practice, a slight suction (partial vacum) of the order of 5 cm. W.G. is arranged in front of the grate. This helps reduce or eliminate the emission of smoke or flame from the fire door and overheating of the furnace front that might be caused by a very slight excess of pressure.

The amount of draught depends upon:

(a) the nature of the fuel,

(b) the depth of the fire to be maintained,

(c) the rate of combustion desired,

(d) the design of the boiler and that of the fuels and

(e) the combined resistance of the ancillary plant such as the economisers, air heaters, regenerators etc.

Some fuels require more draught than the others. Low volatile matter fuels like coke, anthracite coal etc., require that most of the air for combustion must be drawn through the fuel bed as primary air; this is subject to the resistance of the fuel bed. With high volatile matter fuels, a considerable proportion of the combustible matter of the fuel is distilled off, passing away without burning. Hence, this must be burned with the help of the secondary air. Since secondary air is drawn through openings that offer virtually no resistance to flow, the draught required to burn the high volatile fuel is less than that needed for low volatile fuel. Further, the fuel bed resistance increases as the size of the fuel decreases. So, a coal which contains a large proportion of fines, requires a stronger draught than a graded coal.

The quantity of air that can be drawn into a fuel furnace is governed by :

(a) the (cross) sectional area of the fuels and chimney,

(b) the draught provided and,

(c) the combined resistance of dirty flues and other similar obstructions.

Of the above three, the dimensions of the furnace, its flues etc., are all fixed and so to improve the combustion characteristics, only the draught can be varied.

Natural draught

The chimney conducts the hot flue gases outside into the atmosphere. The air intake, the furnace and the chimney together can be regarded as making up a U-tube. The gases in the chimney being lighter due to their being hot, there will be a tendency of a higher thrust from the atmosphere into the furnace. This is called natural drought. The amount of air that can be provided by natural draught is governed by :

(i) the height of the chimney,

(ii) the average temperature of the gases within the chimney.

The taller the chimney and the hotter the gases in it, greater is the resulting draught.

Mechanical draught

Mechanical draught is provided by fans. This may be increased by providing larger fans. While designing a fresh installation, provision should be made so that the fan can be overloaded if necessary. The advantages of mechanical draught are :

(i) cheaper low-grade fuels can be used and the rate of evaporation can be increased,

(ii) efficient combustion is attained and smoke is avoided because of the greater ease of air control,

(iii) furnace control is simplified,

(iv) smaller chimneys can be used,

(v) heat transmission efficiency can be increased.

Primary and secondary air

Air is admitted into a furnace to provide the oxygen necessary for the combustion of the fuel. The air admitted through the fuel bed so that it gives up its oxygen to effect the preliminary part of the combustion of the fuel is known as the primary air. For pulverised fuel and liquid and gaseous fuels, primary air enters the furnace, mixed with the fuel itself. In the case of solid fuels however, it passes through the fuel bed. The remainder portion of the air necessary to complete the burning is introduced separately, generally just above the fuel bed and is known as the secondary air. Secondary air helps complete the combustion of the volatile matter and smoke expelled from the solid fuel during the preliminary stages of combustion (Fig. 3.2).

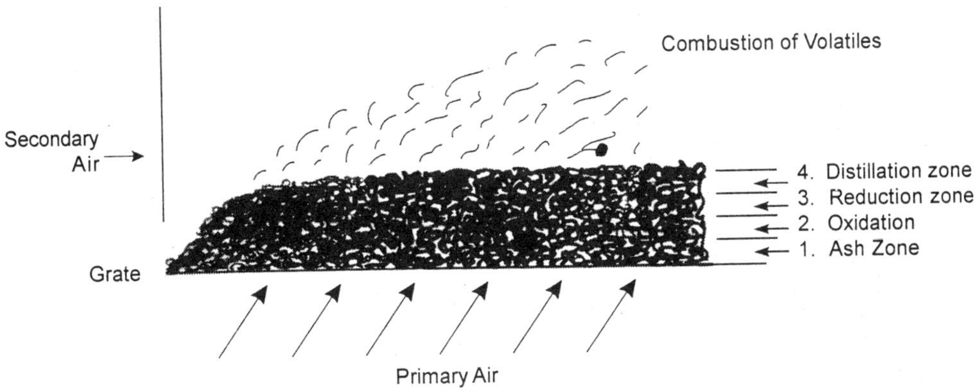

Fig. 3.2 Coal Bed on a Grate.

The fuel bed itself can be divided into various zones. At the bottom of the bed lies the zone of ash. Above this is the zone of primary oxidation in which the reaction between carbon (in the fuel) and oxygen (in the air) occurs.

$$C + O_2 = CO_2$$

If the fuel bed is deep enough, the carbon dioxide, during its ascent through the bed is reduced while passing over the hot coal or coke; forming carbon monoxide;

$$CO_2 + C = 2\ CO$$

Since the carbon monoxide is an inflammable gas, secondary air is required to burn it. Unless the CO burns to CO_2, the fuel does not give out complete heat. Escape of carbon monoxide into the flue gases represents a serious waste of the heating capacity of the fuel. In a shallow bed of fuel however, very little carbon monoxide is formed.

Above this zone, there is the distillation zone, in which the raw coal, heated by the gases rising through it and by radiation from the lower zone, is distilled. This carbonisation gives off tarry gases, vapours and smoke, all of which rise into the combustion space above the fuel bed. They require secondary air to complete their combustion. Though low-volatile fuels like coke and anthracite have little or no distillation zone, nevertheless secondary air is needed to burn off any carbon monoxide formed.

Thus, complete combustion of solid fuels is brought about by the use of primary and secondary air. Efficient combustion takes place when the primary and secondary air are correctly proportioned. The most frequent cause for smoke emission is the inadequacy of the secondary air. So, in order to obtain the maximum efficiency, the secondary air must be so controlled and mixed with the gases leaving the furnace fuel – bed, that complete combustion takes place within the appointed space and with the use of as little 'excess air' as possible.

Excess air

The relative ease with which secondary air is drawn into a furnace emphasises the importance of controlling it. The flue gas composition enables us to calculate the amount of excess air used and the quantity of the flue gases produced. The exact figure will however, depend on the composition of the fuel.

If carbon monoxide or any other gas which is combustible reaches the flue unburnt, it is an indication that there is a recurring loss of the potential heat. This should not be allowed to happen. In a good boiler practice the carbon dioxide percentage should be within the limits of 12-14 % in the flue gases.

The effect of using too much air or too little air on the furnace efficiency is one of lowering it. In an experiment conducted on a Lancashire Boiler, it was noted that maximum efficiency of 72% was obtained using 34% excess air. On increasing the excess air to 40%, the efficiency fell to 60%. The same drop in efficiency was recorded on decreasing the excess air to 15%.

However, a certain amount of excess air is unavoidable and for all practical purposes can be regarded as essential.

The heat carried away by the flue gases depends upon their heat capacity, i.e., their specific heats, quantities and temperature. Of them, mainly the quantity and temperature are of importance, useless excess air adds to the quantity of the flue gases, thereby leading to loss of heat.

Combustion of coal on the grate of a furnace

Once the correct quantity of air required for the combustion of the fuel is calculated and divided into two parts – as primary air and the secondary air, the combustion of the fuel is dependent upon three important factors :

1. turbulence,
2. time, and
3. temperature.

Turbulance

In the furnaces fired with coal, volatile matter is evolved from the coal during burning. The secondary air sometimes tends to pass over above the volatiles but not mixing with them. When this happens, the mixing of the volatiles and the secondary air is accomplished by using a jet of steam or air directed at an angle. The idea behind is to create turbulence in the zone of secondary air and get the volatiles and the secondary air mixed properly.

Time for combustion

All chemical reactions require certain time for their completion. The inherent nature of the reaction, the temperature and the difficulty of mixing the reacting substances intimately, add up to the effect of time requirement. With solid fuels, a bed that is too thin or thin in relation to the size of the fuel, lets the air pass through it without consuming it. This leads to inadequate contact between the air and the carbon of the fuel.

Temperature

Combustion cannot occur until the temperature of ignition of the fuel concerned is not only reached but also exceeded. When there are cold surfaces close to the grate, it is particularly necessary to mix the secondary air with the volatiles as quickly and as completely as possible. Sometimes it is advisable to preheat the secondary air. But, where long flames are required (like in kilns), this practice is not however, recommended.

The speed of combustion reactions increases much more rapidly than does the rise of temperature at which combustion occurs.

The chilling effect of the cold surfaces is also very important and can not be ignored. A chill surface, in contact with the flame may lead to soot formation. Soot formation, not only leads to a loss of the combustible constituent in the fuel, but also hinders heat transmission due to its being a bad conductor. In metallurgical furnaces where the charges are generally cold, this becomes an important consideration. Chilling in furnaces results from :

(i) heavy charges at infrequent intervals,

(ii) excessive air supply; prolonged opening of the furnace doors,

(iii) long flame,

(iv) thermal features that force the burning gases into intimate contact with cooler metals, and

(v) bad design of the plant.

In order to attain a good degree of mixing of the fuel and air, it is advisable to use a coal of a uniform size. Small-sized-graded fuel gives the best air distribution leading to the fullest use of the primary air.

The caking properties of the fuel control the combustion characteristics. The caking nature increases with the fineness of the fuel. Caking coals tend to form lumps and lead to improper air distribution in the fuel bed.

Smoke

Smoke in a furnace largely consists of tarry distillation products. When the volatile matter in the coal is less, the quantity of tar evolved from the coal becomes less. This is the reason for anthracite and the like (low volatile matter coals) to yield less smoke.

The smoke is mainly of two forms :

1. The brown smoke which is mainly tarry matter. The tarry matter is given off at relatively lower temperatures immediately after the coal is charged on the hot grate.
2. Black smoke – this consists of particles of carbon derived from the 'cracking' and subsequent quenching of hydrocarbons at a high temperature.

Brown smoke is easy to consume, whereas the black smoke is less easy to deal with. The excess air, even if pre-heated, is sometimes unable to react with the black smoke. To consume smoke there must be sufficient quantity of secondary air, with the volatiles and a sufficiently high temperature zone in the combustion space to ensure that the combustion takes place rapidly before the gases come into contact with any cold surfaces.

The amount of carbon present in the smoke is small. The real danger of waste due to smoke lies in the possible presence of unburnt invisible volatiles. On the other hand, attempts to avoid the smoke production by using unnecessarily large quantities of air, can cause more heat losses and reduce the efficiency of the fuel.

Formation of clinker

Clinker is defined as masses of ash and sometimes cinder, partly compacted by local melting.

One of the main difficulties in maintaining a uniform resistance of the fuel bed to the air is the formation of clinker. The masses of clinker prevent the air flow to those portions of the grate which they cover. Thus, the remaining area of the grate has to admit more air than it is designed to.

The ash formed when coal is burned is a complex mixture. The combustible material derived from the plants from which the coal is formed, the combustible mineral material with which the plant remains had reacted and the stony material mined along with the coal; each of these substances contributes its own quota of ash. Any one of them may possess a relatively low melting point. When it melts, the adjoining pieces of ash may become cemented together with them.

Sometimes, though none of the portions may have a low melting point, two or more of them, when intimately mixed, may form a complex with a low melting point.

The coal may produce clinker only under certain conditions and not under other conditions. Slack coal may produce clinker more readily than large sized coals.

The behaviour of individual chemical constituents of the ash is interesting. The higher oxide of iron (Fe_2O_3) does not tend to produce clinker. But, the lower oxide of iron (FeO) however, will flux with SiO_2 and form a low melting constituent which will finally lead to clinker formation.

The FeO is formed under reducing conditions. The intermediate oxide of iron Fe_3O_4, behaves somewhat as FeO and furthermore, itself has a low melting point.

Though it is very difficult to underline any fixed pattern for clinker formation of the ash, an indication of the tendency to form clinker can be had by knowing the melting point of the ash. Precisely speaking, it is finely powdered and P.C.E.* is determined. From the temperature obtained, the coal can be predicted to behave as follows :

Ash P.C.E. over 1400 °C	- No clinker formation
Ash P.C.E. 1200 °C - 1400 °C	- Clinker may form but may not lead to firing troubles.
Ash P.C.E. below 1200 °C	- Clinker troubles are likely.

Pulverised coal

Pulverised fuel firing is a method in which finely crushed fuel, generally reduced to a fineness of 200 mesh B.S. sieve, is carried forward by air through pipes, directly to burners. When discharged into the combustion chamber, the mixture of air and fuel burns in a manner very similar to that of the combustion of a gas.

Pulverised fuel firing has become a very important procedure because a large proportion of coal mined comes out as fines from the mine. This is true, especially with machine mining.

The following are some of the advantages claimed for pulverised fuel firing practice :

(i) efficient utilisation of the low grade coal,

(ii) flexibility in firing, with ability to meet fluctuating loads,

(iii) elimination of banking losses,

(iv) better adaptability to automatic control,

(v) ability to produce a high temperature flame at the correct position,

(vi) high availability, and

(vii) ability to use preheated air and obtain higher temperatures,

Preparation

Though bituminous coals were the first of the fuels used for pulverised firing practice, nowadays, the whole spectrum of coals is being used; of course, excepting peat and lignite. The most important consideration in the selection of the fuel for pulverising is its moisture content. The coal should be thoroughly dried. This applies more particularly to the low-volatile fuels. If the coal is initially too wet, the material may clog in the hoppers and feeders or even in the mill which will suffer a reduction in output. The moisture responsible for these deleterious effects is the surface moisture.

---

* Refer testing of 'Refractories' eleswhere in this book

The main types of plant used for the pulverising of coal are :

(a) Ball, tube or rod mill,

(b) Roller or table or bowl mill,

(c) Ball and track mill,

(d) Impact or beater mill, and

(e) Ring and ball pulveriser,

Ball or Roller mill

The ball or roller mill consists of a steel drum charged with steel balls or rods. The drum is rotated at speeds varying between 20-40 rpm. The rods or balls are carried upto a position by centrifugal force, from which they fall down on to the material being pulverised. The mill is air swept with preheated

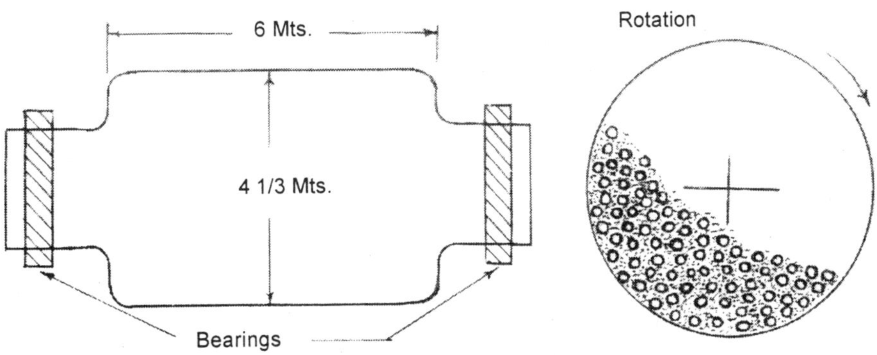

Fig. 3.3 Ball mill (or schematic diagram).

primary air. The length-diameter ratio of the mill is maintained between 2 and 1.5. The total power consumption for pulverising bituminous coal to the required average fineness, including the exhaust fan is 40-50 Kwh/ton.

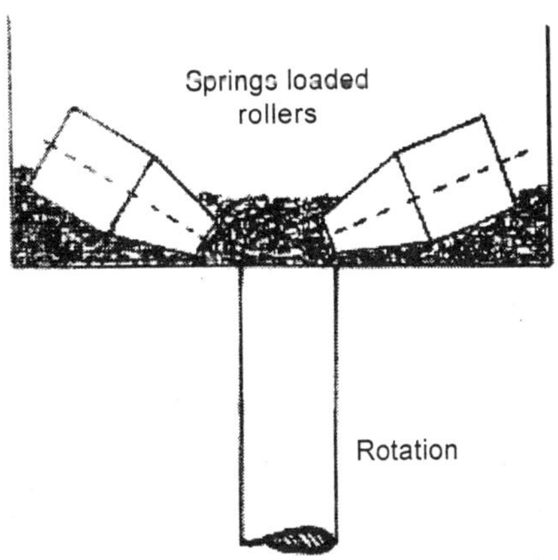

Fig. 3.4 Roller and table mill.

Medium speed mills

The coal is ground between rotating or fixed rollers on a fixed or rotating table. The rollers are spring loaded and adjustable. These mills are air swept. The product is conveyed to a classifier. The oversize is rejected and returned to the mill. These mills are cheaper in operation and are not sensitive to moisture. Their drawback is however, their inability to grind anthracites effectively.

High speed mills

These mills, referred to under c and d type above, effect size reduction mainly by attrition and impact. Hammers or pegs rotating inside the casing at very high speeds apply the impacts. These machines require more careful maintenance. They also suffer from the drawback that they are not suitable for pulverising anthracite or coals high in ash.

The installation should consist of a magnetic separator to remove any tramp iron from the feed coal. The mills should be easily accessible for maintenance and repair and a classifier should be installed at the output end to ensure the oversizes return to the mill.

Ring and ball pulveriser

Ring and ball pulverisers are the latest in the pulverising of coal. In fact, these pulverisers have become popular due to their capability to grind ores and fluxes, also besides coal and coke.

A sectional diagram of the mill is shown in Fig. 3.5. The diagram is self-explanatory regarding its method of operation. Coal enters the mill through the central feed pipe. It is carried to the grinding rings by centrifugal action. Air is admitted below the yoke and passes upwards picking up the ground coal. Primary classification occurs here itself because the coarser particles of coal are not carried upwards by the air and settle down. The air carries finer particles to the classifier unit, the coarse classifier discharge falling back into the mill.

The grinding rings are made of Ni- hard alloy and the balls are made of cast steel and suitably hardened. An optimum number of balls from the point of view of power economy during running idle and efficiency in grinding is arrived at and is fixed at 10.

Grindability of coal

The term grindability is a vague term. It is the number of revolutions required for a standard ball mill to reduce the size of the coal to pass BS 200 (IS 75 μm mesh). But in burning the pulverised fuel, it is not the fineness that matters but the uniformity of size of the product. It is measured by measuring the amount of coal ground to +200 BS. 75 micron sieve size, from a standard larger size. Fines are to be ignored.

Method of test

This method is used to determine the relative grindability or ease of pulverising coals in comparison with a coal chosen as 100 grindability. It is based on Rittinger's law, which states that "the work done in pulverising is proportional to the new surface produced". A prepared sample receives a definite amount of grinding energy in a miniature pulveriser and the new surface is determined by sieving.

The grindability machine (Fig. 3.6) consists of eight 1 inch (25mm) dia balls rolling on a stationary ring and are driven from the top by a rotating ring. The action of the rolling balls causes an increase in the surface of the sample being tested. A definite pressure of $64 \pm \frac{0.5}{2.2}$ Kgf on the balls is obtained

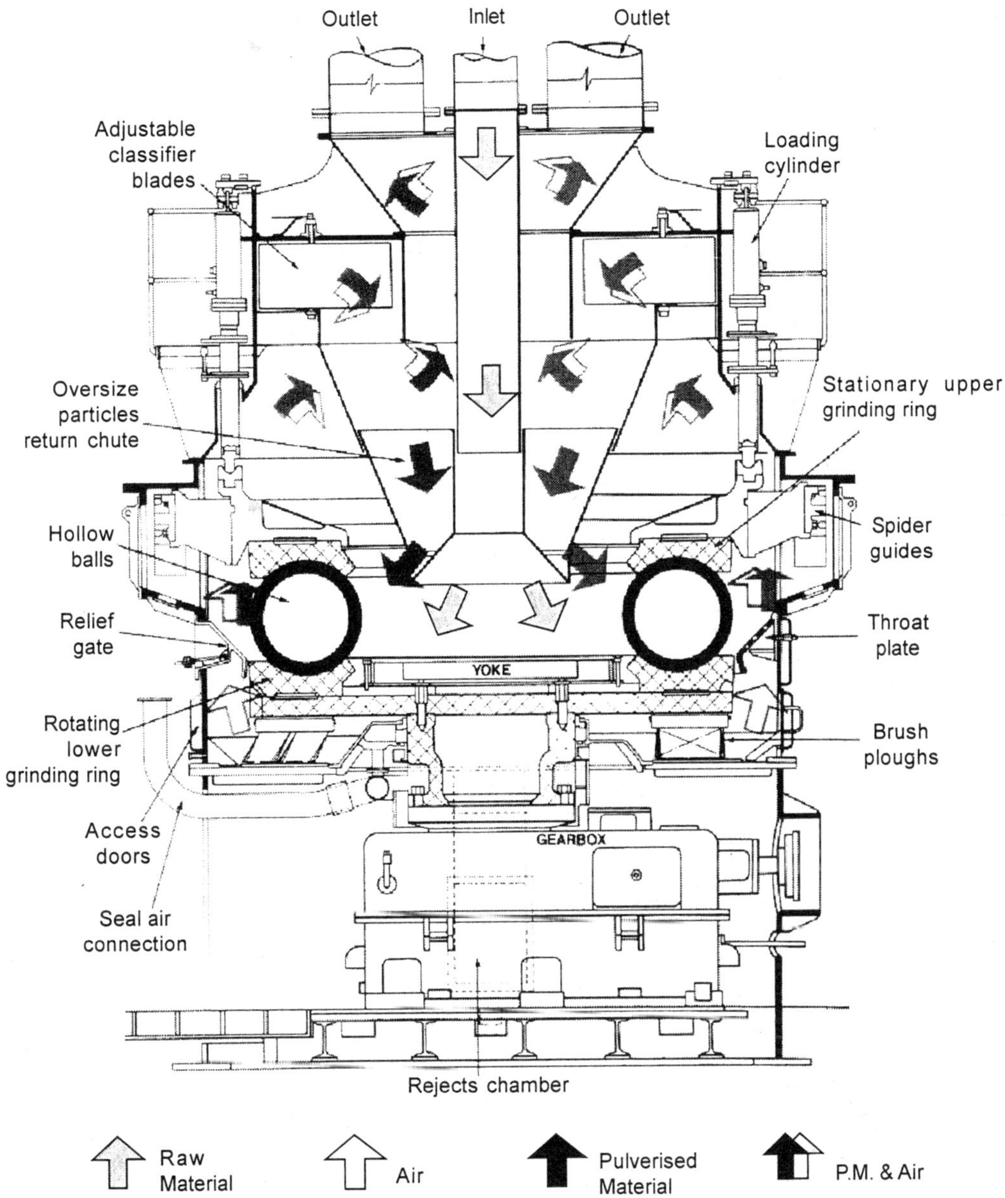

Fig. 3.5 Ring and ball pulveriser.

by the weights, shaft, top grinding ring and gear. A rotation counter is fitted to the machine which stops the motor as soon as the vertical shaft of the grindability machine has made exactly 60 revolutions.

The sample used is 50 gm of the coal under test. Weighing accuracy of 0.01 gm is sufficient. The sample shall be of the size (– 1190 micron) sieve No. 16 – (+ 595 micron) sieve No. 30. The sample is air-dried until the loss of weight is not more than 0.1 per cent / hour. The sample is ground in the

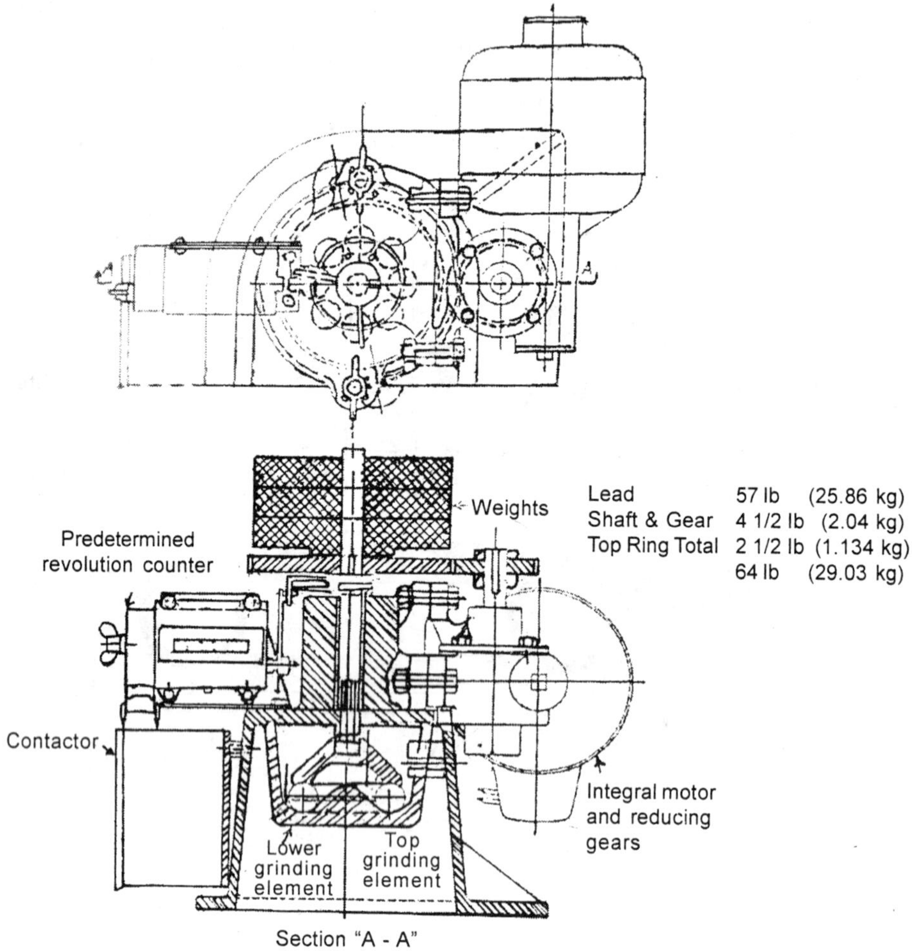

Fig. 3.6 Hardgrove grindability machine.

grindability machine for 60 revolutions and the sample collected for sieving. The sample is sieved on a (74 micron) No. 200 sieve for 10 minutes using a mechanical sieve. The sieve is cleaned with a brush and sieving is continued for another 10 minutes; in stages of 5 minutes, each time cleaning the sieve with a underside or bottom of the sieve is brushed clean. The material passing through the 74 micron sieve is discarded. The material retained on the sieve is weighed to an accuracy of 0.1 gm and the weight is recorded to give W in the formula.

The permissible variation between two or more determinations is 2 per cent in case of testing in the same laboratory or 3 per cent in different laboratories.

The grindability index, called the Hardgrove index is commonly used to express the grindability nature of coals and coke. This test eliminates the cumbersome sieve analysis. The Hardgrove grindability index is found out using the correlated formula.

$$\text{H.I.} = 6 - 93\ W + 13$$

where W = Wt. of the material in gms.
passing the 200 B.S. sieve (75 micron I.S. sieve) being fed into grinding mills.

Pitch

Hard pitch is an excellent fuel for pulversing. It has a low-ash and high calorific value and does not pick up moisture, if stored in lumpy form. But the pulverising of pitch suffers from the practical difficulty that it softens at very low temperature — as low as 1000 °C. So, care should be exercised in the pulverisation of the pitch so that the material does not get heated up due to friction. It is customary to make the pitch into 1" size pieces in spiked roll crushers and store in lumps before.

Combustion of pulverised coal

The time required for the combustion of a particle of coal is governed by the coal properties such as its rank, size, temperature and the aerodynamic conditions in the furnace. Studies on the ignition and combustion of the coal particles injected into a furnace indicate that the combustion takes place in 3 stages,

(i) Pre-ignition stage. During this stage, the size and shape of the particle will change. Some volatile matter is released,

(ii) Ignition and combustion of volatile matter, and

(iii) Ignition and combustion of the residual carbon.

The behaviour of the particles of caking, non-caking and anthracite coals differs greatly during the initial stage. Caking coal particles become very soft or plastic and they get blown into tiny balloons having very thin walls. These are termed cenospheres. Weakly caking or non-caking coals, low-volatile coals and anthracites do not form cenospheres on heating. Some fragmentation occurs due to the rapid rate of heating in the ignition zone. The solid residue from these coals is much more reactive.

It is also probable that the coal particle ignites at a lower temperature and combustion of the solid residue may take a longer time. The overall burning time of a coal particle is mainly dependent upon the time required for burning out the solid residue remaining after the evolution of the volatiles. The rate of burning is governed by its temperature above a certain temperature (800-1100 °C) which however, varies depending upon the character of the residue. The rate of combustion depends upon the rate of diffusion of oxygen through the surface of the particle. Below this temperature, the rate of combustion depends upon the rate of reaction between carbon and oxygen, which is found to rapidly decrease as the temperature decreases. Therefore, if the particle is cooled rapidly much below 800 °C by the surroundings, the rate of burning decreases.

During combustion, the particle is surrounded by an atmosphere of combustion products. The oxygen should diffuse through these, to reach the carbon.

The solid residue from low volatile coals and anthracites is relatively unreactive. So, it is difficult to burn these varieties of coals than those of the lower rank.

The pulverised fuel burners

The main requirements of a burner are :

(i) it shall ensure that the fuel and air get intimately mixed, and

(ii) it shall ensure an adequate supply of air surrounding each particle of the fuel until the combustion is complete.

Burners designed to obtain a turbulent flow of the fuel powder and the air, work giving stress on the first point referred to above. The pulverised fuel and air-mix is charged through a rotating worm and an air stream, generally pre-heated, is admitted through a central pipe. These burners produce a short flame. (Fig. 3.7).

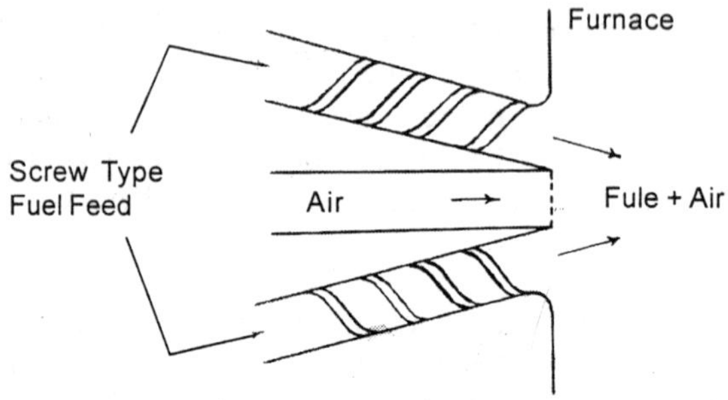

Fig. 3.7 Turbulent flow burner.

The parallel flow burner (Fig. 3.8) uses a mixture of air and the fuel, discharges into the furnace as strata of jets. These jets are interposed with the secondary air.

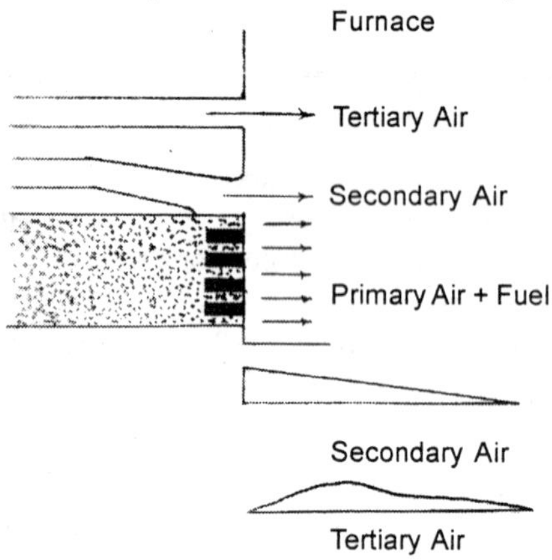

Fig. 3.8 Parallel flow burner.

In the designing of the burners, it is assumed that the coal/air ratio can be correlated to the rate of flame propagation. Any lack of balance between these two will either lead to loss of ignition or back firing. It can be seen from the curves (Fig.3.9) that the maximum rate of flame propagation of low volatile coals is when the air/coal ratio is low. This must be still further reduced for anthracite coals.

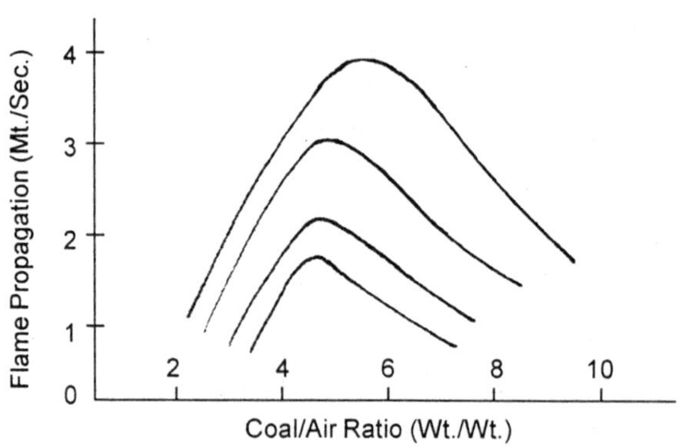

Fig. 3.9 Variation of flame length with coal - Air ratio.

Metallurgical application of pulverised fuel firing

Use of pulverised fuel has many applications in the metallurgical field. It has resulted in economy, improved control of the furnace temperature and atmosphere and better quality of the finished product. Some applications are listed below :

1. annealing furnaces for malleablishing,
2. small forge and drop stamp furnaces,
3. heavy forge furnaces,
4. continuous furnaces,
5. melting furnaces, and
6. in the manufacture of non-ferrous metals.

Most reverberatory furnaces for copper smelting, pot furnaces for lead manufacture and the flash smelting furnaces of copper ore are designed to operate on pulverised coal.

4 Storage of Coal

Coal is stored for various reasons. Stocks of stored coal will help overcome the lean seasons of supply. Transport irregularities, like delay arising out of diversions climate etc., are prone to effect the industries dependent upon coal and in such eventualities, the stored coal buffers the situation. Further, the seasonal price fluctuations can be avoided by maintaining huge stocks of coal in the months when the off-take is less.

Storage of coal is associated with certain difficulties :

1. deterioration of the coal during storage,
2. dangers of spontaneous oxidation leading to ignition and the consequent fire hazards,
3. spontaneous oxidation, occurring to an extent not leading to ignition, may lead to loss of calorific value of the coal,
4. coal deteriorates by weathering, and
5. loss of caking power.

All the above are due to spontaneous oxidation taking place in the coal heap. Oxidation process occurs due to the absorption of oxygen by the coal, leading to the evolution of combustible carbon monoxide, which, under favourable circumstances like an elevated temperature, ignites. Thus, the whole heap of the coal burns.

The various precautions followed to store the coal are based on the above mechanism and are directly or indirectly aimed at preventing the spontaneous oxidation.

Size of the coal

Assorted coal sizes are more prone to local heating. Uniformly sized coal will have pores left between different pieces stacked and is less likely to heat. Fines should be avoided in coal heaps – even the fines resulting from handling and chutes.

Ventilation

Ventilation is a ticklish proposition during the coal storage. There should be either a proper and thorough ventilation or it should be totally suppressed. The latter is more easy because, howsoever carefully stocked, there can never be a good ventilation in a coal heap, especially when it is large.

Ventilation is minimised by storing the coal in bunkers which can be flooded with water. But this type of underwater storage is difficult in practice. It is advisable to store the coal in sized-heaps, the larger side of the leap lying in the direction of the atmospheric wind. Further, it is advisable to have a small wall across the wind direction. This stops the wind reaching the bottom portion of the heap from where usually the ventilation current starts. Another method is to pack the coal surface and sides with the coal breeze which seals off the pores.

Height of the stack

Coal stored in tall heaps is likely to suffer from a temperature increase in the bottom regions. A safe limit to the height of the stock can be taken as 1.5 metres. However, taller stacks can be maintained, by making the heaps in stages. It is suggested to lay a heap of about one metre height and increase its height by a quarter metre after about 3 months. However, the temperature of the coal in the heap's lower strata should be ascertained to be satisfactory before laying the additional stratum. Thus, coal heaps of about 2 metres height also can be built up gradually.

Places suitable for coal storage

Coal storage area should be far from heat sources. If possible a concrete flooring is recommended. Or else, the ground should be prepared firm and free from organic materials. Small storages upto 500 tonnes can be made by constructing 0.25 metre brick wall, about 30 metres long and partitioning it into 3 metres U-shaped bays. This provides an access to the trucks which transport the coal to and out of the storage. A pictorial representation of a coal storage is given in Fig. 4.1.

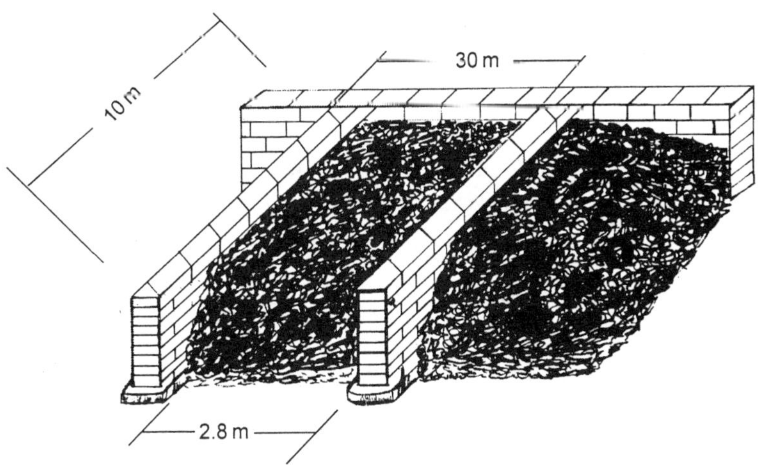

Fig. 4.1 Coal storage bay.

Activity of the coal

It is established by experience that the freshly mined coal is more prone to spontaneous oxidation than old coal. The first four weeks after mining constitute the first dangerous period and the next four months, in general, are the next dangerous months. Hence, it is advisable to go in for an 'old' coal to make the stocks or heaps for storage.

Maintenance

Whether a coal heap is satisfactory or not can be judged by periodic determination of the temperature of the lower layers of the coal heap. Metallic pipes about 30 mm dia, preferably of wrought iron or steel, closed at its bottom are thrust vertically at distances of 4-5 metres on a coal heap. The depth to which they are thrust depends upon the height of the coal stack, but in any case, they should be long enough to project a metre upwards. The bottom temperature can be measured periodically with the help of a thermometer. At no time the temperature should exceed 50 °C; 70 °C is a danger signal.

In general it is observed that coals with lower percentages of moisture and volatile matter i.e., anthracites and hard bitumenites, are less prone for damage or ignition during storage. Soft coals such as lignites and bituminous coals are found to be more susceptible to spontaneous oxidation.

5 Manufacture of Metallurgical Coke

Manufacture of metallurgical coke

Coke is manufactured by the carbonisation of coal. Carbonisation is defined as the process of distillation of coal without contact with the air so as to give a solid residue – coke; and liquid and gaseous products. The latter are mostly comprising of the volatile constituents and are treated as by products.

Coals have varying caking powers – the ability to form coke – the ability to form a hard coherent mass on heating, varies from zero with lignites to a maximum with a coal of about 88% C and starts to decrease to zero as the carbon content increases further to 93%. Thus, the coal required for the manufacture of coke should contain about 83-90% C.

Process

Coke is manufactured by the horizontal retort process. The Beehive type ovens which were used until recently are obsolete nowadays. The modern by-product ovens are made of rectangular chambers, length 10-12 m, 4 m in height and 1 m in width and closed at both the ends. Charging is performed from one end and the coke is discharged from the other. A number of such retorts are built one next to the other and the whole unit is known as a 'coke oven battery'. The older plants were employing side flues which were horizontal and the hot gases were passing through the coal bed from end to end, two or three times. Nowadays, preference is given to vertical flues, in which it is found that the rate of heating is more uniform.

The heat in the outgoing gases is recovered by passing them through regenerators. The chambers are heated by a mixture of blast furnace gas and air, preheated in the regenerators. The chambers are lined with silica brick. The temperature of carbonisation is about 1200-1400 °C. The carbonisation takes about 72-96 hrs.

By-product recovery

The recovery of by-products is a very important economic factor in the manufacture of coke. Tar, benzol and gas bring invaluable returns. Ammonia is either recovered in the form of sulphate or liquor so that benzol is later recovered from the gas. Ammonia recovery itself is not an economically viable process but a must.

Mechanism of coking

During the process of coking, there will not be any air available, for burning or oxidation of the coal. The coal will only decompose partly. The volatile matter contained in the coal will be expelled yielding various hydrocarbon gases like CH_4, C_2H_4, C_6H_6, H_2, NH_3, tar etc. The residue contains the fixed carbon and ash together with some volatile matter which was not totally expelled.

If, on the other hand, some air is allowed into the process, obviously much less than that required for the complete combustion of the coal, the volatile matter is driven out just as in the above mentioned case. Besides this, there occurs partial oxidation of the volatile matter and some fixed carbon. Some carbon monoxide is also obtained.

When the analysis of the coal is mentioned, carbon reported is partly existing as fixed carbon and partly as compounds in the volatile matter. The hydrogen is also shared, but its proportion existing in the coal is negligible. Whatever oxygen is present, is present as H_2O and it takes part in chemical reactions during coking, as follows :

$$C + H_2O = CO + H_2$$

$$C + 2H_2O = CO_2 + 2H_2$$

Traces of oxygen remain in the coke in spite of the above reactions.

A portion of whatever nitrogen is present in the coal, forms ammonia. But ammonia is unstable at such high temperatures and in turn decomposes. Thus, all the nitrogen present in the coal, goes out as nitrogen only. It is fair to assume that all the sulphur present in the coal gets gasified and forms H_2S. Some sulphur also remains in the coke. Ash remains entirely as it is, unreacted.

Properties of coke

Physical properties desired in the coke vary with the purpose for which the coke is meant to be used. Blast furnace coke must be hard whereas the domestic fuel coke should be highly reactive and smokeless in firing. In general, however, the cokes should contain a low moisture and ash contents. Further, certain constituents like sulphur and phosphorous should be present within a specified limit.

Density and porosity

During the carbonisation, coal swells and looses its volatile matter. This followed by shrinkage during the heating at the higher temperature, results in an increase in density. The more the coal is devolatilised the more its specific gravity approaches that of graphite. The value of 2-3 (of graphite) is however, never reached since the coal contains mineral matter.

The density is determined by grinding the coke to pass the IS 212 μm mesh sieve. This breaks down the cellular structure. The powder is dispersed in water to displace the air, and the density is determined.

True density is calculated from the above observed value, by assuming the specific gravity of ash as 2.5, as follows,

$$\text{True density} = \frac{(100\,d - 2.5\,a)}{(100 - a)}$$

Where d = observed density,

a = percentage ash.

The apparent density of the coke depends upon the development of its cellular structure. All the pieces of coke are immersed in boiling water. This drives off the air in the open pores by expansion. The pieces are allowed to cool. The weight of the pieces with water in the pores and after drying are found out and the apparent density is calculated as follows :

$$\bullet\text{Apparent density} = \frac{w}{(w_2 - w_{1})}$$

Where W = weight of a dried sample of coke,

W_1 = weight of the coke in water after boiling in water for 2 hours and cooling,

and W_2 = weight of the coke in the same condition as per W_1 but in air.

The porosity of the coke is calculated from the values of true and apparent densities, as a percentage:

$$\%\ \text{Porosity} = \frac{(\text{Difference between density values}) \times 100}{\text{True Density}}$$

Bulk density is the weight of unit volume of the material. This depends upon many factors like size, grading size of the measuring vessel, shape of the pieces, method of packing and moisture content.

Hardness

Hardness of coke is its surface hardness. This is a measure of its resistance to abrasion. The Cochrane test consists of tumbling a 12 kg sample of 75 mm coke in a welded steel drum of 450 mm internal diameter. The drum is fitted with 2.5° angle iron lifting plates welded to the inside drum surface at an angle of 17° to the axis. The speed of rotation is 18 rpm. For one test, 1000 revolutions are performed and the sample is screened on a 12.5 mm sieve. The abrasion index is the amount of material (percentage) remaining on the sieve. Thus, a high value of index means – a high resistance to abrasion.

For coke to be used in the blast furnace the abrasion index is of paramount importance. The value should be above 75.

Strength

Strength of the coke can be defined as its resistance to breakage on impact during handling. The strength is expressed as shatter index. A 50 1b (22.7 kg) representative sample of coke is taken of the size 50 mm. This is kept in a box 28 × 15 (70 × 46 cm) size and dropped on to a steel plate from a height of (183 cm) 6 ft.,

After the test, the coke in the box is screened on 2, 38 mm, 25.4 mm and 12.7 mm sieves. A good blast furnace coke should show 75% over 50 mm, 85% over 38 mm and 92% over 12.7 mm. Foundry coke (for use in cupolas) should show 85% over 50mm.

Reactivity

Reactivity, in relation to coke, is broadly defined as its ability to react with the oxygen, carbon dioxide or steam, depending upon the purpose for which it is to be employed. If used as a fuel, its reactivity with respect to air or oxygen is only of importance. When the coke plays a part in gas/solid reactions as in the blast furnace, reactivity may or may not be of much importance.

In the cupola, high temperature oxidation zone is large and so unreactive coke in large piece is preferred. On the other hand in the blast furnace the formation of carbon monoxide is favoured at the hearth and so coke should possess a high reactivity.

Reactivity is measured in many ways. For metallurgical cokes, Mott and Wheeler have suggested a method to measure the combustibility. A fuel bed of 350 mm depth, consisting of 25-40 mm sized coke is employed, covering an area of 9.3 decimeters. The experiment consists of determining the compositions of gases at a series of 8 points in the fuel bed at 40mm intervals from the grate. The bed is fed with air under controlled conditions. At the same levels, the temperatures are also determined using an optical pyrometer. The results are expressed as reactivity with oxygen expressed as the distance above the grate at which the gases contain more than 20% carbon monoxide, the reactivity is expressed as the reactivity with carbon dioxide (Fig. 5.1).

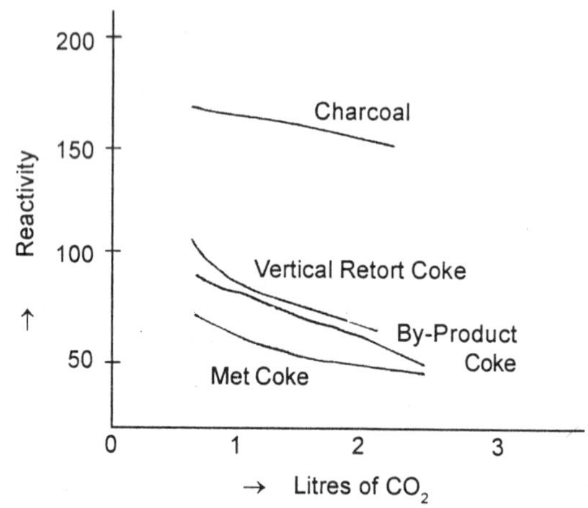

Fig. 5.1 Reactivity curves of different solid fuels.

Factors affecting the coking

The coke obtained by carbonisation is influenced in its quality by many factors. The following are a few important of them :

(a) the nature of the coal,

(b) method of preparation and size,

(c) the moisture content,

(d) method of charging,

(e) rate of heating, and

(f) method of quenching.

In the olden days when Beehive coke ovens were in use, very fusible coking coals were demanded. But, the modern coke oven plant cannot employ them for, they give rise to a very soft and porous coke which is not suitable for blast furnace use. Nowadays, blending of various coals is performed in order to control the ultimate physical properties of the coke. Blending of weakly coking coals with strong coking coals is done in certain proportions. This also helps in the utilisation of the coals of poorer coking qualities. An invariable constituent of the blended coal is fusain dust to a proportion of 3.0%. Of late, coke breeze is being substituted for fusain. The addition of fusain dust or coke breeze is found to yield a coke of good hardness and larger size.

It is reported that coke of good bulk density is obtained by adding 0.5% tar oil to the coal blend (when added to the dry coal) while the bulk density of the coke produced suffered if the same oil addition is made to wet coal (charge). In our country Durgapur and Rourkela Steel Plants are having the required facilities for oil injection to the coal charges in their coke oven batteries.

Further, blending is practised by mixing two coals, one of high and the other of low ash contents, of course, taking into account their coking characteristics. As our coals are of high ash varieties, all the coal coked is treated for ash reduction either by washing in water-sand emulsion or by floatation; the former process being cheaper is more common. It should be noted that the coal charged into the coke oven should not contain more than 16% ash.

Selective crushing of coal is a well known procedure for the preparation of the coke oven charge. In this process, the easily crushable vitrain portions of the coal are subjected to milder crushing. The other harder constituents are given a good grinding. As the vitrain portion of the coal contributes to the coking and plastic properties of the coal, the final product i.e., coke is found to possess a fine grained structure and good hardness.

Selective crushing consists of crushing the coal (preliminary crushing to 2-3 mm size) when the different petrographic constituents are liberated. Screening the crushed coal separates the softer vitrains (as –2 mm material) and the over sizes are further crushed. Subsequently, the screened undersizes and the second crushed finer product are mixed together to make up the charge to the coke ovens. The charge size is quite reasonably established. More than 80% of it should pass through the 3 mm screen; no over sizes at all.

The percentage of moisture in the coal charged into the coke oven is important, not only from the coking point of view but also from the fuel consumption angle. The time of coking is found to be longer if the moisture in the charge is more. It is not necessary to allow more than 5% moisture in the coal.

Recent trends are towards dry charging and preheating. In these, the coke oven charge is subjected to a thermal treatment. The process eliminates the excess moisture. In addition to just drying, the practice is to preheat the charge as well. Preheating is claimed to increase the oven throughput by about 35% besides reducing the costs by 10%. In addition to these advantages, the conservation of good coking coals contributes to another 10% savings in terms of costs as low grade coals can be successfully employed for coking by this practice. At present these techniques are practised in U.K., U.S.A., Russia, West Germany, France, Canada, Australia and Japan.

Recent trends in charging indicate a favourable tilt towards what is called, the stamp charging. The method consists of designing a small chamber in the pusher machine itself and the charge is stamped in this chamber before it is introduced into the oven. Stamping is found to increase the dry bulk density of the coal charge from 740-850 kg/m^3 to 930-1000 kg/m^3. The coke obtained is found to possess better physical strength even when low grade coals are used for coking.

The coke which is pushed out of the oven is quenched with water to avoid atmospheric oxidation. Quenching is also experimented with an inert gas with an idea to minimise if not avoid the moisture in the coke but the process is too costly. Thus, water quenching remains to be the most common method of quenching of coke. The finished product should not contain moisture in excess of 1.0%. Every additional one percent moisture in the coke is found to increase the coke consumption in the blast furnace by 1.0% in turn.

The process of quenching consists of pushing the red hot coke into open wagons which are moved into the quenching shed where sprays of water are made to fall on the red hot coke (Figs. 5.2 and 5.3). The quantity of water used for quenching is predetermined, keeping in view the moisture, the coke should finally contain.

Fig. 5.2 Coke ovens pushing of coke.

Fig. 5.3 Coke ovens after quenching.

Courtesy : Bhilai Steel Plant

Formed coke :

In spite of the many coal washeries presently working and the other few contemplated, our demand for washed coal will be about 12 million tonnes more than the installed capacity by 2000-2010. This is based on the assumption that all the coal washeries (as on that date) work at 80% of their rated capacity giving 60% yield (clean coal); and the steel plants attain their full rated capacities.

With the limitations, both natural and production-wise, many researchers have made vigorous efforts towards synthesising the coke. Experimental work in this direction in many advanced countries including our country has given encouraging results. As a result the work has reached the pilot plant stage. The processes reported fall mainly into three categories, as follows :

(i) non-coking coal is devolatalised to produce char and tar. The two products are later briquetted (tar in the mix acts as a binder) and the briquettes are subsequently treated thermally,

(ii) non-coking coal is briquetted with a bituminous binder. Some coking coal may also be added to the mix and the briquettes are devolatilised, and

(iii) non-coking coal is devolatilised to produce char and tar. The char and tar are then mixed with a small proportion of coking coal and briquetted at 450 °C. The briquets are later thermally treated.

The work in our country is based on the first category process. A demonstration plant with an annual production capacity of 88,000 tonnes was set up at Talcher (Orissa) at a cost of 20 crores of rupees. The work was conducted under the auspices of the Central Fuel Research Institute, Dhanbad. Formed coke technology has a bright future in our country as our voluminous coal deposits, as already mentioned, are of non-coking type. Some coal washeries and their capacities in our country are given in Table 5.1.

Table 5.1 Coal Washeries in India.

S.No.	Name of the place.	Rated annual capacity (Million tonnes of raw coal input)
1.	Bhojudih	2.0
2.	Chasnala	2.0
3.	Dugda I	2.4
4.	Dugda II	2.4
5.	Durgapur (H.S.L)	1.5
6.	Durgapur (D.P.L)	1.35
7.	Giridi	2.84
8.	Jamadoba	1.44
9.	Kargali	2.72
10.	Kathara	3.00
11.	Lodna	0.40
12.	Sawang	0.75
13.	Tatherdih	2.00
14.	West Bokaro	0.57

6 Petroleum

Petroleum

Petroleum is a dark coloured liquid that occurs in the earth. Like coal, petroleum is also the product of ages of chemical action in deep earth. However, the base ingredient in coal formation is thought to be wood material; the exact source for petroleum is yet doubted. In all probability, it is not one but marine animal bodies and woody material together may have acted as the prime source. The mechanism of formation is also complicated and not fully established. The liquid state of the material makes it migrate and so the place of its occurance and surroundings often fail to give any idea regarding its co-products or environment of formation. High pressures coupled with temperature might be the conditions responsible for a vacuum distillation – like process of the organic substances.

The rocks in the oilfield are found to be sedimentary in nature. The rock serves as the casing for the oil reservoir. The oil is found floating on a water layer. In folded rock formations, deep wells are found. A map of a typical oil deposit is given in Fig. 6.1.

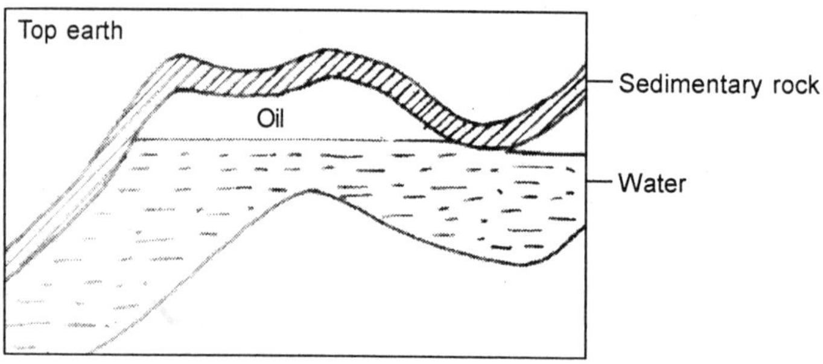

Fig. 6.1 Oil well.

Oil is tapped by using pipes after drilling to the depth of the field. As depths are increasing, the diameter of the drill hole (pipe) decreases. Depths as much as 7000 meters are already reached. Once the pipeline penetrates the top rock layer, oil flows out under pressure, like a fountain. The as-mined oil contains a lot of hydrocarbon gas in solution (upto 200 vols/vol). This gas is removed at the well-head. Partial reduction of pressure is the common method adopted at the well head, employing multistage separators. The gas obtained consists of considerable moisture which is further treated (either by charcoal absorption or compression) to recover some fuel.

Prospecting for oil

Prospecting for oil is a complicated geological process. Aerial photographs of the earth are taken to study the earth formation. Recent advances in satellite technology have further helped this aspect of study. Next step in the prospecting is the geophysical survey. Changes in the acceleration due to gravity of the specific regions are studied. An increase indicates the existence of a heavy rockdome and the region requires further probing. In seismic studies, the velocity of sound propagation through the earth (strata) is studied. Again in this direction, underground nuclear explosions are found to be quite beneficial. The precise methods are of a much complicated nature and become out of the scope of this volume.

Composition of petroleum

Petroleum is comprised of the following four major elements ;

Carbon	-	79.0 - 87.0 %
Hydrogen	-	11.5 - 14.8 %
Sulphur	-	Upto 5 %
Nitrogen, Oxygen	-	0.1 - 0.5 %

The sulphur is present as organic sulphur and is the most problematic. The petroleum from Kuwait and Iraq consists sulphur upto 4% while the Mexico crude consists upto 5%. Desulphurisation is a big problem in the processing of the crude. Sulphur as well as its compounds are corrosive agents and present problems with the refining machinery. If present in the fuel or lubricants produced, sulphur corrodes the engines and machinery wherever the fuel or lubricant is used. Effective desulphurisation techniques are evolved with the advance of technology, however. But the cost of the process is to be reckoned with.

Indian production

After independence, the consumption of kerosine, diesel and petrol as well as the industrial oils has steeply risen in our country. The advances made industrially are but the direct reason for this steep rise. Our reserves of crude are very limited. Assam oilfield was the only one which was tapped and its yield was barely sufficient to feed 10% of our actual consumption. Consequently, vigorous prospecting was taken up by the Government of India. An oil field at Ankaleswar in Gujarat was struck and went into production during the fifties. Off-shore prospecting for oil was taken up during the later sixties and during 1970 oil was struck off Bombay coast. Commercial exploitation of the reserve started from 1974. With all this, we are still importing about 70% of our total requirement. The production of crude in our country during the last decade is illustrated in a graphical form in Fig. 6.2. A list of various oil refineries in our country is also given below;

1. Barauni = 1
2. Bombay = 2

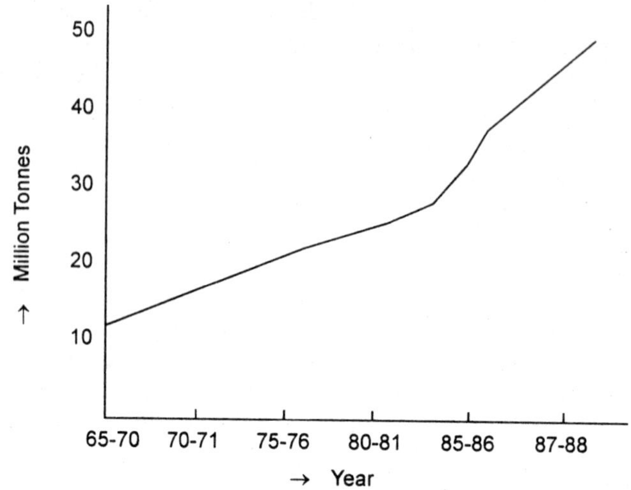

Fig. 6.2 Crude throuput to refineries.

3. Bongaigaon = 1
4. Cochin = 1
5. Digboi = 1
6. Gauhati = 1
7. Haldia = 1
8. Koyali = 1
9. Chennai = 1
10. Mathura = 1
11. Visakhapatnam = 1

Characteristics of petroleum

Generally petroleum is classified into three varieties. This classification is based on the type of residue obtained after the distillation of the petroleum, as follows :

1. paraffin base,
2. asphat base, and
3. mixed base.

The paraffinic base crudes are generally low boiling (30° - 60 °C). The asphaltic base crudes have higher boiling points. Further, the paraffinic type petroleum yields a large proportion of low-boiling point constituents on distillation. The asphaltic base petroleums, while possessing a higher boiling point (80 - 180 °C), distil higher boiling point constituents. The following example testifies the statement :

Property	Iranian crude	Mexican crude
Specific gravity	0.845	0.988
Boiling point	30 °C	125 °C
% of sulphur	1.08	5.18
Type	Paraffinic	Asphaltic

Refining of petroleum

As seen above, crude petroleum consists of carbon and hydrogen in a highly concentrated form. A large number of hydrocarbons can be separated from it by fractional distillation and chemical treatment. The paraffin family of hydrocarbons, the olefine family, the napthene family and the benzene family are the most common.

A hydrocarbon family should be understood as a series of compounds between carbon and hydrogen, governed by the same general formula.

Family	Formula
Paraffin	$Cn\,H_{(2n+2)}$
Olefine	$Cn\,H_{2n}$
Napthene	$(CH_2)\,n$
Benzene	CnHn

Next in the order come a series of hydrocarbon gases. These gases are of the condensable type. Later come the stable liquid and next, solids - ending up with paraffin wax.

Earlier (upto 1915) distillation was the simplest of its type in which only gasoline and fuel oil were produced. The internal combustion engine is the first to demand a change in the distillation technique. Simple fractional distillation technique was replaced by catalytic polymerisation techniques, after 1920. With the advent of II world war and the development of aircraft engineering, the oil refining techniques became more and more complicated. Catalytic cracking has supplemented polymerisation in the oil refineries. No refining, nowadays, can have a fixed flow sheet set products of manufacture. It can be said with good authority that the refineries will have to alter their techniques depending upon the raw material to be treated and the products required.

The following table shows, broadly, the physical properties of important petroleum distillates;

Product distilled	Distillation range °C	Specific gravity
Motor spirit	40 - 180	0.7 - 0.75
Naptha	110 - 170	0.8 - 0.82
Kerosine	140 - 250	0.78 - 0.83
Diesel oil	250 - 340	0.85 - 0.88
Light fuel oil	200 - 320	0.88 - 0.92
Heavy fuel oil	Above zero	0.92 - 1.00

The actual distillation, depends upon the type of the petroleum being treated. The two main petroleum types yield the products as shown below :

- Paraffinic Crude
  - Distillate
    - Gas
    - Gasolene
    - Kerosene
    - Diesel oil
  - Residue (Fuel oil)
    - Wax
      - Lubricating oil
      - Wax
    - Residue (Lubricating oil)

- Asphaltic Crude
  - Distillate
    - Gas
    - Gasolene
    - Kerosene
    - Diesel oil
  - Fuel Oil Residue
    - Diesel
    - Lubricating oil
    - Bitumen
  - Refined Lubricating oil

Refining process fundamentals

Thermal cracking

The basic process in the preparation of crude petroleum for further refining is fractional distillation. The aim is to remove dirt, water and natural gas. The whole process is made up of three stages viz.,

1. Separation 2. Conversion, and 3. Treating.

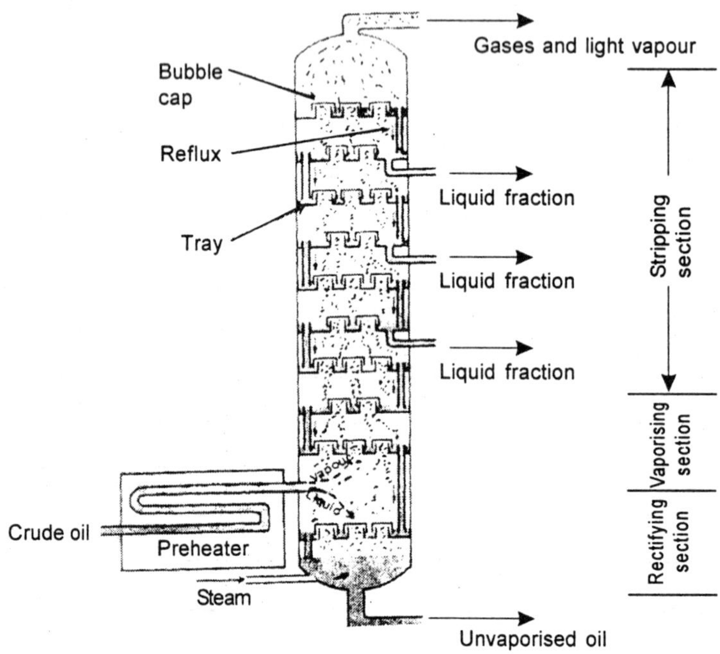

Fig. 6.3 Primary distillation of petroleum.

Separation

This is the primary separation process universally adopted. Essentially the process is fractional distillation. The reactor chamber is a tubular preheater through which crude oil is pumped at a slightly higher (than atms pressure) pressure 350 kgf/cm^2 and fractional distillating column. The fractional distillating column is in the form of a tower, divided into compartments by perforated trays. (Fig. 6.3). The preheated crude oil (to 300-350 °C) enters the fractionating column as a spray. The vapourating chamber as it is called, is the lower part of the set-up. The crude expands due to the reduction of pressure to near atmospheric and the vapours pass upwards the 'column'. The residue comes down. The residue is reheated and returned to the column below the vapourising chamber. Steam is introduced into the lower section of the column to evaporate any fractions still not vapourised. The fractionating column thus consists of three zones - stripping zone, vapourising zone and rectifying zone.

The condensed fractions are removed from column as side streams. The rising vapours are thus made to bubble through the condensed liquid in every tray by an arrangement of baffles, called bubble caps. Thus each of the trays is the place of continuous condensation and (partial) reevaporation (Fig.6.4).

The scheme of primary distillation of crude oil is extended to a process of preliminary distillation. This process involves preheating the crude oil to a relatively low temperature 150 °C and at a pressure of 350 Kgf/cm^2 and passing it through a simple fractionating column. The process is arranged to yield two fractions - namely the unvapourised part and the minor, vapourised part. The dissolved gases and liquids of low boiling point (propane butane etc.,) are removed from the crude to a large

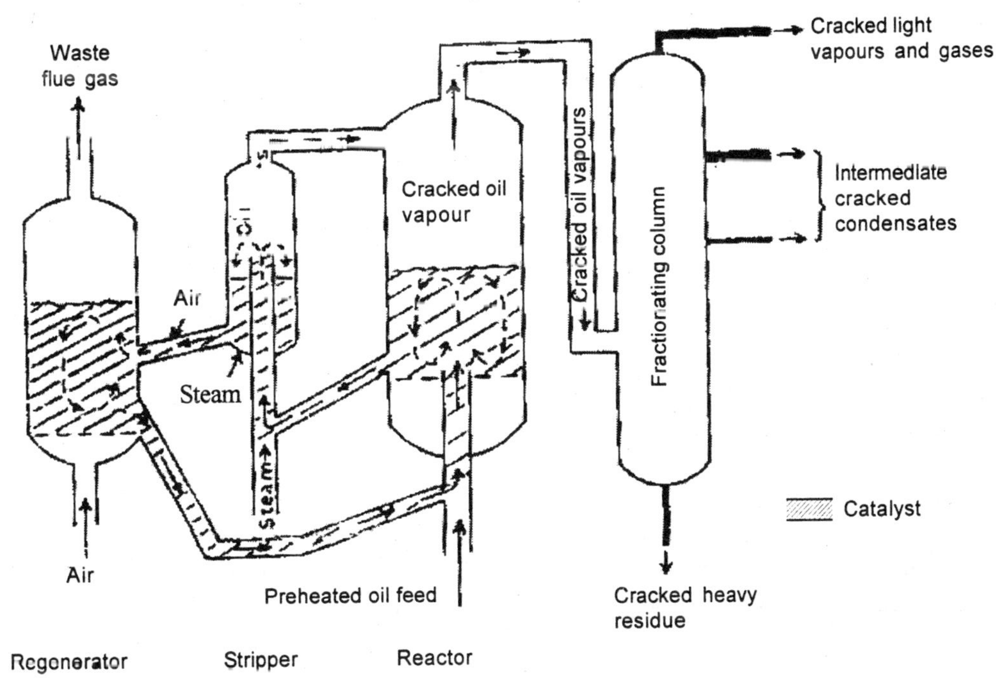

Fig. 6.4 Fluid catalytic cracking.

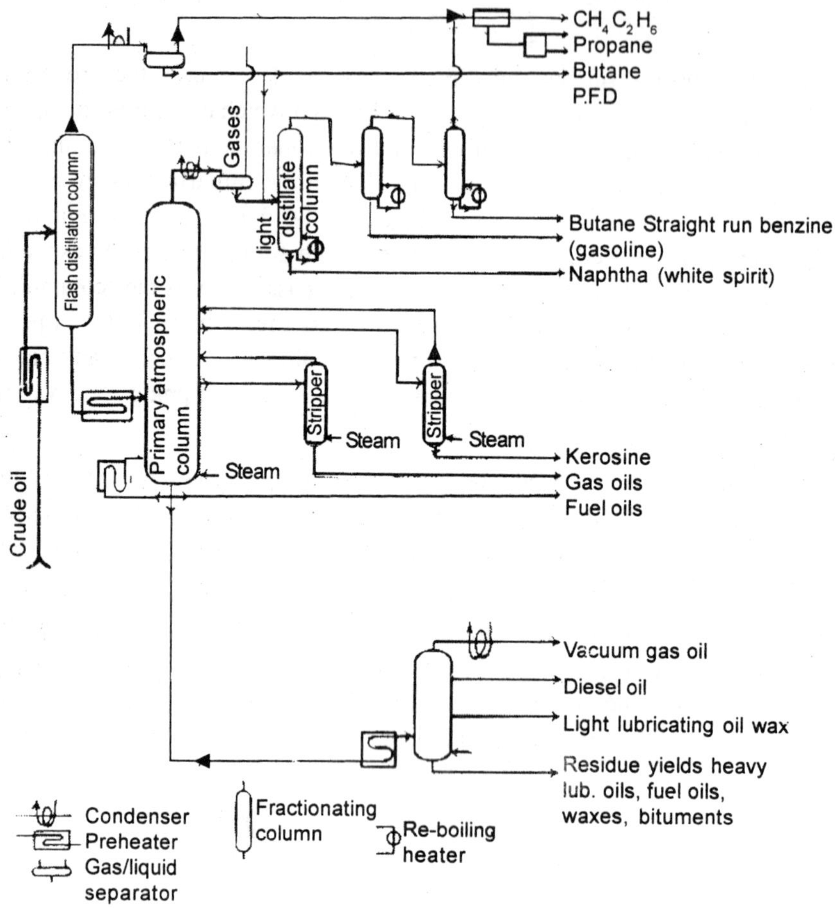

Fig. 6.5 Fractional distillation of petroleum.

extent. The unvapourised part of the crude leaving the base of the primary column passes to the main preheater-redistilled. The volatile liquid condensed from the outlet of the primary column is called primary flash distillate (PFD) which is further refined to give a chain of valuable products.

Catalytic Thermal Cracking

In this process high boiling point fraction is heated to a temperature much above its boiling point under high pressure. Eg. A fraction having a boiling point of 200 - 300 °C may be heated to as high a temperature of 500 °C, the pressures ranging from 700 - 3500 Kgf/cm^2. The treatment ruptures large hydrocarbon molecules and produces free carbon liquids of relatively low boiling point and hydrocarbon gases (Fig. 6.5). Thus, a variety of hydrocarbons namely ethylene, propylene and butylene. The unsaturated hydrocarbons produced by the pyrolysis process are seperated and converted into desired chemical products- a wide range of polymers. A simple example is given below,

$$CH_3\,CH_2\,CH_2\,CH_2\,CH_2\,CH_2\,CH_2\,CH_2\,CH_2\,CH_3 \qquad \text{yields}$$

n-decane.

$$CH_3\,CH_2\,CH_2\,CH_2\,CH_2\,CH_3 + CH_2 \ldots\ldots\ CH\,CH_2\,CH_3$$

n-hexane butane (1)

The free carbon obtained in the cracking process is called petroleum coke : It is generally aimed to reduce the yield of petroleum coke and run the cracking operation effectively at economically lower temperatures and pressures. Catalysts are used to achieve this. High grade gasolenes are produced from the component.

The carbon precipitation was also found to occur on the catalyst. The catalyst was frequently withdrawn and oxidised away, in oxygen. The regeneration of the catalyst itself is a complicated process.

The gasolene produced has a high octane number. But the combustion characteristics are found to leave a gummy residue in the internal combustion engines. The anti-knocking characteristics can be improved by the addition of tetra-ethyl lead.

Thus, we get primary gasolene and a distillate. There are a number of processes by which the distillate which also contains gasolene is treated. The aim is to get a variety of hydrocarbons in addition to gasolene. Methods like polymerisation, catalytic polymerisation, alkylation etc., are some and their treatment is beyond the scope of this book. The reader is advised to refer to some organic chemistry or petroleum technology literature, if further interested.

Tar sands

Petroleum-like liquid is found impregnated into sand and such sands are called tar sands. A large deposit of this nature is found in Alberta district of Canada. Unofficial estimates put the availability of oil from the reserves at 75,000 million metric tons. The oil is of high-sulphur type, with specific gravities over 1.00.

Various methods of treating the sand for the recovery of oil are tried but not sincerely. The reason may be the ready availability of petroleum elsewhere at a reasonably cheap rate. But the recent price-hikes in the crude by the Middle-Eastern countries may force a serious research by the Canadian scientists towards exploitation of their own tar sands.

Shale oil

Shale is also found to contain sufficient quantity of oil. Large deposits of shale are known to occur in Scotland, U.S., and U.S.S.R., of which only the Scottish shale was worked. Oil production was started from Scottish shale in the 19th century itself and by 1964, a million tons of oil production per annum was reached. Since 1964, the production was discontinued. Much is yet to be done to locate oil yielding shale in many countries. As such, the exact world reserves are not available.

Coal tar fuels

When coal is distilled i.e., heated for the production of coke or gas, coal tar is obtained. It is a liquid which can yield a series of products on distillation or further treatment. The further treatment consists of generally hydrogenation, to produce automobile fuel.

The products obtained from coal tar distillation are not exactly the same as those obtained from petroleum. Yet, these also find a useful place in the industry; especially in fertiliser production.

Coal tar is not produced as it is. It is only a by product in some other process like coking. Yet, it is not left untreated, as mere coking, without utilising the by-products, becomes uneconomical.

The products obtained on the distillation of coal-tar are :

1. Hydrogenation spirit
2. Motor benzole
3. Benzole
4. Creosote oil
5. Anthracene oil
6. Cresylic acid
7. Phenol
8. Tar fuels
9. Road tar

Serial numbers 4 to 8 are called C.T.F., oils (coal tar fuel oils) and are numbered starting from 50 in multiples of 50. Eg. CTF 50, CTF 100 etc., The numbers indicate the temperatures in degrees Fahrenheit to which they are heated for effective atomisation for combustion. Road tar is the black solid residue which is the final product and used for road laying.

Hydrogenation of coal

As already mentioned above, coal contains primarily hydrogen and carbon. The ratio C/H is 15/1. The idea behind hydrogenation is to reduce the carbon and hydrogen ratio to 8 : 1; in cosonance with that of petroleum. Very high temperatures and pressures are required for the process. The process was successfully adopted by Germany during the II world war when petroleum supplies to that country were completely cut off by the Allied Forces. Under such circumstances, the cost of production is of no consequence and the sole idea was of service.

A similar situation, though not due to war, is arising nowadays due to the multifold increase of the crude price by the predominantly oil producing, Arab countries. But, the cost of production of coal as well as the industrial overheads are so high due to inflation that, inspite of the six-fold increase in the price of petroleum after 1973, coal hydrogenation may not match the petroleum, in economics. Yet, it cannot be just ruled out and remains a powerful weapon from the strategic point of view.

The coals suitable for hydrogenation are not strictly specified. It is observed that low-grade coals are better suited for the process. It is found that as the percentage of carbon in the coal increases, higher temperatures are required for hydrogenation. The best suited are the higher peats and lower bitumenites. Thus, even in employing the process in emergencies, high-grade coals need not be used.

The preliminary attempt in the hydrogenation of coal was Bergius process. Fine coal is mixed with the coal tar in a 20 : 8 proportion with some one part of iron-bearing luxmasse. The mixture, of the texture of a paste was pumped through a series of three horizontal retorts, at 450 - 480 °C. Each retort or convertor is 2 meters long and 20 cm in diameter. The walls are 60 cm thick to withstand the high pressures of operation. The retorts are fitted with stirrers to promote hydrogenation. Pressures employed are as high as 200 - 250 atmospheres. The coal is hydrogenated and leaves the last convertor in the form of a thick liquid. The average time of treatment is 2 hours.

Hydrogen

The hydrogen requirement of the hydrogenation of one ton of coal is about 12 cubic mts. This is produced by either of the following methods.

1. Catalytic cracking of gaseous hydrocarbons,
2. Liquifaction of coke oven gas, and
3. Coke.

Oil synthesis

This method is an oblique hydrogenation. Coal or coke can be gasified using a mixture of hydrogen and carbon monoxide in a ratio of 2 : 1 in the presence of a catalyst;

$$n\,CO + 2n\,H_2 \rightarrow Cn\,H_{2n} + n\,H_2O$$

$$n\,CO + (2n + 1)\,H_2 \rightarrow Cn\,H_{(2n+2)} + n\,H_2O$$

The process named after its discoverers Fisher and Toopsch has the advantage of operating at atmospheric pressure and lower temperatures, in the range of 200 °C.

The catalyst employed is either nickel or cobalt oxide. The process is similar to catalytic cracking of petroleum described above in that the catalyst used is in a granular state and forms the bed through which the gases are circulated. The catalyst is cooled by a network of water pipes.

The process is very much modified nowadays, by improving the efficiency of cooling, and the catalyst. Iron has replaced cobalt oxide.

Further details of the process and of distillation as already mentioned are beyond the scope of this volume.

7 Combustion of Liquid Fuels

Burning of liquid fuels

The common liquid fuels used in industrial furnaces and boilers can be classified as :

(i) Gas oil,

(ii) Light fuel oil,

(iii) Heavy fuel oil,

(iv) Coal tar fuels.

Fuel Grade	Viscosity Redwood-1 at 75 °C	Pour Point °C	C.V. Gross J/gm	C.V. (Net) J/gm
Gas oil - D	45 Sec.	−9	10,350	40813
Light medium Fuel Oil - E	250 Sec.	−9	19,300	40643
Heavy Fuel	1000 Sec.	−2	10,200	40018

Petroleum liquid fuels

Coal tar fuels

A variety of coal tar fuels can be obtained starting from light distillate oils to heavy residuals. The intermediate grades can be regarded as the mixtures of these two extremes, in varying proportions. Most of them can be used as substitutes for petroleum fuels. However, certain precautions like washing with a light grade tar oil and necessary adjustments in the burners are recommended in their use. The coal tar fuels contain a higher C/H ratio than the petroleum oil fuels.

Coal tar fuels of the heavier categories i.e., 150, 300 and 400 grades, need preheating because they are very viscous or solid at atmospheric temperature and pressure.

Burning

Though the liquid fuels contain traces of moisture (0.1% Max.), when the fuel is stored in bulk, the water settles to the bottom. This should be removed, using a suitable drain cock. In the coal tar fuels, the accumulation of water would be at the top and the removal is performed by the use of a suitable draw off arrangement. Filters used in the system may also contain some water after some usage and this should be removed.

Heavier oils require heating or mild 'cracking' to break up the heavy hydrocarbon chains to make them thinner. This facilitates easier pumping and ensures a correct viscosity at the burner.

Liquid fuels are supplied to the furnace from a central storage through pipelines. If, however, a single furnace is required to be fired, a small tank near the furnace itself supplies the fuel. The tank is located at a higher level and the oil flows due to the difference in the head.

Burners

Essentially four types of mechanisms are used for burning the liquid fuels :

(i) the fuel spray is produced by mechanical means,

(ii) the fuel is broken down into a spray by physical impact with an atomising medium,

(iii) a combination of the spinning cup and blast,

(iv) in which the fuel is vapourised.

For many ordinary applications, the burners employing pressure jet principle are used. Using distillate liquid fuels, one can burn 4.5 Lit per hour. (0.0045 m^3 per hour) at a minimum rate. At –7MPa/Sq. cm atomising pressure, the orifice and swirl grooves will be very small i.e., 0.025 mm. Very special filtering techniques are necessary to avoid choking.

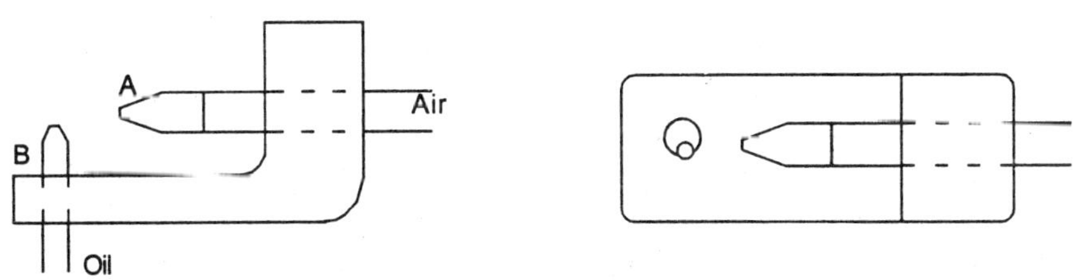

Fig. 7.1 Scent spray type burner.

Atomisation

The oil and air should be throughly mixed to the extent physically possible. The oil stream can be broken up by directing a high velocity air jet onto it. A simple type is of the scent spray mechanism. This is shown in Fig. 7.1 and is meant only to understand the process. In practice, a weir type burner is more commonly used, shown in Fig. 7.2. A thin weir is used to supply the oil and air is injected onto the oil from an oil feed of equal width. The weir type burners are used in locomotive diesel engines.

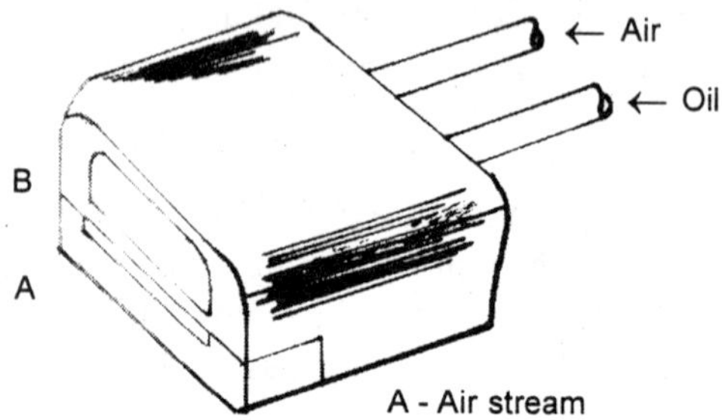

Fig. 7.2 Weir type burner.

Other modifications for specific combustion purposes are rotary cup oil burner and the steam atomiser. In the former, an electric motor rotates as cup, through the periphery of which the oil is spilled due to the centifugal force. High velocity air completes the atomisation. The speeds of rotation of the cup and the quantity of oil admitted per second vary depending on the specific design. In the steam atomiser, steam is employed instead of the air. This finds its application only in the firing of steam boilers.

Pressure jet burner

The pressure jet burner is of universal application in industries like power generation and ships. Large quantities of oil fuel are burnt by employing this type of burners. The burner has a conical swirl chamber with an air core. Heated oil is forced into the conical swirl chamber, which rotates at a high speed. The tangential grooves make the oil leave at peripheral velocities as high as 10 Km/sec. The oil, by the time it reaches the orifice, develops into a fast swirling annulus about the central stream of air. When it leaves the orifice, it forms into minute droplets suspended in the air. So fine is the droplet that its diameter will be as small as 20 or 30 microns. The air pressure being high (upto 20 atm) a thorough mixing of the air and oil occurs.

Secondary air

The proper distribution of the secondary air in the combustion region is of paramount importance. On weight basis, the air requirement for the complete combustion of a liquid fuel is 20 times the height of fuel. The proper regulation of this quantity with respect to both the distribution as primary and secondary air and the pressure with which it is supplied, especially the latter, will have a remarkable effect on the size and quality of the flame obtained. It is the practice to admit about 10-40% of this quantity of air as the primary air.

Assuming that the atomisation is perfect, the quantity of the secondary air admitted should be so controlled as to ensure the complete combustion of the fuel. For this to be achieved, the direction and the velocity of the air should be such that a perfect mixing occurs with the cloud of atomised fuel. An indication of the degree of efficient burning is given by analysing the exhaust gases. The exhaust gases should contain 12-13 % CO_2.

Metallurgical furnaces

Fuel oil combustion is applied in many fields including metallurgical industry. The billet heating furnaces, soaking pits, openhearth furnaces, crucible furnaces, annealing furnaces are a few examples of the application of liquid fuel. In all these applications, the secondary air admission is very important and needs a regorous control. The air should only be sufficient for and used up in the combustion of the fuel. Any excess tends to scale the metal in case of solid stock and oxidise the metal in case of liquid charge (except in the case of crucible furnace).

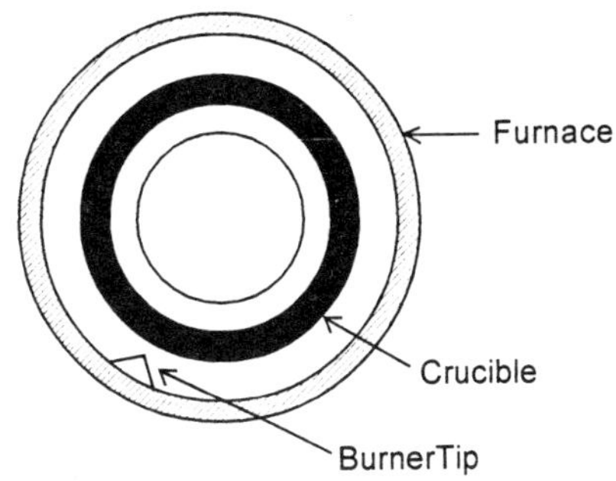

Fig. 7.3 (a) An oil-fired furnace (tilting type). **Fig. 7.3 (b)** A cross section of the furnace.

Courtesy : Morganite thermal designs Ltd. Stourport-on-seven, Worcestershire U.K

Openhearth furnaces were fired by using a mixture of coke oven gas and blast furnace gas. In some instances when the supply of natural gas is available in plenty, it replaces the coke oven gas. With the increases in the capacity of the openhearth furnaces effected, arose the necessity to have a higher heat-input and oil is introduced into the openhearth furnace ports through suitable burners. Generally, heavy coaltar fuels are utilised for this purpose.

Foundries employing crucible furnaces haye only two alternatives for fuel, namely coke and oil. When coke is used, the furnaces are of pit type. The heat loss in a pit furnace is so much that as far as possible the economics forces the foundry operator to discard this furnace in favour of an oil fired furnace. For alloys of a medium melting range – brasses and bronzes, the oil fired furnace is most universal. A photograph of the furnace is given in Fig. 7.3 (a). The furnace employs an oil burner which is placed in such a way that the flame practically envelopes the crucible inside as can be seen from the sketch shown seperately. In cases where the crucible capacity is large, two burners located diametrically opposite can also be employed. The location of burner with respect to the crucible is schematically shown in Fig. 7.3 (b).

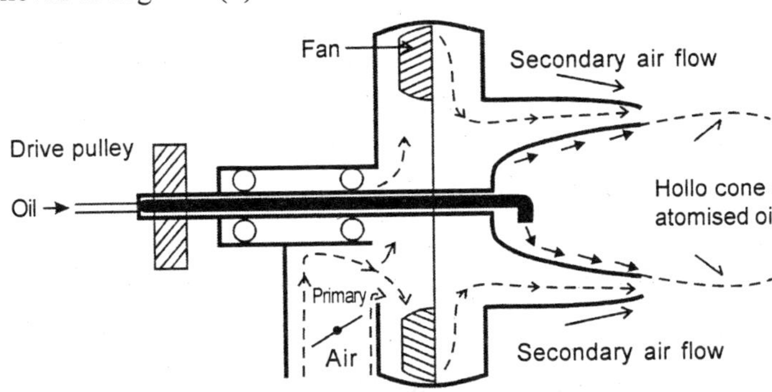

Fig. 7.4 Rotary cup burner.

The soaking pits and annealing furnaces operate with oil when electric power becomes scarce. Again, the billet heating furnace or soaking pits (for ingots) are more economically fired by coke oven and blast furnace gas mixture in a composite Iron and steel works. But in the small units undertaking steel rolling, a bye-product fuel as mention above is not available. So, they employ oil-firing or electrical heating.

The most important requirement in the firing is the control of the secondary air. The billets or ingots should not develop scale. Medium pressure burners are used and the burner is supplied with 50% of the total air requirements; the balance 95% being supplied as the secondary air. A sketch of a bell type furnace is shown in Fig. 7.5 for sheet annealing.

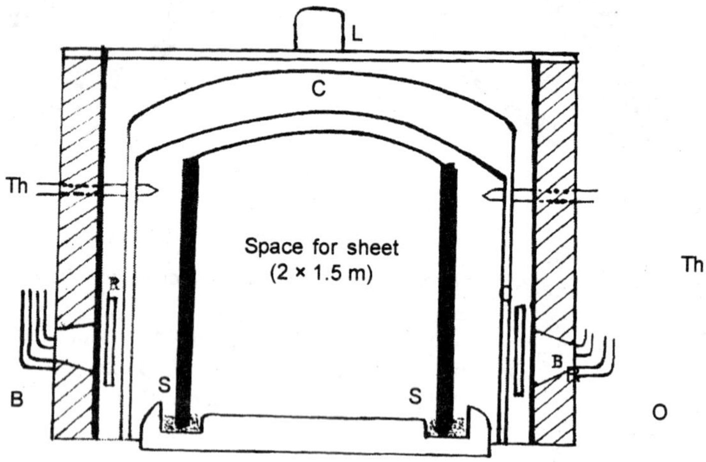

O - Oil inlets
Th - Thermocouple
B - Burner
C - Heat-resisting inner lug
R - Radiant Tile
L - LIfting lug
S - Sand seal

Fig. 7.5 Sheet annealing furnace.

A sand seal is used at the bottom in the sheet annealing furnace. The sheet, arranged on an open wagon enters the furnace and the bell is lowered over the loaded wagon. The burners are situated on either side. Secondary air supply is by forced draught. A number of thermocouple hot junctions note the temperature of the inside of the furnace.

Advantages of Liquid Fuels

1. the quality will be consistent with the specifications,
2. a uniform calorific value can be obtained,
3. easy and compact storage,
4. easy control over the feeding to the furnace,
5. can be easily metered,
6. ash or clinker disposal problems will not be there.

Disadvantages

1. difficult to obtain a reducing atmosphere without smoke,
2. certain deleterious substances like sulphur are present.

8 Fuels in Transport – Petrol, Diesel and Kerosene

The motor car has revolutionised the engineering industry as a whole. As a chain effect, steel and other industries had also to undergo improvements both technologically and production wise. Mass production has replaced batch production.

The production of motor cars, motor cycles and even the airplanes has registered a hundred fold increase in the past quarter century. Aviation fuel has also changed from petrol to kerosine. With these developments, the regorous specifications for petrol and kerosine of various qualities have come into existence. Motor spirit or gasoline as it is called, the petrol remains as the most outstanding fuel for the automobile and motor cycles. Again, dieselisation of the rail, ship and lorry engines has taken place. The so-called 'high speed diesel' has came to be manufactured as an important distillate fraction of the petroleum.

Gasolenes

The gasolenes consist of mixtures of complex hydrocarbons, depending largely on the type of petroleum from which they are distilled. See Table. 8.1. But their boiling points are close in a given range of temperature. The ultimate analyses of these, are, however, such that their total carbon is about 85.0% and hydrogen 14.5-15.0%. Sulphur content should be below 0.1%. Their specific gravities range from 0.723 to 0.733.

The calorific values of all the gasolenes vary from 36775-43770 KJ/kg – a very narrow range. Again, there is not much difference between aviation spirit and motor spirit in respect of composition or calorific value but the former has a lower boiling range – about 10- 15°C less than the motor spirit.

Table 8.1 Analyses of gasolenes.

Normal Paraffin Type			Napthalene Type		
Constituent	**Formula**	**Vol.%**	**Constituent**	**Formula**	**Vol.%**
Pentane	C_5H_{12}	0.5 - 1.0	Cyclo - Pentane	C_5H_{10}	1.0 - 2.0
Hexane	C_6H_{14}	5.0 - 12.0	Cyclo - Hexane	C_8H_{12}	5.0 - 15.0
Heptane	C_7H_{16}	–	Cyclo - Heptane	C_6H_{14}	–
Octane	C_8H_{18}	–	Cyclo - Octane	C_7H_{16}	–
Nonane	C_9H_{20}	–	Cyclo - Nonane	C_9H_{18}	–

Combustion of petrol is accomplished by injecting the petrol vapour and air into the cylinder. The mixture is taken, compressed and ignited by an electric spark. That is how an automobile petrol engine operates.

The process of mixing the petrol and air is accomplished by an instrument called carburettor. The air is sucked by the engine stroke itself through the carburettor when the volatile constituents of the petrol get readily vapourised and join the air. Some of it will remain in a finely divided state and the suspended petrol gets vapourised, almost instantly, after entering the hot cylinder. Sectional views of a carburettor to be used alongwith a petrol engine are shown in Fig. 8.1. Various parts are labelled. It consists of the main petrol jet (G) while the choke tube (k) provides the main air supply for petrol disintegration. The correct air petrol ratio is automatically maintained by the use of a calibrated jet (a) called the air correction jet. Petrol from the tank is led into the float chamber (0) via the needle valve (P) making the float (F) to rise. The float (F) holds the needle valve at a pre-determined level on its seating and thus the petrol level is held constant.

Petrol from the float chamber passes through the main jet (G) into the well (II) in which the emulsion tube (et) is suspended. When the throttle is opened, the increasing depression in the choke tube (K) causes air to be drawn through the calibrated correction jet (a), into the emulsion tube (et) and then passing out through small holes drilled in the lower end of the emulsion tube. The air emulsifies the rising column of petrol in the well (II). The emulsion of air and petrol rises to the top of the well (II), wherefrom it is carried away by the high velocity air passing through the choke tube (K) and via the throttle valve (V) reaches the inlet manifold. At this point, the petrol gets vapourised and enters the engine (Cylinder) as petrol vapour / air mixture.

When the throttle (V) is completely closed, the by-pass orifice (BB) is on the atmospheric side and acts as an air bleeder. Thus, atomisation is not only assisted but also the over-riching of the mixture is prevented. With the throttle (V) gradually opening, the by-pass orifice (BB) is progressively through the idling orifice (GL), thereby, proportionately enriching the output at the transfer position between the idling and main circuit supplied.

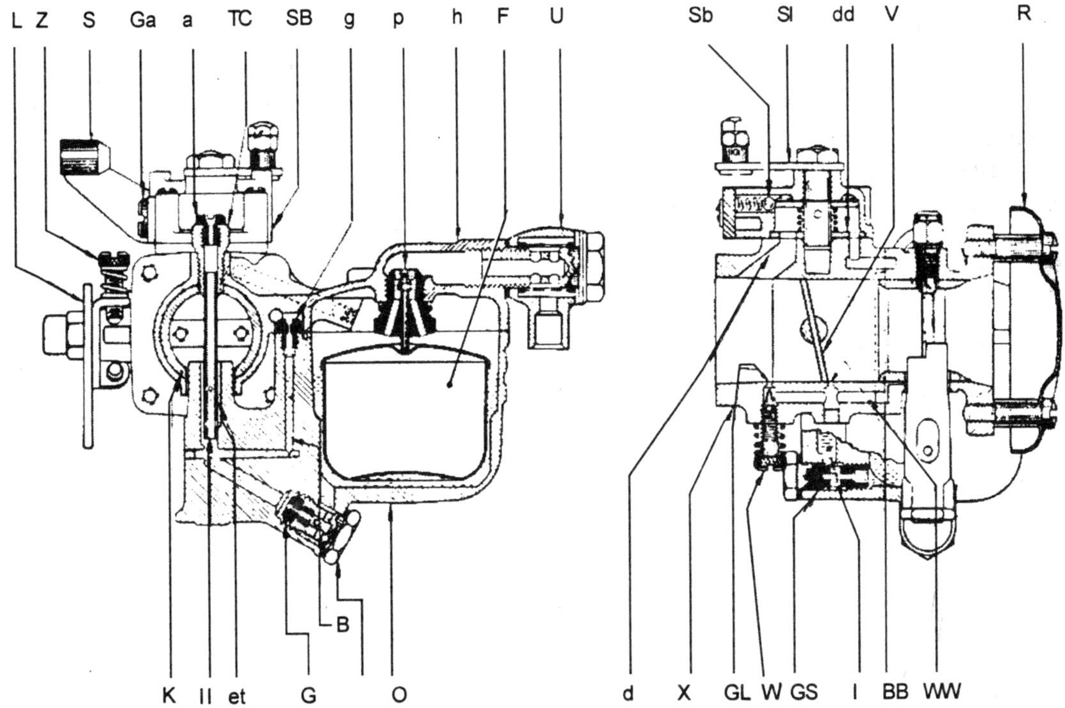

a	Air correction jet	**Ga**	Starter air jet	**L**	Throttle lever	**TC**	Emusion tube holder
B	Pilot jet well	**GL**	Idling orifice	**O**	Float chamber	**t**	Main jet holder
BB	By-pass orifice	**GS**	Starter petrol jet	**P**	Needle valve	**U**	Petrol union
d	Starter outlet channel	**g**	Pilot jet	**R**	Air bell	**V**	Throttle
dd	Starter valve assembly	**h**	Float chamber cover	**S**	Starter cable support	**W**	Volume control screw
et	Emulsion tube	**I**	Starter well	**SB**	Starter body	**WW**	Idling channel
F	Float	**II**	Main reserve well	**Sb**	Spring ball chamber (bi-starter)	**X**	Throttle
G	Main jet	**K**	Choke tube	**Sl**	Starter lever	**Z**	Idling adjustment screw

Fig. 8.1 Sectional diagram of an automobile carburettor.

Courtesy : Zenith carburetors Ltd

Considering the above, it can be appreciated how the various volatile fractions in the petrol are necessary. Some proportion of low-volatile material should be present in the petrol so that the engine starts in a cold condition. Again high distillation temperature constituents should not be more. In such a case, complete combustion may not be achieved leading to excessive carbon deposition on the piston and cylinder heads. Water and acid materials should not be present in the petrol, for they lead to corrosion of the cylinder.

All petrols contain some quantities of unsaturated hydrocarbons which under the conditions of the temperatures consequent to the ignition, will polymerise and form a gummy substance. This substance, like ash in the combustion of a coal, is inevitable. But, unlike the ash in the case of coal, gum formation can be inhibited by adding some chemicals like catehol, ortho-aminophenol traces etc.

Compression Ratio - Its Significance

As seen above, the petrol-air mixture is compressed in the engine cylinder and then it is ignited by a spark. In all the engines, this compression before ignition is important. The degree of compression is expressed as 'Compression ratio' – a ratio between the volumes of the mixture before after the compression. Obviously, the higher the compression ratio, the higher the power developed. This is true only upto a certain limit, called the Highest useful compression Ratio (H.U.C.R). If the compression ration exceeds the H.U.C.R. value, the petrol air mixture gets ignited by itself. This is called spontaneous ignition and is found to occur before the 'spark'. Then, the effect of the spark will lead to what is known as knocking. A sort of an ugly sound is produced in the engine operation and in the long run effects the other parts of the engine – both mechanical and electrical. Knocking is also known as 'detonation' or 'pinking'. Further discussion about knocking will be a deviation from the scope of this volume.

This difficulty has led to the research and development of what are called the anti-knocking compounds which are added to the petrol. Anti-knocking compounds commonly used are tetreathyl-lead and tetramethyl - lead. They are used in small quantities 0.6 - 0.8% by volume. As these compounds are poisonous, the petrol mixed with these compounds is given a distinctive colour.

The anti-knocking characteristic of petrol is expressed in terms of what is commonly known as octane number. The anti-knock value of iso-octane (2 : 2 : 4 trimethyl pentane C_8C_{18}) is taken as 100 and that of n-heptane (C_7H_{16}) as 0, the octane number of every fuel is fixed as a number. This number numerically denotes the percentage of iso-octane contained in the fuel by volume. It is interesting to note that during the recent years, the octane number of petrol has considerably increased due to the improvements in the engine design. Nowadays, the aviation fuel octane ratings are above 100. The values are obtained by reference to the various blends of iso-octane and tetraethyl-lead after considerable testing.

Kerosene

This is a light paraffin oil obtained as a second distillate fraction. The boiling point ranges between 140-280 °C.

Kerosene oil should have less than 0.1% S and an octane number of over 50 and the flash point above 27 °C. By analysis, it contains carbon 86.5% and hydrogen 13.5%.

Previous to 1950, the largest use of kerosene was for village home lighting, for which it is still employed in considerable quantities in developing countries. Kerosene stoves are designed for cooking and many middle-class families employ it as their domestic fuel. Jet propulsion in the aviation industry has made kerosene an important aviation fuel, during the last two decades. Of course, the aviation kerosene is a fraction intermediate between the gasolene and kerosene. Further discussion of the jet engine or combustion of kerosene in jet engines falls outside the purview of this work.

Diesel Oil

The invention leading to the development of diesel oil fuel for use in an automobile cylinder in the early part of last this century is another revolutionary step. It is found that the diesel oil and air mixture compressed to a high pressure of about 3500000 N/m^2 (3.5 MPa)ignites by itself (without an external spark) at temperature of over 500°C. This has led to the development of the diesel engine. The engine is generally a four stroke type. The normal four stroke engine operates as follows;

The first stroke draws the air in and the valve closes, the second stroke compresses the air into the clearance volume of the cylinder into which the atomised diesel fuel is injected. The third stroke is the power stroke when the mixture explodes when all the valves remain closed. The fourth stroke is the one during which the exhaust valve is opened and the products of combustion are forced out. Thus, there will be one power stroke (the third) for each cycle of two revolutions of the crankshaft. In the two stroke engine, all the above four strokes are arranged to occur in one revolution of the crankshaft itself.

Fuel injection is attained by using a separate pump and injection nozzles. This mechanism, in fact, replaces the carburettor of the petrol engine.

From the above it can be seen that the essential requirement of the diesel fuel is that it should posses a suitable boiling range so that ignition is effected easily and without delay at the end of the compression stroke. This is expressed as what is called spontaneous ignition temperature (S.I.T) This is determined by determining the flash point of the diesel oil in an atmosphere of oxygen.

Cetane Number

The ignition quality of a diesel oil is expressed in terms of the cetane number. This is calculated by actual combustion tests, called Aniline point.

Aromatic hydrocarbons in the fuel are found to possess the property of ready ignition, because they mix readily with air even at room temperature, But paraffins do not require heating. Thus 'Aniline point' denotes the ignition quality of the fuel.

Cetane is a paraffin hydrocarbon, hexadecane (C_{10} H_{34}). This has high ignition quality and is given an index number 100. On the farther side, a methyl nepthalene has the lowest ignition character known amongst the petroleum fuels and is indexed as 0. The cetane number, thus has come to represent the ignition quality of the diesel fuel. It ranges from 18 to 70, in the commercial grades of diesel oil. It can also be calculated as follows:

$$\text{Cetane No.} = 2 / 3 \text{ Diesel Index} + 0.068 \text{ mid B.P. } (^{o}\text{F}) - 22$$

$$\text{or} \quad 175.4 \log \text{mid B.P. } (^{o}\text{F}) + 1.98 \text{ API Sp.Gr} - 496$$

$$\text{where Diesel Index} = \text{Aniline point } ^{o}\text{F} \times \frac{(\text{A.P.I. Sp. Gr.})}{100}$$

Oils with cetanc numbers about 20 can be used in large slow moving engines (about 300 rpm) as in ships. But in engines requiring high r.p.m (about 4000 r.p.m) like those to be fitted in motor vehicles, the diesel should have a cetane number of about 60.

Advantages of Diesel Engine

1. Occupies less space for the power it developes.
2. Cooling water can be circulated.
3. Fuel Economy.
4. High thermal efficiency (upto 40%)
5. Cold starting is possible.
6. Full power output can be attained, almost instantly.
7. Electric generation system (in transport vehicles) can be coupled to the engine very efficiently.

9 Analysis of Liquid Fuels

Liquid fuels are analysed for the following important properties :

1. specific gravity,
2. viscosity,
3. flash point,
4. pour point,
5. calorific value and sulphur content, and
6. carbon residue.

Sampling

The process of taking a representative sample from liquid fuel in bulk for subsequent laboratory examination or reference purposes is known as sampling. The idea behind any sampling procedure is to see that the sample taken is a close representative of the total contents of the main container. If the container is small i.e., upto 50 litres capacity, it is advised that the volume is thoroughly agitated and sample is taken. If the volume of the container is more than 50 litres, it is the custom to take three samples – one each from the top, middle and bottom portions, viz. at points $1/6^{th}$, $1/2$ and $5/6^{th}$ of the depth of the liquid. Later, these three samples are mixed together to obtain an average sample. A sample of at least 500 cc is taken and divided into two parts. One part is used for the analysis and the other, kept as a reference sample.

Specific gravity

This is determined directly by using a hydrometer. Gravimetric methods like using a specific gravity bottle are also employed. It is expressed along with the temperature at which it is determined.

Viscosity

A liquid which flows with difficulty is said to be viscous. The property which determines the internal resistance to flow is known as its viscosity.

Resistance to fluid flow is caused by friction. Fluids in motion are in contact with the surfaces of the pipes in which they move. The layer of fluid in immediate contact with the surface is stationary. The force acting between solid surfaces in contact does not operate in the same way as between moving fluids and the surfaces by which they are bounded.

The particles of moving fluids do not move with a uniform velocity throughout. Immediately against the surface, there is a stationary layer – may be one molecule thick. Subsequent layers move with velocities increasing with their distances from the surface. The work that is expended in order to produce this relative motion represents frictional forces that come into play in the interior of the liquid. This force tends to retard more rapidly moving layers and accelerate those moving less quickly. The force which is required to cause this relative motion under standard conditions is known as viscosity.

The fuel oil flow is determined by their viscosities – higher the viscosity, slower their flow would be. The number of seconds taken by 50 ml of the oil to flow through a standard orifice in a viscometer of standard design at a specified temperature is measured to give the viscosity of the oil. Redwood viscometer No.1 type is a common instrument used for this purpose. It is used for oils with Redwood viscosities from 30 secs. to 2000 secs. For still thicker oils, Redwood viscometer No.2 is employed. This instrument is having a much wider orifice and gives a time of flow which is 1/10th of that on Redwood No.1 type.

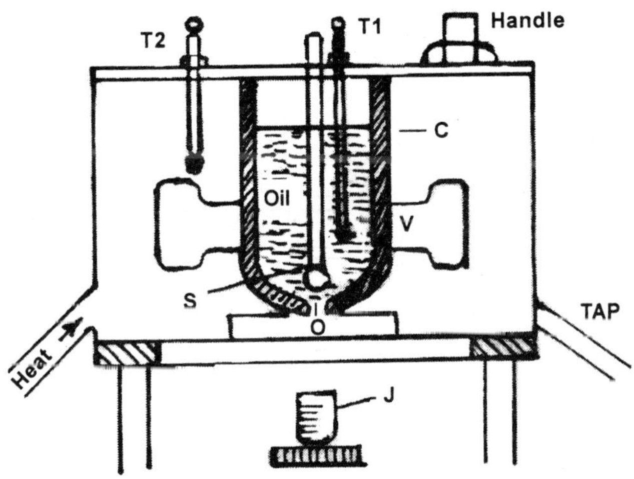

O Orifice
S Stopper
T1 T2 Thermometers
C Cup
V Vane
J Graduated jar

Fig. 9.1 Redwood viscometer.

The instrument consists of a metal cup surrounded by a heating bath and provided at the bottom with an agate plug. The orifice in the agate plug is closed or opened by a ball valve.

Usually the viscosities are determined at 37.5 °C for (centistokes) and 37.5 or 50 °C for furnace oils and expressed in metric units.

100 centistokes = 1 stoke
= 407 Sec. Redwood I
= 460 Sec Saybolt Universal
= 46 Sec Saybolt Furol
= 13.3° Engler
= 0.1 Pas

Saybolt viscometer is the standard instrument used in the U.S. Two types are in use, one saybolt universal and the other Saybolt Furol. Confusion in the test values is avoided by expressing viscosity in centistoke.

The absolute viscosity unit is Poise which is the product of specific gravity and Kinematic viscosity (in stokes). This unit is rarely used in petroleum technology except for pipe line calculations (transport of oils).

Flash point

The flash point of an oil is defined as the temperature at which the vapour of the oil just 'Flashes' in the presence of an open fire. The instrument consists of a test cup marked with the fuel oil level. The cup is enclosed in a heating arrangement. There is provision for stirring the oil and measuring its temperature by inserting a thermometer.

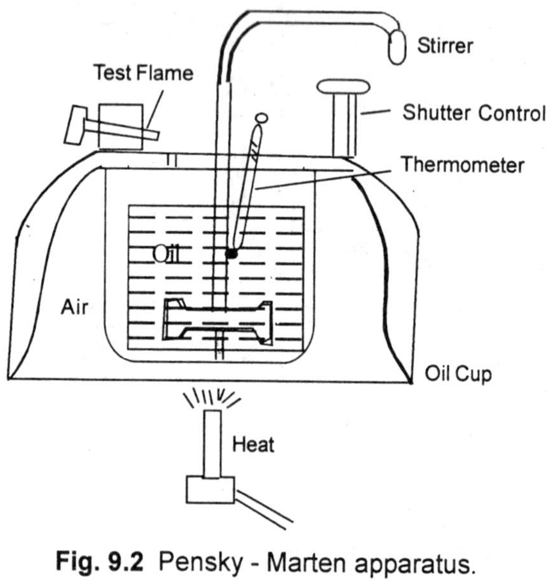

Fig. 9.2 Pensky - Marten apparatus.

The oil should be heated at a rate of about 5 °C per minute. The stirring should be in one minute. The flame should be applied for observing the flash at every degree rise of temperature.

Two models (designs) of apparatus are available. One named after Abel is used for oils having flash points upto 50 °C and the other named Pensky Marteins for oils with flash points over 50 °C.

Pensky Martens apparatus

This consists of a closed cup (see Fig. 9.2) in which dried oil is filled the cup with lid on, is heated in air bath. The oil is stirred and is exposed to a small flame at every 1 °C rise is temperature. The temperature at which a distinct flame appears inside the cup by the test flame is taken as the flash point.

The following points are to be observed during the test,

(a) Oil should be filled in the cup to the indicated level.

(b) Heating should be in such a way that the oil temperature rises by 5 °C per minute.

(c) Stirrer is worked at a rate of 1-2 r.p.m.

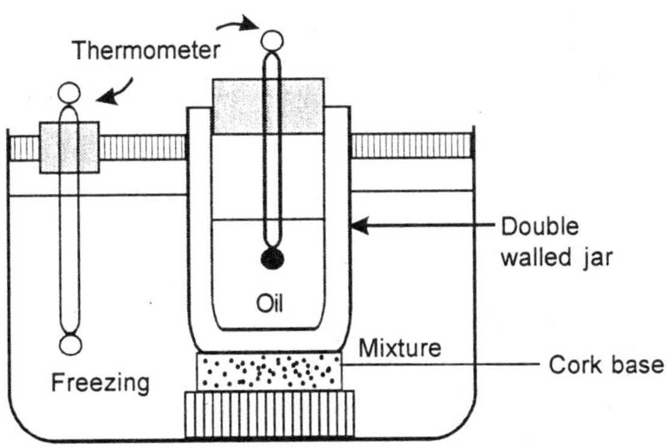

Fig. 9.3 Pour - point test.

The test flame is introduced at every 1 °C temperature by momentarily opening the shutter in the lid. The process is continued for some more time after noting the flash point. The temperature at which the oil continues to burn for 5 secs. (When the test flame is applied is recorded as the fire point of the oil.

Or flow, when chilled without disturbance, is called the pour point. The pour point is determined in an apparatus which consists of a 1¼ inch, dia test tube carrying a thermometer and mounted in a wider tube to provide air space. The outer tube is immersed in ice water or freezing mixtures.

The oil sample is taken in the inner test tube and heated to 115 °F. It is slowly cooled and at intervals of 5 °F temperature, the tube is removed from the cooling bath and held gently titled. Ultimately a temperature is reached when the tube can be held horizontally for 5 seconds without any movement of the oil. The pour point is taken as 5 °F. above this point of solidification.

Calorific value and percentage of sulphur

A weighed amount of oil, usually 1gm is contained in a small platinum or silica crucible. This is placed in a stainless steel calorimetric bomb in such a way that the bomb can be charged with compressed air and the oil ignited electrically. The quantity of oxygen used is sufficient to burn the oil completely. The sulphur in the oil is burnt to sulphuric acid. The bomb is immersed in before and after firing and the temperature rise of water is recorded very accurately from which the calorific value is calculated.

In many cases, the determination of sulphur is not called for. If necessary, a small quantity of water (about 2 cc) is also placed in the bomb so that sulphuric acid is formed after ignition. The amount of sulphuric acid is estimated by volumetric or gravimetric methods.

Carbon residue

This test determines the amount of carbonaceous residue that remains when an oil is evaporated under specified conditions. This is designed to give an idea regarding the coke forming tendency of the oil at higher temperature.

Ramsbottom test

A tarred glass bulb with a small capillary which permits the ascent of oil vapours is taken and 2 or 4 gms of oil under test is placed in it. The bulb is heated in a molten metal bath maintained at 550 °C. The temperature is raised to red heat after the oil vapours cease coming off. After heating at red heat of 7 minutes, the bulb is allowed to cool and then weighed. The carbon residue is expressed as a percentage of the weight of the oil used.

10 Producer Gas

Producer gas is manufactured by blowing air and steam through a bed of incandescent solid fuel, under such conditions that the combustible matter of the fuel is converted into combustible gases.

In thc olden days, only air was being passed through a bed of coke of sufficient depth and at a high temperature. The gas, mainly consisting of CO and N_2 was obtained (CO : N_2 = 1:2). When coal was used, the gas contained some hydrogen and hydrocarbons also, besides CO and N_2. Such a production of gas does not provide the conditions of maximum thermal efficiency. The heat liberated during the combustion of carbon to carbon monoxide is very high and much more than is required just to maintain a suitable temperature of the fuel bed. The additional or extra heat thus produced leaves out along with the gases as sensible heat. Further, the high temperature results in the partial melting of the ash and consequent clinker formation.

In the recent days, steam is added to the air blast. This, moderates the temperature of the fuel bed and improves the thermal efficiency. Steam reacts with the Carbon as follows :

$$C + H_2O \rightarrow CO + H_2$$

This reaction, being endothermic, temperates the bed reactions as a whole.

Sometimes, it is found that the output gases also contain some carbon dioxide; may be due to the reaction,

$$CO + H_2O \rightarrow CO_2 + H_2$$

There is no loss of the calorific value for, each volume of CO converted into CO_2, is followed by the generation of an equal volume of hydrogen which itself has an equal calorific value as the Carbon monoxide.

Gas producer

The gas producer is essentially a reaction chamber, made of steel plate and lined inside with refractories. There is a water sealing arrangement at the bottom and air is admitted from the bottom only. Coal is charged from the top and an exhaust is provided for the gas formed, from the side near the top (Fig. 10.1). The fuel bed can be thought of to be divided into a number of horizontal zones. They are:

1. The ash zone
2. Oxidation zone
3. Reduction zone
4. Distillation zone

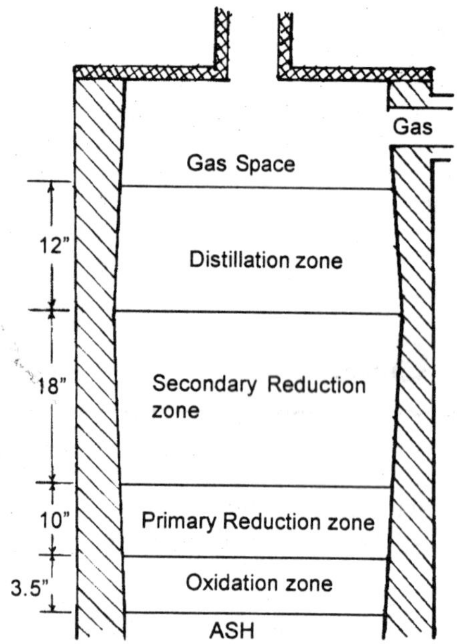

Fig. 10.1 Gas producer.

As the fuel travels down the bed, the carbonaceous matter from it is removed. The air and steam, entering the producer from below, get gradually transformed into a mixture of combustible gases.

The Ash zone

This extends from the grate level to a certain height, say about 20 cm. There is no hard and fast rule for the thickness of the ash bed – it varies depending upon the quantity removed from the producer. However, it is always advisable to maintain a certain thickness of the ash zone, for the hot ash preheats the air steam gas mixture and also prevents the grate from unduly heated up.

The Oxidation zone

The this zone, the oxygen of the air blast reacts with the carbon in the coal. This layer will be about 10-15 cm thick (about 3-5 times the size of the coal charged). Samples of gas analysed from this zone show that the main product of combustion is carbon dioxide. The topmost parts of the zone also show same carbon monoxide. Probably, the first formed gas is CO which, in the presence of liberal quantities of air gets oxidised to carbon dioxide.

Reduction zone

The extends from the level at which no significant quantity of free oxygen is present in the gas, upto that level where no further reaction of fixed carbon with CO_2 and steam occurs. The gas entering this zone from below has a high CO_2 content and water vapour and is at a high temperature (1100-1200 °C).

The following reactions take place in this zone.

$$H_2O + C \rightarrow H_2 + CO$$

$$CO_2 + C \rightarrow 2CO$$

The reactions are very rapid. As the gases pass through this zone, fall of CO and H_2 contents rise rapidly. These reactions are however endothermic. So, the temperature of the gases zone, as rapidly as the gases rise in this zone.

The drop in temperature and progressive decrease in the CO_2 content and steam slow down the gasification reactions. At above 20- 30" above the combustion zone, a level is reached at which the temperature of the fuel is about 300 °C.

Distillation zone

Fresh fuel charged at the top of the bed comes into contact with the fuel that has already become red hot and the gases leaving the bed. The charge is dried, preheated and carbonised successively. Thus, water vapours, tarry vapours and carbonisation gases are added to the gas leaving the producer.

The successful operation to the producer depends upon the maintenance of the fuel bed. The fuel bed should be of a uniform permeability to the gas. The various zones should be well distributed – horizontally across and uniformly.

The composition of the producer gas is as follows;

CO_2 : 3-9%

CO : 20-30%

H_2 : 11-20%

CH_4 : 0 - 3%

N_2 : 46-55%

Cleaning of the gas

The gas coming out of the producer needs to be cleaned. Coal and anthracite gas is cleaned in a water cooler. The great portion of the dust and tarry matter are removed by passing through a tower charged with coke on which water is sprayed. Later, the gas is passed through a box containing (packed with) wood chippings, wood wool and sisal fibre. Last traces of dust are thus removed. If the fuel contains sulphur, the cleaning box may also be charged with iron oxide so that any hydrogen sulphide in the gas is decomposed as iron sulphide.

The cleaning and purification of the gas made from bituminous coal is more difficult. The gas contains a light volatile tar. Dust should be removed before the tar vapour is allowed to condense.

A large well- insulated dust catcher is used for this purpose before the cooler. The washer coolers are not packed with coke. The filter boxes are replaced by electrostatic precipitators. Electrostatic precipitators remove fine dust and tar fog very effectively. In many cases the removal of H_2S is not necessary. If needed, it is removed by using Fe.

Pressure gas producer

In this, the inlet gases – air and steam are supplied at a higher pressure. These producers are of various types but the principles of operation and performance are the same. These varieties are principally designed to supply gas for industrial heating and hence are located near the furnace or some other plant for which the gas is meant. The feature of the gas is that it contains the tar vapours in it; thus enriching its calorific value. Cleaning devices like filters for dust removal are used but are maintained at higher temperature.

Use of oxygen in producer practice

Oxygen addition to air supplied to the producer is an effective method to reduce the percentage nitrogen in the producer gas. This naturally decreases the amount of the 'idle' constituent present in the producer gas thus increasing its calorific value. Steam addition is only to keep the temperature in the producer moderate. The process is a good move but for the high cost of pure oxygen. Once effective and economic oxygen producing methods are developed, oxygen enrichment of the air is bound to be followed. Every 25% addition of oxygen yields producer gas 10% of higher calorific value.

Producer fuel

Non-coking and other lower grades of coal are preferred for use in the gas producers. But, the actual operation of the gas producers demands a non-coking, non-clinker forming and well-vented bed for its smooth operation. While these are the basic requirements, fuels used actually in the gas producers vary considerably from anthracite to colliery waste with almost 40-50% ash.

The ratio of hydrogen to oxygen in the fuel should not exceed 0.55. They should be of a uniform size so that they present a large interstice volume for the free passage of gas. The fusion point of the ash of the fuel used should be well above the operating temperature of the producer. Practically, it should be above 1400 °C.

Coal and coke breeze have also been employed as fuel successfully – the only difficulty being increased proportion of dust in the producer gas.

Uses of producer gas

1. heating furnaces, coke ovens and gas retorts,
2. operating gas engines, and
3. diluting the town gas.

11 Water Gas

The term water gas is given to a mixture of Carbon monoxide and hydrogen obtained by passing a stream of dry stream over incondescent coal bed.

$$C + HO \rightarrow CO + H_2 - 175435.3 \text{ J}$$

Industrially, water gas is produced from coke. A deep coke bed is used in a plant resembling the gas producer. The unit has controls for blowing in air and steam, through the coke bed, in either of the directions. First air is blown and then steam is blown in opposite direction successively. The water gas is directed out, the stream supply is cut off and air blowing is performed. The cycle repeats itself. A sectional view of the water gas generator is shown in Fig. 11.1.

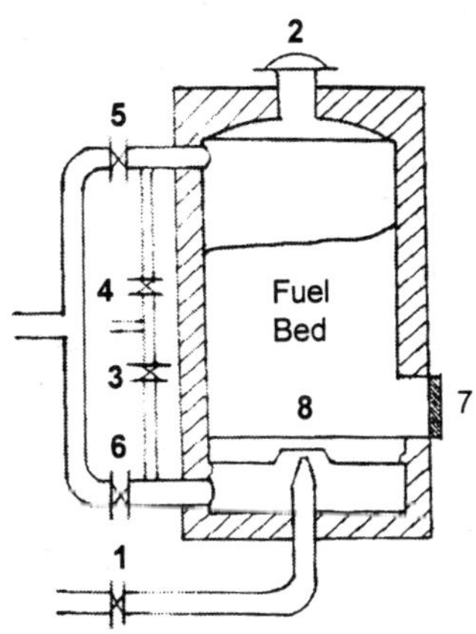

1. Air valve
2. Air outlet valve
3.& 4. Steam inlet valves
5. & 6. Gas inlet valves
7. Clinker door
8. Grate

Fig. 11.1 Water gas generator.

In modern plants, the water gas generator is associated with a combustion chamber for burning the blow gases. A waste heat boiler is also installed for utilising the heat in the hot gases. The procedure for operation as detailed in the preceeding paragraph is controlled mechanically. An electric or electronic timing device may also be used for controlling all the operations. The charging of coke and discharging of clinker is also made automatic.

Water gas composition is as follows :

Hydrogen	: 48-50%
Carbon monoxide	: 40-42%
Carbon dioxide	: 3-6%
Nitrogen	: 3-6%
Methane under	: 0.1%

Such a gas has a calorific value 35400 J/m^n

Applications

Water gas is used for industrial heating, It is preferred where intermittent and quick heating is warranted. But, it cannot outweigh the producer gas for, the latter is continuous in production and cheaper, though less heat producing. The main application of water gas is in the manufacture of pure hydrogen and ammonia.

The only disadvantage with the water gas is that a mixer cum holder is necessary to attain a uniform composition and continuous supply.

Carburetted water gas

This is water gas mixed with some hydrocarbons derived by cracking a fuel oil. The equipment for producing carburetted water gas, thus consists of the usual water gas generator and an additional superheater for cracking the enriching oil. Generally tar is used as the fuel to supply the additional hydrocarbons.

The calorific value of the carburetted water gas is around 41686 J/m^3.

Developments in the water gas production

Instead of cracking a liquid fuel seperately and mixing the products with the water gas, charging the oil itself on to the coke bed was experimented in the U.S. and found to be a success. Oil is sprayed on to the top fire in the generator.

Coal was tried as a replacement for coke in the generator. In actual practice, the process was a gasification of coal cum production of water gas. In Germany, complete gasification of the local brown coals was attained. The object however was to produce synthetic oils from coal. Oxygen was employed instead of air and it was also found that all the coke formed was not consumed for the production of water gas. A part of it was discharged for other uses. Many processes known by their different inventors are in vogue. One important process, the Lurgi Process, is described below.

A gas generator of 2.75 m dia. and 7 m. tall employs brown coal. The coal is sized in the range 2-10 mm., and a miximum moisture content allowed was 20%. The generator operates on steam and oxygen mixture at a high pressure of 20 atms.

A fuel bed about 1.5-2.0 m depth is always maintained in the generator. The operating pressure may go up to 50 atms and the steam / oxygen ratio 7 : 1 by volume. The calorific value of the gas produced is around 39600 J/m^3.

Town Gas

As the name suggests, it was used mostly for street lighting and as a domestic fuel in Europe and U.K. Essentially it is a hydrocarbon gas by composition. Coal is carbonised and the hydrocarbons evolved (volatile matter) are carefully led out and marketed by pipelines and metering.

The replacement of coal gas lights by electric lights has led to the diminishing usage of town gas for public lighting. The advent of producer gas has led to almost total extinction in its applications. Yet the existing pipelines and other accessories are used to market the gas, whatever is produced either in its own form or by combination with natural gas or producer gas.

The process of carbonisation is similar to the manufacture of coke. The retorts employed are generally vertical and more than one are employed. The temperature employed are low – 600 to 700 °C. The raw material employed is sized non-coking coal.

The recent trend is to crack the oil also alongwith the coal - on similar lines as the production of carburetted water gas.

The approximate volumetric analysis of town gas is as here under,

	CO_2	-	2.00-1.5%
	CO	-	6.5-7.5%
(Unsaturated Hydrocarbons)	C_XH_Y	-	6.5-1.0%
	H_2	-	60.0-40.0%
(saturated Hydrocarbons)	C_nH_{2n+2}	-	25.0-40.0%
	N_2	-	4.0%

The calorific value is high – of the order of 56275-62530 J/m^3.

12 Combustion of Gaseous Fuel

The main applications of fuel gases on our country are :

1. Domestic and Laboratory heating
2. Industrial heating.

Domestic gas is the liquified petroleum gas and the laboratories use petrol gas. The burners used work on the principal of Busen burner. The gas is fed in to a fine orifice. The primary air is admitted through a circular hole which can be opened or closed by using a concentric tube, also containing a hole of equal size. By rotating this outer tube the overall opening can be adjusted thereby controlling the quantity of air admitted (Figs. 12.1 & 12.2). The air enters the burner due to the suction provided on account of the height of the burner (by natural draught).

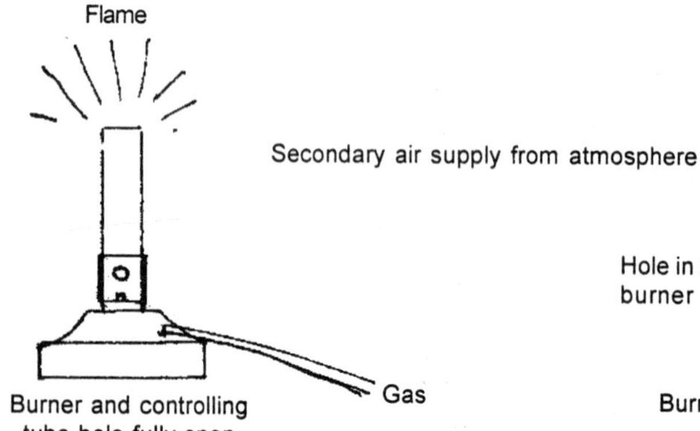

Fig. 12.1 Primary air (max.).

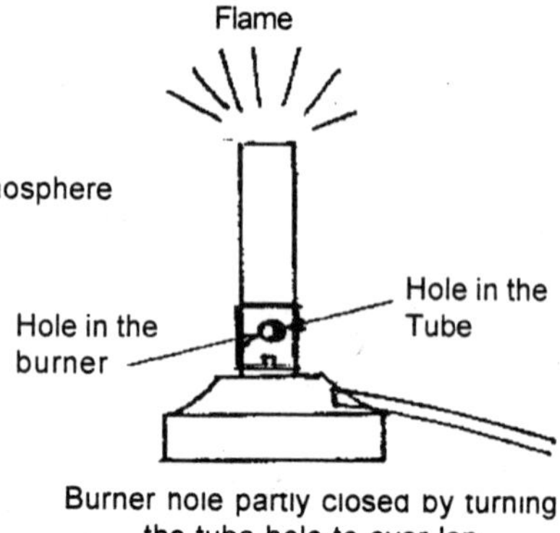

Fig. 12.2 Primary air (restricted.).

A domestic gas burner is illustrated in (Fig. 12.3). A fine orifice supplies the gas into a tube which is bent into the shape of a L. The primary air also enters the tube. The air and gas mix thoroughly and reach the top of the burner upwards. The secondary air is supplied through very fine openings circumferentially situated at the top of the burner.

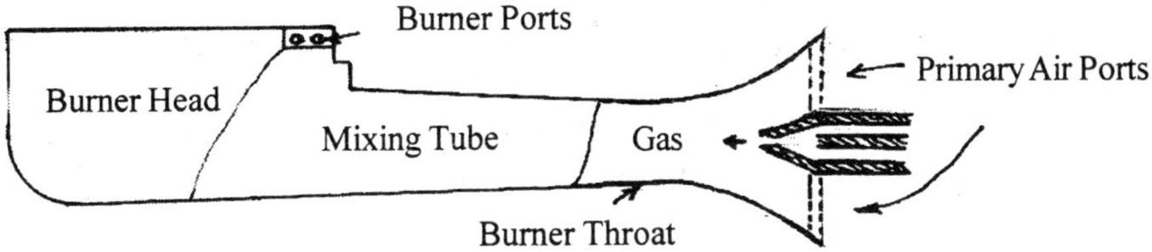

Fig. 12.3 Domestic gas burner.

The greater the quantity of primary air allowed, the shorter the flame obtained – more is the combustion. When the air/gas proportions become equal, the combustion is totally complete and the flame character becomes independent of the gas/air velocity.

Domestic cooking warrants complete combustion and the length of the flame required is also less. But in the industrial heating, the requirements differ depending upon the type of furnace being fired. A high temperature may be required to be developed in a confined space, a high temperature may be required over a large area, not a very high temperature may be required over a large area or the temperature should be developed intermittently. Thus, the various requirements warrant different types of burners which may be of any of the following :

1. Gas admitted through an opening and air by induced method (Fig. 12.4)
2. Gas admitted through an opening and air, both primary and secondary, by forced injection (Fig. 12.5)
3. Gas and air admitted into the ports separately so that they mix at a distance and burn over a large space (Fig. 12.6)
4. Special gas burners in which a stream of air is introduced in to a gas stream (Fig. 12.7).

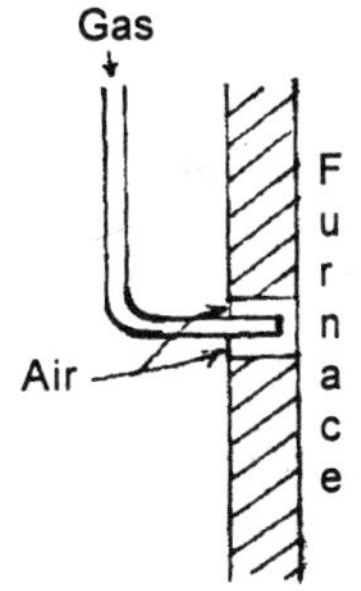

Fig. 12.4 Induced air burner.

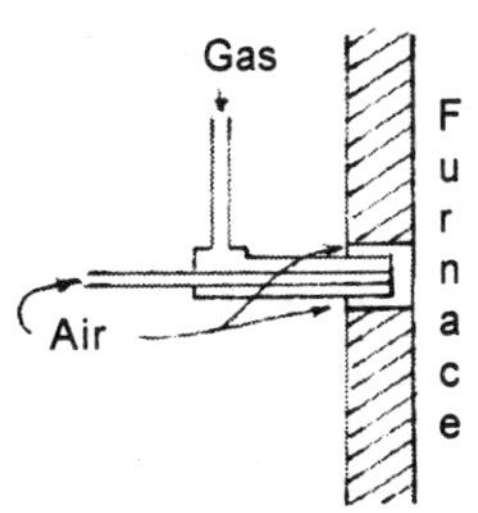

Fig. 12.5 Burner arrangement using forced primary air and induced secondary air.

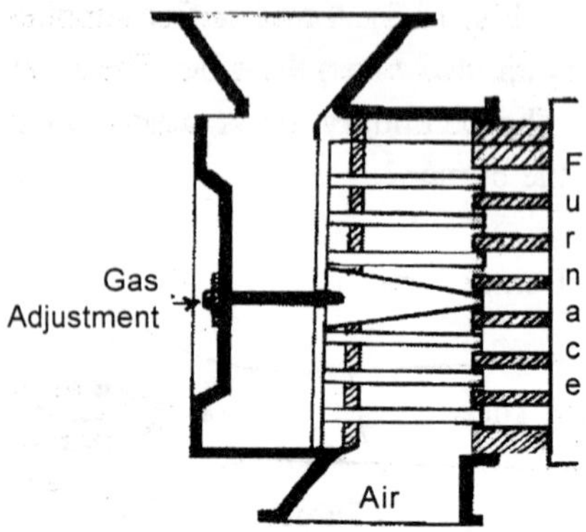

Fig. 12.6 Producer gas burner with compressed air.

While the first two types are commonly used in commercial burning of the fuel gas in flues, the burner of the type mentioned in (3) is more universal in its application. The fact that the gas and air are let in seperately will help to produce heat over a large space. The separate inlets of the gas and air can be controlled by providing dampers at each of the inlets. A further development of this type of burner is the so-called – Fuel Research Gas burner which can be used with any type of gas. The air stream is introduced into a gas stream by a separate inlet. The quantity and velocity of the air stream can be controlled depending upon the type of flame desired.

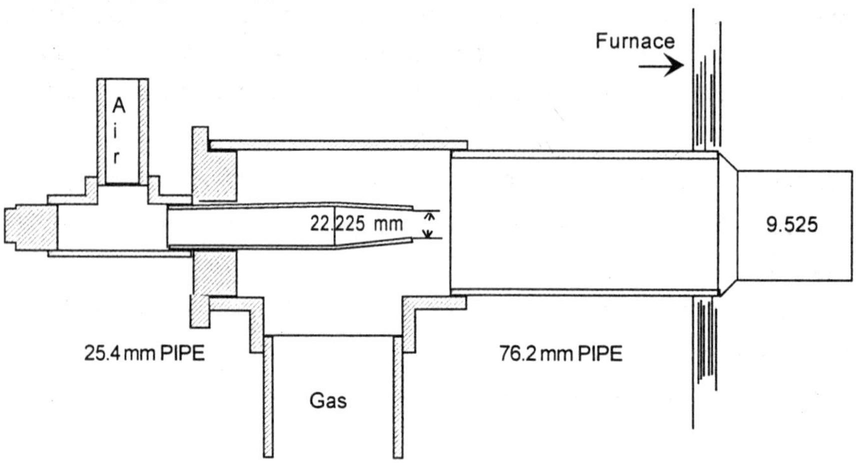

Fig. 12.7 Fuel research gas burner.

The fourth type of burner (Fuel research gas burner) is employed when the fuel gas used at low pressure and a definite type of flame is required.

Combustion characteristics of a gas

If we examine the flame of a gas, three distinct regions can be identified :

(i) ***The luminous cone***

In this region, air / gas mixture burns. Complete Combustion is not attained and a portion of combustible gases are still available. This region extends from the tip of the burner upto a small distance.

(ii) ***Inner Envelope***

This region is the portion in which complete combustion occurs. Secondary air is drawn in and the CO is oxidised to carbon dioxide. At the end of this region, maximum temperature is developed.

(iii) ***The Outer Envelope***

This is the extension of the flame where no combustion occurs. Yet, the products of combustion will be around the above two zones and depending upon the relative quantities of the fuel and air, control the atmosphere in the furnace. In highly oxidising types of combustion, however, this region is not visible to the eye.

If the proportion of the air is increased in the air fuel mixture, the flame becomes oxidising and if the proportion of the gas is increased the flamè becomes reducing.

The composition of the fuel gas plays a very important part in its combustion. Hydrogen burns faster than any other constituent. Hence the percentage of hydrogen in a fuel gas controls the rate of combustion as well as the stability of the flame.

In an aerated burner, the quantity of primary air required will decrease with the increase in the percentage of hydrogen. Flame stability is defined as the range between the minimum rate of supply of the gas and the maximum rate. When the gas supply is minimum, it causes the light back and when it is maximum, the flame blows off. Sometimes there occurs what is called flame lift – the combustion starting from a distance away from the burner tip. The flame stability and flame lift are important in the industry for, on them depends the rate of heat produced.

Fluidge and his followers have plotted combustion curves. A simple burner in which the proportions of gas and air can be independently varied was employed, with a gas of high calorific value. Further, different fuel gases were found to yield different sets of curves (Fig. 12.8).

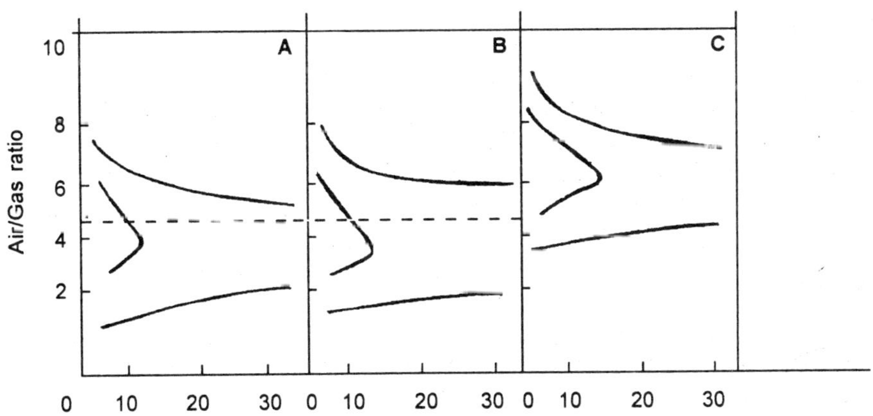

Fig. 12.8 Heat input.

The above curves can be studied in the light of the following index.

(i) the disappearance of the flame luminosity is represented by the curve C,

(ii) the theoretical air required for complete combustion is indicated by the dottel line,

(iii) the blow-off point of the flame is represented by the curved,. and

(iv) the area to the left of the curve A, B is the back fire area.

Basing on this data, a standard burner 19.04 mm called Aeration Test Burner 63.5 mm is designed, in which the inner luminous cone of the flame is 3/4" mm when the gas pressure is 2.5" mm W.G. With this the air supply needed for any particular gas for the aforesaid flame characteristics is determined. Further work led to the standardisation of the burner size and its orifice and provision of a micrometer arrangement to the air baffle. The so-called TECLU uses a 304.8 mm size 10.26 mm I.D and an orifice of 0.9906 mm dia. so that the luminous cone obtained in the flame is 63.5 mm. (Fig. 12.9).

Though the A.T.B. Number of a fuel gas controls the performance of a burner in the form of the heat input, the gas requirement, for example, in an emergency or at peak load cannot be exactly predicted. The Wobbe Index which is a quotient obtained by dividing the calorific value of the gas by the square root of its specific gravity, is developed to give a fairly accurate method of the gas quality to be employed.

$$\text{Wobbe Index} = K \frac{C.V}{V.d}$$

where K = a proportionality constant

d = density of the gas.

The basis for the wobbe index appears to be the relation between the specific gravity and calorific value of a fuel gas. They are found to be directly proportional to each other under constant pressure.

For two gases of the same calorific value (in B.T.U.) of say 500, one with a specific gravity of 0.4 and another with 0.625, it can be seen that the Wobbe index will vary. With the former it's value is about 750 and with the latter, it is around 600 (value of K = 0.3). Thus we can attain the same rate of heat input with a gas of lower calorific value by decreasing its specific gravity also proportionally.

Special burners

Special burners in which all the air required for the combustion of the gas is introduced at the flame are also available. The Hypact burner and the Bray burner are typical examples of the types of non-aerated burners. The gas is introduced through a fine nozzle and depending upon the design of the burner, made to deviate in a pre-calculated direction or spread on a wire mesh so as to present more of itself to the air. The advantages of these burners are their capacities for high rates of fuel burning (thereby higher heat inputs) and short and noiseless flames.

Swirl type burner

The burner consists of an air swirler inside which the fuel gas is led. Due to the swirling action the gas fuel mixing will be thorough. The flame will be confined to a small region at the burner itself. Temperature as high as 1600-1700 °C are attained. The air pressure is 8" W.G. The burners are commonly used for produce gas burning and the sizes are specified by the volume of the gas burnt per hour.

Whatever may be the type of the burner, in a gas combustion process the efficiency of the burner is the degree of nearness to which the flame temperature obtained approaches the theoretically calculated maximum, of course, making due room for the gas dissociation etc., which are indespensable at the higher temperatures. With burners of conventional types in which the gas and air enter the burner in stream-lined flow, the maximum efficiency of combustion possible is 70%. However, with burners in which the air and gas are mixed (pre-mixing and swirl type burners) and pre-heated air is used, efficiency values of 100% are attained.

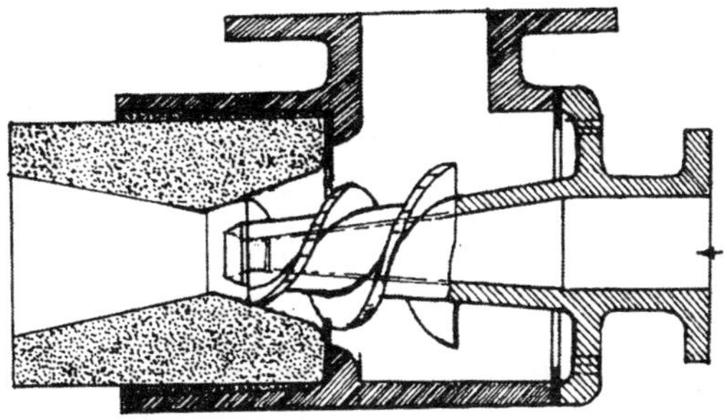

Fig. 12.9 Eddy ray burner for producer gas.

Analysis of Combustion Gases

Analysis of combustion gases is commonly performed in an apparatus called Orsat's apparatus (Fig. 12.10). This consists of a graduated burette A. The graduations are 100 divisions, starting from the bottom. An aspirator bottle B is partially filled with water and helps to move the gas in the apparatus. There are three pipettes D_1 D_2 and D_3 each containing an absorbent to absorb one constituent of the gas. The first pipette contains a solution of KOH to absorb CO_2 (and SO_2). The second pipette contains a freshly prepared solution of alkaline pyrogallol to absorb oxygen. The third pipette contains a solution of coprous chloride in ammonia. This is capable of absorbing CO (and also CH_4). The pipettes are usually filled with glass tubes so as to present a large surface to be moistened with the particular absorbent. The stainer pipette achieves the same objective by forming innumerable bubbles of the gas throughout the absorbent liquid, each stainer pipette is connected to the absorption pipette by a U tube.

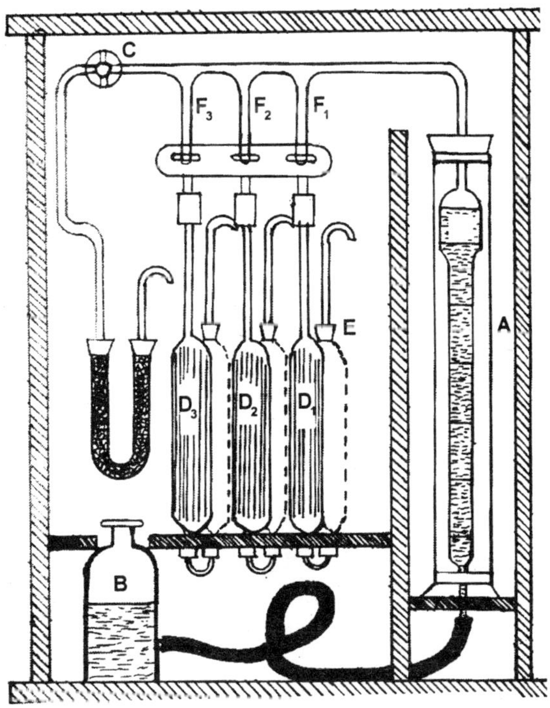

A Graduated burette
B – Aspirator bottle
C – Stop cock for letting in gas sample
D1,D2 ,D3 – Absorbent Liquids
E – Displacement reservoirs
F1,F2,F3 – Stop cockes for burettes.

Fig. 12.10 Orsat"s Apparatus.

Procedure

The aspirator bottle B is raised so that the burette is filled completely with water. The 3-way stopcock C is turned so as to allow the gas to be analysed into the apparatus. There is smoke filter in the form of a U tube, through which the gas is passed, before it enters the apparatus. Gas gets into the apparatus (burette) when the aspirator bottle is lowered. The gas is admitted and purged out twice or thrice so as to completely drive out the air in the burette. FInally, 100 units of volume of the gas is admitted into the burette.

The 100 units of gas is passed into the first pipette by opening the stop cock F_1 and raising the aspirator bottle. By lowering the bottle the gas is brought back into the burette.

Thus the gas is made to pass through the absorbent twice or thrice. The decrease in volume of the gas denotes the quantity of CO_2 in the flue gas. The process is repeated with the absorption in D_1 and later D_3. Further reduction of volume occurring after absorption in the pipette D_2 gives the quantity of O_2 present in the gas and that in D_3 gives the quantity of CO. While measuring the volume of the gas after each absorption, the aspirator bottle should be held alongside the burette and the level of water in the bottle and the burette equalised.

The volumetric analysis arrived at as above gives us the volumes of the gases measured over water.

13 Combustion Characteristics of Fuel

Any fuel is used to give heat. The heat is evolved only when it burns. Burning is total oxidation and hence the combustion characteristics of a fuel are studied in the light of the total oxidation of the particular fuel.

Fuels generally consist of carbon and hydrogen. Both these elements burn with oxygen of the air. Some fuels contain oxygen within and this also assists in the process of oxidation. In other words, while calculating the total oxygen requirement for combustion, the quantity of oxygen that is needed to be suppled is arrived at by substracting the oxygen in the fuel from the total oxygen required for combustion.

Air is a mixture of oxygen and Nitrogen. Volumetrically, their proportions are $N_2 : O_2 = 79 : 21$. By weight basis, they are $N_2 : O_2 = 76.8 : 23.2$.

When we calculate the requirement of air for a particular combustion process, it should be remembered that, only the oxygen part of the air is useful. Nitrogen does not take any part in combustion but only acts as a dilutant. In fact, the large quantity of nitrogen also gets heated up to the maximum temperature developed in the firing system and carries away considerable quantity of heat along with it, as sensible heat, in the exhaust.

During combustion, carbon, hydrogen and carbon monoxide are the constituents which burn. Their products of combustion are carbon dioxide and water. Since the process of combustion takes place in air, the carbon dioxide and water produced also contain, alongwith them, large quantities of nitrogen. The products of combustion are referred to as flue gases or waste gases or exhaust gases. Traces of sulphur contained in the fuel is oxidised to sulphur dioxide which is also present in the exhaust gases.

The combustion of a fuel can be studied both qualitatively and quantitatively by chemistry. The fuel analysis is taken into consideration and the individual constituents' complete oxidation is put down.

$$C + O_2 \rightarrow CO_2$$

$$2H_2 + O_2 \rightarrow 2H_2O$$

The equations indicate the relative proportions in which the individual elements combine. If we examine the equation, $2H_2 + O_2 \rightarrow 2H_2O$, it can be seen that two molecules of hydrogen react with one molecule of oxygen to give two molecules of water. In other words, 4 atoms of hydrogen and 2 atoms of oxygen combine to give 2 molecules of water.

Now, we bring into picture the atomic weights of the reactants and the products. The atomic weight of hydrogen is 1 and that of oxygen is 16. So, we can say that 4 (4 × 1) parts of hydrogen (by weight) combine with 32 (2 × 16) parts of oxygen (by weight) to give 36 parts of water (by weight). Parts by weight means grams or kilograms - the same unit being employed throught.

Volumetrically, one volume of oxygen burns with two volumes of hydrogen to give rise to two volumes (not three volumes) of water.

Air consists of 21 percent of oxygen by volume. So, one volume of oxygen is accompanied by 79/21 = 3.76 volumes of nitrogen, inevitably. Thus, when air is employed for combustion, the above equation can be written as follows :

$$2H_2 + O_2 + 3.76\ N_2 \rightarrow 2H_2O + 3.76\ N_2$$

Thus, as it is mentioned above, nitrogen is just a copassenger to oxygen and does not take part in any chemical reaction.

The above example of combustion of hydrogen is given assuming that the volumes of oxygen, hydrogen and water vapour are determined at the same temperature and pressure. However, if they are not, the values should be corrected by using the formula.

$$\frac{PV}{T} = \text{Constant}$$

where P = Pressure absolute

and T = Absolute temperature

Chemistry shows that equal volumes of gases contain equal number of molecules. So, the weights equal to the molecular weights of all gases, occupy the same volume. It is experimentally determined that the weight of a gas equal to its molecular weight occupies a volume of 22.4 Lit at 0 °C and 760 mm (Hg) pressure. These weights are referred to as the gram molecular weights.

Some atomic and molecular weights of common gases and compounds are listed in the Table 13.1.

Table 13.1

Sl. No.	Name	Mol. Symbol Mo. Formula	At. Wt	Mol. Wt.
1.	Hydrogen	H_2	1	2
2.	Carbon	C	12	-
3.	Nitrogen	N_2	14	28
4.	Oxygen	O_2	16	32
5.	Sulphur	S	32	32
6.	Water vapour	H_2O	-	18
7.	Carbon Monoxide	CO	-	28
8.	Carbon dioxide	CO_2	-	44
9.	Sulphur dioxide	SO_2	-	64
10.	Methane	CH_4	-	16

In all the combustion calculations it is the practice to take the atomic and molecular weights of the reactants and products. It is also assumed that all gases behave like perfect gases i.e, obey the gas laws. Then it becomes simple to calculate. Throughout the calculation, it is recommended to work with weights of each chemical identity expressed in units of its molecular weight. The weight is given as a certain number of mols. In the above example of oxidation of hydrogen, the calculation takes the following pattern;

2 gms of hydrogen = 1 mol of hydrogen (the molecular wt. of H_2 is 2)
32 gms. of oxygen = 1 mol of oxygen (the molecular wt. of O_2 is 32)
18 gms of water = 1 mol of water (the molecular wt. of H_2 is 18)

If we examine the chemical reaction

$$2H_2 + O_2 \rightarrow 2H_2O$$

(4 gm. of H_2 + 32 gm. of O_2 - - - - - 36 gm. of H_2O) Or
(2 mols of H_2 + 1 mol of O_2 - - - - - 2 mol of H_2O)

Again, if we take the atmospheric air, the proportions of oxygen and nitrogen are, by volume, 21 : 79. Because we have seen that one mole of any gas occupies a space of 22.4 lit at N.T.P., if we express the ratio of oxygen and nitrogen in the air in terms of mols, still it will be 21:79. Thus, the volumetric proportion is equal to the mol. proportion. Thus, the calculations become very easy.

Example.

1. Calculate the quantity of air required for the complete combustion of 1kg of coal of the following composition.

   Chemical composition of the coal Kgf (by Wt) :

   Carbon - 72.0 % (by wt.)

Hydrogen - 6.0%
Oxygen - 5.0%
Nitrogen - 1.0 %
Sulphur - 1.0 %
Moisture - 10.0%
Ash - 5.0%

Solution

Let us consider 1 kg. sample of coal.

Constituent	Wt.kgf	Mols / kgf	Reaction	Mols of O_2 required
C	0.72	$\frac{0.72}{12}=0.06$	$C+O_2 \rightarrow CO_2$	$1 \times 0.06 = 0.06$
H_2	0.06	$\frac{0.06}{2}=0.03$	$2H_2+O_2 \rightarrow 2H_2O$	$1/2 \times 0.03 = 0.015$
O_2	0.05	$\frac{0.05}{32}=0.00156$	--	0.00156 (inherently available)
N_2	0.01	--	--	--
S	0.01	$\frac{0.01}{32}=0.00031$	$S+O_2 \rightarrow SO_2$	$1 \times 0.00031 = 0.00031$
H_2O	0.1	--	--	--
Ash	0.05	--	--	--

Total Oxygen required = 0.07375 mols.

$$\text{Wt. of oxygen required for 1 kg} = 0.07375 \times 32$$
$$= 2360 \text{ gmf or}$$
$$= 2.36 \text{ kgf} = 23.15 \text{ N}$$

Alternatively,

$$\text{Volume of Oxygen required} = 22.4 \times 0.07375 \text{ lit,}$$
$$= 1.65 \text{ m}^3$$

$$\text{Volume of air} = \frac{1.62 \times 100}{21} = 7.7 \text{ m}^3$$

Volume of air required for 1 kgf = 7.7 m^3

Example

2 : In the above process of combustion, calculate the volume of the exhaust gases and its analysis ?

Consider 1kg. of the Coal

Constituent	Wt. kgf	mols / Kgf	Reaction	Product	Mols of product Kgf
C	0.72	0.06	$C + O_2 \rightarrow CO_2$	CO_2	$1 \times 0.06 = 0.06$
H_2	0.06	0.03	$2H_2 + O_2 \rightarrow 2H_2O$	H_2O	$2 \times 0.03 = 0.06$
H_2O	0.1	0.005	--	H_2O	0.005
N_2	0.01	0.0007	--	N_2	------ 0.0007
S	0.01	0.00031	$S + O_2 \rightarrow SO_2$	SO_2	$1 \times 0.00031 = 0.00031$
					Total 0.096

Total exhaust gases $= 0.099$ mols

Volume $= 0.099 \times 22.4$

$= 2.218\ m^3$

In addition to the above, the nitrogen accompanying the oxygen (in the air)

$= (7.7 - 1.62) = 6.08\ m^3$

Total Volume $= 8.23\ m^3$ / kgf of fuel

Analysis

The exhaust gases can be converted into volumes individually as follows:

Wt. of the fuel - 1kgf.

Constituent	Mol.Wt.	Volume
Carbon dioxide produced	0.06 mols $= 22.4 \times 0.06$	$1.344\ m^3$
Water vapour	0.035 mols $= 22.4 \times 0.035$	$0.784\ m^3$
Sulphur dioxide	0.0003 mols $= 22.4 \times 0.0003$	$0.00672\ m^3$
Nitrogen in the fuel	0.0007 mols $- 22.4 \times 0.0007$	$0.01568\ m^3$
Nitrogen in the air		$6.08\ m^3$
		Total 8.23040 m^3

$$CO_2 = \frac{1.344}{8.23} \times 100 = 16.33\ \%$$

$$H_2O = \frac{0.784}{8.23} \times 100 = 9.526\ \%$$

$$SO_2 = \frac{0.0067}{8.23} \times 100 = 0.08141\ \%$$

$$N_2 - \frac{6.09568}{8.23} \times 100 = 74.06\ \%$$

Example

3. The analysis of a coke oven gas by volume and on moisture- free basis is as follows :

H_2	----	56.00 %
CH_4	----	28.00 %
C_2H_4	----	3.00 %
C_6H_6	----	0.90 %
CO	----	5.4 %
CO_2	----	2.5 %
NH_3	----	1.4 %
N_2	----	2.8 %

Find the carbon in kilograms contained in m^3 of the gas ?

Solution

Let us take 1 m^3 of the gas.

It contains, CH_4 – 0.28 m^3

22.4 m^3 of CH_4 contains – 12 kgf of carbon

1 m^3 of CH_4 contains – $\frac{12}{22.4}$ kgf.

So, 0.28 m^3 contains – $\frac{12}{22.4} \times 0.28$ kgf.

= 0.1501 kgf = 1.472 N

Similarly the gas contains 0.03 Cu.m. of C_2H_4.

22.4 m^3 of C_2H_4 contains – 2 × 12 kgf of Carbon

1m^3 of C_2H_4 contains – $2 \times \frac{12}{22.4}$ kgf.

So, 0.03 m^3 contains – $2 \times \frac{12}{22.4} \times 0.03$ kgf

= 0.03215 kgf = 0.3154 N

Similarly the gas contains 0.009 Cu.m^3 of C_6H_6

22.4 m^3 of C_6H_6 Contains – 6 × 12 kgf of Carbon.

1 m^3 of C_6H_6 contains – $6 \times \frac{12}{22.4}$ kgf.

So, 0.009 m^3 contains – $6 \times \frac{12}{22.4} \times 0.009$ kgf.

= 0.02894 kgf = 0.2839 N

The gas contains	–	5.4 % CO = 0.054 kgf.
22.4 m^3 of CO contains	–	12 kgf of carbon.
1 m^3 of CO contains	–	$\frac{12}{22.4} \times 0.054$ kgf.
	=	0.02894 kgf = 0.2839 N
The gas contains	–	2.5 % CO_2 = 0.025 m^3
22.4 m^3 of CO_2 contains	–	12 kgf Carbon.
1 m^3 of CO_2 contains	–	$\frac{12}{22.4} \times 0.025$ kg
	=	0.01334 kgf = 0.1309 N

Total Carbon	= Carbon in CH_4	–	0.1501
	Carbon in C_2H_4	–	0.0321
	Carbon in C_6H_6	–	0.0289
	Carbon in CO	–	0.0289
	Carbon in CO_2	–	0.0133
			0.2533 kgf = 2.4849 N

Alternatively, we can proceed to solve the same by adding the carbon percentages of all the carbon bearing gases, as follows :

CH_4	–	0.28 × 1	=	0.28 m^3
C_2H_4	–	0.03 × 2	=	0.06 m^3
C_6H_6	–	0.009 × 6	=	0.054 m^3
CO	–	0.054 × 1	=	0.054 m^3
CO_2	–	0.025 × 1	=	0.025 m^3
Total				**0.473 m^3**

$$0.473 \times \frac{12}{22.4} = 0.473 \times 0.536$$

$$= \mathbf{0.254\ kgf.} \approx \mathbf{2.511\ N}$$

Example

4. If the above gas has resulted from a coal of the following analysis, find the volume of gas produced per metric ton of coal ?

Coal Analysis			Coke Analysis		
C	-	79.00%	C	-	91.0%
H	-	7.00%	H	-	1.2%
O	-	6.4%	O	-	0.6%
N	-	1.4	N	-	0.4%
S	-	1.0	S	-	0.8%
Ash	-	3.2	Ash	-	5.0%
H_2O	-	2.0			

Solution :

$$\text{Wt. of ash in 1000 kg. Coal} = \frac{3.2}{100} \times 1000 = 32 \text{ kgf.}$$

$$\text{Wt. of ash in coke} = \frac{5}{100} \times \text{wt. of Coke} = 32 \text{ kgf.}$$

$$\text{(Wt. of Coke} = \frac{32 \times 100}{5} = 640 \text{ kgf / Tonne.)}$$

Thus 640 kgs. of coke contains 0.91 × 640 = 582.4 kgf. C.

The carbon give in the gas and Tar = 790 – 582.4

Total Carbon amount **207.6**

Assume the Carbon going into the gas is 2/3 of the total Carbon available.

$$\text{The C going in the gas} = 207.6 \times \frac{2}{3}$$

$$= 138 \text{ kgf.}$$

0.254 kgf of C yields – 1 m^3 CO gas

$$\text{For 138 kgf of carbon, the gas} = \frac{1}{0.254} \times 138 = 543.3 \text{ m}^3.$$

Example

5. The coal used in a gas producer analyses as follows :

C	-	74.3
H	-	6.7
O	-	8.6
N	-	1.4
S	-	1.7
H_2O	-	1.6
Ash	-	5.7

The producer is supplied with 8 m^3 of air and 1 kg of steam. It is established that only 85% of the steam is decomposed. The air supplied carries 15 mm. of water vapour. The ashes of the producer discharge contain an equivalent of 2.5% of coal. Of the 74.3% Carbon in the coal 60% represents fixed (non-volatile) carbon and the remainder 14.3% in contained in the volatile matter which may be assumed to enter the gases as CH_4. Of the carbon burned by air, $1/5^{th}$ goes to CO_2 and $4/5^{th}$ to CO.

Find

1. The percentage of fixed carbon burned by air and steam.
2. Volume of gas produced per kg. of coal.
3. Percentage composition of the gas.
4. Percentage of heat generated by oxidation of carbon which is absorbed by steam decomposition.

Solution :

1. The air is moist with 15 mm Hg water vapour / 8 m^3

Every 8 m^3 of air contains $\frac{15}{760} \times 8 = \frac{120}{760} = \frac{12}{76}$

$= 0.158$ m^3 of water.

Assume this also decomposes alongwith the steam.

0.158 m^3 of water vapour weighs $0.158 \times \frac{18}{22.4}$ kgf

$= 0.127$ kgf.

Thus the air + steam mixture consists of

$8.000 - .158 = 7.842$ m^3 of air (dry)

7.842 and 0.127 kgf. of steam.

Steam decomposed $= 85\%$

$= 0.127 \times 0.85$

$= 0.096$ kgf.

Oxygen in the air $= 7.842 \times 0.21$

$= 1.65$ m^3

This Oxygen reduces Carbon in the following fashion,

CO_2 - 1/5 th $C + O_2 \rightarrow CO_2$

CO - 4/5th $2C + O_2 \rightarrow 2CO$

$C \rightarrow CO$ reaction should be multiplied by 2 so that if the two reactions are added, the C in $C \rightarrow CO$ reaction will be 24 times to that of C in $C \rightarrow CO_2$ reaction.

$$C + O_2 \rightarrow CO_2$$
$$4C + 2O_2 \rightarrow 4CO$$
$$5C + 3O_2 \rightarrow CO_2 + 4CO$$

This reaction represents the combustion of Carbon in the particular case.

We have 1.65 m^3 of O_2 available.

The wt. of C oxidised $= 1.65 \times \frac{60}{3 \times 22.4}$

$= 1.47$ kgf.

Carbon oxidation by steam is represented by the reaction

$$C + H_2O \rightarrow CO + H_2$$

The H_2O oxidising = 0.96.

C reacting with 0.096 kg. of H_2O

$$= \frac{0.096 \times 12}{18} = 0.064 \text{ kgf.}$$

Thus the air/steam mixture burns 1.47 kg. C (by air) and 0.64 kgf. C (by steam).

Proportions $1.47 + 0.064 = 1.534$ kgf

C Burned by air $= \frac{1.47}{1.534} \times 100 = 95.83\ \%$

C Burned by steam $= \frac{0.064}{1.534} \times 100 = 4.17\ \%$ (2) and (3)

2% Carbon is lost in the ashes

So, Net Carbon oxidised = 60 – 2 = 58%

Or 0.58 kg. of C / kgf. of coal.

There is 0.086 kg. of oxygen in the coal which also takes part in the oxidation. It can be assumed that this oxygen also oxidases carbon in the same 4 :1 ratio as the oxygen of the air. Sulphur is also oxidised by the oxygen.

Sulphur present in 1kgf. of coal = 0.017 kgf.

0.017 kg. of S requires $0.017 \times \frac{32}{32}\ O_2$

$= 0.017$ kgf.

This oxygen is derived from the inherent oxygen.

Balance O_2 available = 0.086 – 0.017 = 0.069 kgf.

0.069 kg. of oxygen oxidies carbon in the above cited 4 : 1 ratio to CO and CO_2

$$= 0.069 \times \frac{60}{96} = 0.043 \text{ kgf. of C}$$

C left for the oxidation by air and steam

$= 0.58 - 0.043 = 0.537$ kgf.

The air burns 69.67% of C

So, 0.537 × 0.6967

$= 0.347$ kgf. C

Steam burns = 0.19 kgf. C

The air reaction states,

$$5C + 3O_2 \rightarrow CO_2 + 4CO$$

0.347 kgf of C requires $0.347 \times \frac{3 \times 22.4}{60}$ m^3 of O_2

$= 0.3886\ m^3$ of O_2

This forms $1/3 \times 0.3886 = 0.1295\ m^3$ of CO_2

Also, $4 \times 0.1295 = 0.5180\ m^3$ of CO

The steam reaction states,

$$C + H_2O \rightarrow CO + H_2$$

0.19 kgf. of C requires$= 0.19 \times \frac{22.4}{12}$

$= 0.354\ m^3$ of steam

This forms $0.354\ m^3$ of CO

$0.354\ m^3$ of H_2

Undecomposed steam = 15% of the blown - in

$= 0.15 \times 0.354 = 0.05295\ m^3$

$= 0.053\ m^3$

N_2 accompanying the blast $= 0.3886 \times 79/21 = 1.462\ m^3$

N_2 from coal $= 0.014 \times \frac{22.4}{28} = 0.0112\ m^3$

H_2O from coal $= 0.016 \times \frac{22.4}{18} = 0.02\ m^3$

SO_2 formed $= 0.017 \times \frac{22.4}{32} = 0.012\ m^3$

CH_4 formed $= 0.143 \times \frac{22.4}{12} = 0.267\ m^3$

$0.267\ m^3$ of CH_4 contains $0.534\ m^3$ Hydrogen.

The coal contains 0.067 kgf. of hydrogen or $0.067 \times \frac{22.4}{2}$

$= 0.7504\ m^3$

Though $0.7504 - 0.534 = 0.2164\ m^3$ hydrogen enters the gas as free hydrogen

Thus the producer gas contains.

CO	-	0.5180 + 0.354	$= 0.8720\ m^3$
CO_2	-	0.1295	$= 0.1295\ m^3$
H_2	-	0.354 + 0.2164	$= 0.5704\ m^3$
CH_4	-	0.267	$= 0.267\ m^3$

H_2O	-	$0.02 + 0.053$	$= 0.073\ m^3$
SO_2	-	0.012	$= 0.012\ m^3$
N_2	-	$0.0112 + 1.462$	$= 1.4734\ m^3$
		Total	$= 3.3973\ m^3$
			$= 3.4\ m^3$.

4. Heat generated by the reaction $C \rightarrow CO_2 = \frac{12}{22.4} \times 0.13 \times \frac{8100}{1000}$

$= 0.564$ k Cals.

Heat generated by the reaction $C \rightarrow CO = \frac{12}{22.4} \times 0.871 \times 2430$

$= 1.132$ k Cals.

Heat generated from the burning of Carbon = 1.926 k Cals.

Heat absorbed by the steam decomposition $= 0.353 \times \frac{18}{22.4} \times 3210$

$= 0.91$ k Cals.

$\therefore$ % heat generated $= \frac{1.128}{1.926} \times 100 = 47.28\%$

Example

7. A furnace is fired with a fuel oil of the following composition :

Carbon	-	82.4%
Hydrogen	-	11.6%
Sulphur	-	0.9%
Oxygen	-	4.1%

Air used is 10% in excess of the theoretical requirements

Find (i) the calorific value of the oil using Dulong's formula

(ii) the volume of air used per kg. of the oil.

(iii) percentage of free oxygen in the products of combustion. and

(iv) the temperature developed in the furnace.

Solution :

(i) The calorific value $= 8100\ C + 34000\ (H - \frac{0}{8}) + 2200\ S - 586\ (9H + W)$

$$= 8100 \times 0.824 + 34000\ (0.116 - \frac{0.041}{8}) + 2200 \times 0.009$$
$$- 586\ (9 \times 0.116 + 0)$$

$= 6674 + 3774 + 19.8 - 612.8 = 9855$ Cal/kgf

$= 9.855$ k.cals / kg.

(ii) 1 kg. oil sample.

Constituent	wt.in kg	mols/kg	reaction	mols of O_2 required
C	0.824	$\frac{0.824}{12} = 0.0687$	$C + O_2 \rightarrow CO_2$	$1 \times 0.0687 = 0.0687$
H_2	0.116	$\frac{0.116}{2} = 0.058$	$2H_2 + O_2 \rightarrow 2H_2O$	$1/2 \times 0.058 = 0.029$
S	0.009	$\frac{0.009}{32} = 0.0003$	$S + O_2 \rightarrow SO_2$	$1 \times 0.0003 = 0.0003$
O	0.041	$\frac{0.041}{32} = 0.001281$		Inherently available–0.0013

Total O_2 requirement = 0.0957

Vol. of O_2 required (theoretical) $= 22.4 \times 0.0957$

$$\text{Vol. of air (theoretical)} = \frac{22.4 \times 0.0957}{0.21} \text{ m}^3$$

$= 10.208 \text{ m}^3$

with 10% excess $= 1.1 \times 10.208$

$= 11.2288 \text{ m}^3$

Total air supplied $= 11.2288 \text{ m}^3$ / kgf. of fuel.

(iii) Oxygen in the 10% excess air $= 11.2288 \times 0.21$

$= 2.358 \text{ m}^3$

Nitrogen in the 10% excess air $= 11.2288 \times 0.79$

$= 8.8708 \text{ m}^3$

Constituent	Product formed in the exhaust gases.	kg. mols	m^3
C	CO_2	0.0687	$0.0687 \times 22.4 = 1.539$
H_2	H_2O	0.058	$0.058 \times 22.4 = 1.299$
S	SO_2	0.0003	$0.0003 \times 22.4 = 0.0067$
O_2	O_2		$= 0.021$
N_2	N_2		$= 0.867$

$$\%O_2 = \frac{0.021}{3.733} \times 100$$
$$= 0.57$$

(iv) To calculate the temperature developed during the combustion, we should strike the heat balance. Thus, calorific value of the fuel + sensible heat in the fuel + sensible heat in the air = Vol. of the exhaust gases × sp. ht. × temp.

In this case, the fuel and the air are not preheated.

So, the calorific value of the fuel = the quantity of the heat in the exhaust gases.

The heat in the exhaust gases = the sum of the heats of the constituents.

Thus, the sensible heat in

$$CO_2 = 1.539\ (0.406 + 0.00009\ t)\ t$$
$$= 0.6247\ t + 0.00013861\ t^2$$

the sensible heat in

$$H_2O = 1.299\ (0.373 + 0.0005\ t)\ t$$
$$= 0.4846\ t + 0.0006495\ t^2$$

the sensible heat in

$$SO_2 = 0.0067\ (0.406 + 0.00009\ t)\ t$$
$$= 0.000272\ t + 0.000000603\ t^2$$

the sensible heat in

$$O_2 = 0.2104\ (0.302 + 0.000022\ t)\ t$$
$$= 0.06384\ t + 0.000004208\ t^2$$

the sensible heat in

$$N_2 = 0.867\ (0.302 + 0.000022\ t)\ t$$
$$= 0.261834\ t + 0.000019074\ t^2$$

(where t is the temp. developed)

Total sensible heat $= 1.435\ t + 0.000814\ t^2$

$= 9,\ 855$ Cals.

Solving the equation for t, we get

$$t = 2729\ ^{o}C$$

14 Nuclear Fuels

Dalton's atomic theory, enunciated a few centuries ago, had defined atom as the ultimate indivisible constituent of matter. This concept of the atom stands out even today but for the modification of the term indivisible as not easily divisible. The atom had attracted the attention of modern science and its structure, well established during the last century.

Nuclear energy is the energy directly released from the nucleus of the atom. Conversion of nuclear mass into energy is consistent with mass-energy equivalence formula $e = mc^2$ in which e is the energy released, m is the mass defect and c is speed of light in vacuum (a physical constant). Release of nuclear energy occurs by any of the three exoenergetic (exothermic) processes.

(i) **Radioactive Decay:** Here, a neutron or proton in the radio-active nucleus spontaneously decays by emitting either particles gamma rays, electromagnetic radiation or neutrinos or all of them.

(ii) **Fusion:** Here, two atomic nuclei fuse together to form a heavlier nucleus and

(iii) **Fission:** Breaking of a heavy nucleus into two (rarely three) lighter nuclei

Present day nuclear power production is by fission.

This had led to the exploration of the possibility of separating the basic constituents of atom and in 1939 scientists were successful in breaking up the nucleus of the atom. The breaking up or splitting of the atom yielded neutrons of tremendous speeds and to describe the process, the word fission is employed. Fig.14.1 gives a schematic diagram of fission reaction.

$${}_{92}U^{235} + {}_{0}N^{1} = {}_{38}Sr^{90} + {}_{54}Xe^{144} + 2{}_{0}N^{1} + \gamma$$

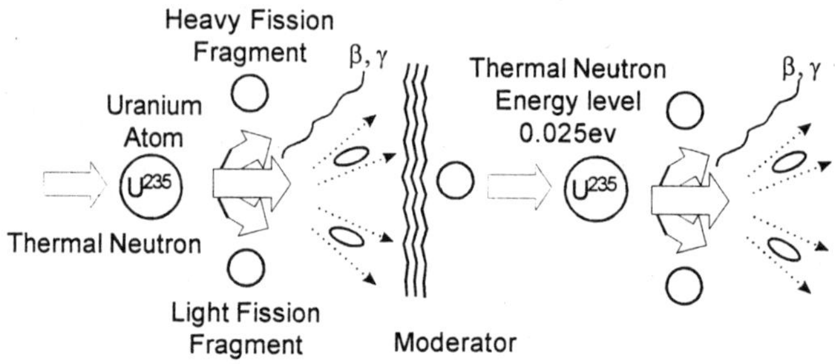

Fig. 14.1 Fission reaction.

Unfortunately, the first use this tremendous energy source put to, was for destruction. Two atom bombs were dropped in Japan on the towns of Hiroshima and Nagasaki in 1944 destroying them completely.

The II world war was won but the entire humanity raised their eye brows at the brutal act. Questions as to why this terrific energy source could not be made proper use of, were raised and research was directed in that aspect. By the year 1950, it was established that the fission of the nucleus can be controlled and the rate of fission slowed down so as to make it a chain reaction and the enormous heat output can be utilized for power generation. This is the essence of utilization of nuclear power for peaceful purposes.

After our country became a sovereign republic in 1950 our national leaders have enunciated the policy of using nuclear energy for peaceful purposes only and the Atomic Energy Commission was established to serve this purpose. It got itself renamed after the first chairman, Homi J. Bhabha and is at present known as Bhabha Atomic Research Centre. Its activities are designed and research about the various nuclear projects and their peaceful applications in various fields like grain storage, medicine etc., in addition to power generation.

Experimental nuclear reactors were built by the center for research and for pilot plant study. The first experimental reactor built by BARC was Apsara which went critical (started to generate power) in 1956. Subsequently four more reactors were built, of different power capacities. The idea behind was developing our own nuclear technology in regard to various aspects of nuclear power. A schematic flow diagram of a boiling water reactor at Tarapur (1969) is shown in Fig.14.2.

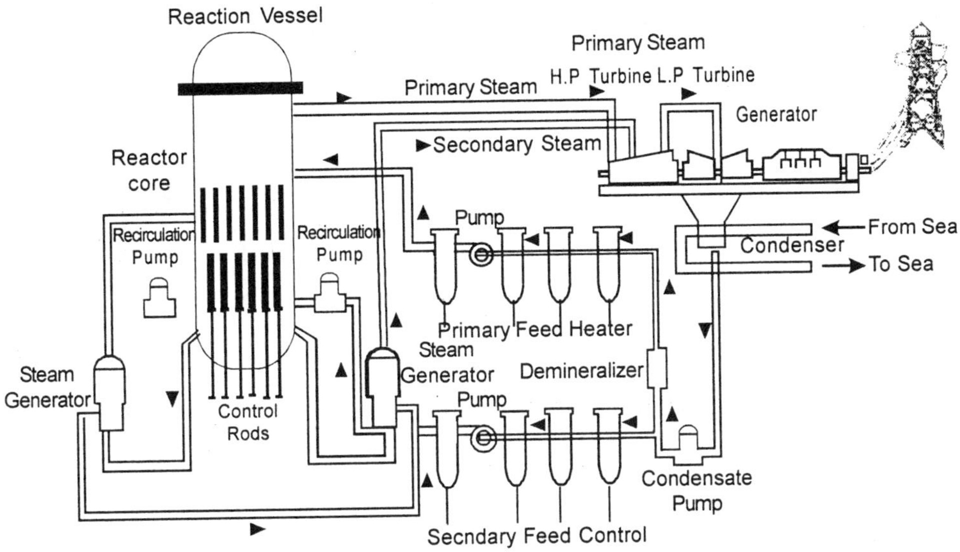

Fig. 14.2 Schematic flow diagram of boiling water reactor Tarapur atomic power station.

We are successful in this aspect and installed more than a dozen nuclear power plants. We are on the threshold of second generation technology, involving use of Plutonium as fuel and liquid sodium as coolant. A couple of nuclear power plants based on this technology are coming up under the aegis of a new company named BHAVANI.

The Nuclear Reactor

Radioactive metals like Uranium are fissible. Uranium occurs as different isotopes with differing numbers of neutrons in its nucleus. When U_{235} is fissioned, U_{233} is formed and a great quantity of energy is released. The energy released is due to the liberation of neutrons of superlative speeds. The neutrons are slowed down by using other materials and the process is called moderation. The moderator employed may be solid, liquid or a gas. The first moderator used was graphite. Subsequent research has established that liquid moderation is more efficient. Ordinary water, heavy water, beryllium and sodium are all successfully used as moderators.

The element whose nucleus is split (fissioned) is called the 'fuel'. Uranium either enriched (to be of the grade of U_{235}) or naturally occurring, can be used as fuel. Besides, thorium is also quite useful as a nuclear fuel.

The planned nuclear power production of our country is shown in the Fig 14.3

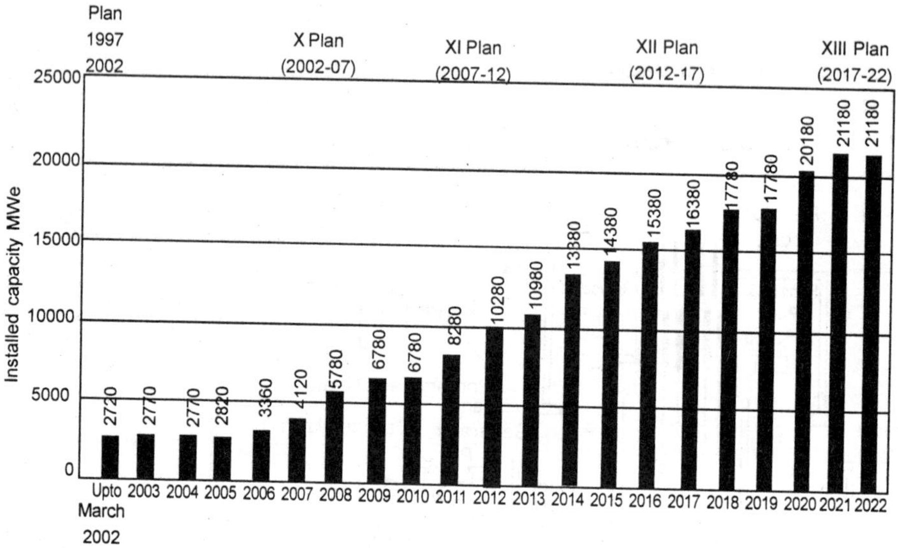

Fig. 14.3 Nuclear power capacity addition planning of Dept. of Atomic Energy.

Nuclear Reactor Fuel

Naturally occurring uranium ore is powdered and is made into cakes. These cakes are called yellow cakes owing to their appearance. The yellow cake is further treated and brought to the required purity to be able to be used as 'fuel' in the reactor.

Fig. 14.4 FBTR fuel subassemblies with cut sections, and PHWR fule assemblies manufactured at Nuclear Fuel Complex.

Reactor is charged with the nuclear fuel as specially standardized (sized and shaped) rods, called fuel elements. Nuclear Fuel Complex at Hyderabad was set up for industrial scale manufacture of nuclear fuel assemblies and zircaloy structural components for power reactors. Zircaloy-4 clad natural and depleted uranium oxide and thoria bundles for pressurized heavy water reactors. Zircaloy-2 clad enriched uranium oxide fuels for boiling water reactors and stainless steel clad thorium and depleted uranium oxide blanket sub assemblies for liquid metal cooled fast breeder reactors. NFC also manufactures zirconium alloy structural components for the above reactors.

Heavy Water

As heavy water is used as moderator and coolant in the pressurized heavy water reactor, seven heavy water manufacturing units are set up in our country. Their performance and safety record has been excellent. Our heavy water production not only caters to domestic requirements, but also exports sometimes.

Indian Nuclear Power Programme

At the time of our Independence in 1947, the total installed generation capacity of electricity was 1363 MW. It rose to 30214 MW by the year 1980-81, to 60086 MW in 1990-91 and 1387390 MW by 2002-03. Thus, the average growth was 8.14% per annum. In spite of such impressive growth, there was an average electricity shortage of 7.8% and peak power demand shortage of 13%. By 2002-03 the shortage has increased to 10% and 15% respectively. This is owing to the rapid industrialization and of course more demand by the domestic consumer sector; also, the increase in population of the country.

The electricity generation in the year 2002-03 was about 532 billion kWH and 104 billion kWH from captive power plants. The pictogram illustrates projected installed capacity of nuclear power generation (Fig. 14.3) and total projected electricity generation. It will be clearly noted that the share of the nuclear power in the total power generation of the country is increasing progressively.

India has five major nuclear power plants besides the experimental reactors at the BARC, Mumbai. Two 200 MW (total power: 400 MW) are operating at Tarapur also near Mumbai. These are employing enriched uranium oxides as the fuel and boiling water as the moderator (BWR -Boiling Water Reactors).

However, the Indian nuclear programmers have chosen technology wherein natural uranium oxide containing 0.07% of U_{235} as fuel and heavy water as coolant. This .nology, referred to as CANDO technology, was obtained from Canada under a mutual pact. Two units each of 200 MW capacity are in operation at Ranapratapsagar (Rajasthan), Kalpakkam (Tamil Nadu), Narora (Uttar Pradesh) and Kakrapara (Gujarat). Another set of such reactors is installed at Kaiga (Karnataka). All these reactors are the fruits of indigenous development over the aforesaid CANDO technology.

There are certain difficulties in our nuclear fuel supply. Our natural resources of Uranium metal are about 30,000 tons. This is meager figure if we have to fuel all our nuclear reactors by Uranium fuel elements. There are plans to substitute the natural uranium with thorium whose Indian reserves are enormous. Further, during use thorium gets converted into U_{233} which itself continues the fission process. U_{233} can also be used by itself. Plans are afoot towards the development of this approach.

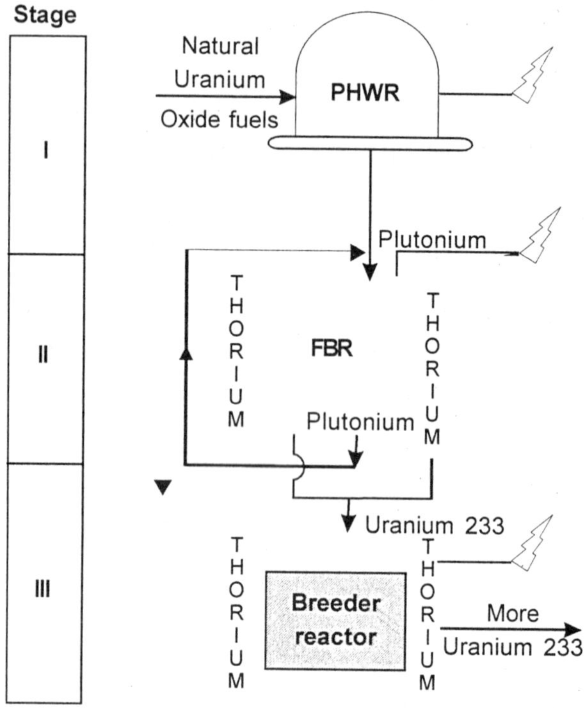

Fig. 14.5 India's nuclear strategy.

The three stage nuclear power programme Fig. 14.5 envisages natural uranium fuelled Pressurised Heavy Water Reactors (PHWRs) in the first stage, Fast Breeder Reactors (FBRs) in the second stage utilizing plutonium based fuel and Breeder Reactors for utilization of thorium in third stage. PHWRs are ideal for first stage on account of higher burn-up and being more efficient producer of plutonium required for the second stage. PHWRs are natural uranium fuelled, heavy water cooled and moderated reactors with on line fuelling. The spent fuel from PHWRs of the first stage will yield plutonium - 239, which will be used as fuel in FBRs in the second stage.

In FBRs, the major proportion of uranium i.e., uranium - 238 will be converted into plutonium-239. Thus in addition of generation of electricity, more plutonium will be generated. By such re-cycling in second stage, significant inventory of plutonium can be generated. Thorium as a blanket material in the second stage will also generate uranium-233.

The third stage reactor system will use uranium-233 as fuel in thorium-232-uranium-233 cycle, providing significantly large energy potential for electricity generation through the use of nuclear resources.

India's long term nuclear power programme is based on ultimately tapping of vast indigenous thorium resources for electricity generation.

BARC's Canadian Indian reactor is illustrated is Fig.14.6 (the entire structure). A schematic diagram of its cross section is shown in Fig.14.7 and a plan of the reactor in Fig.14.8. These figures will give the reader an idea of the principles of functioning.

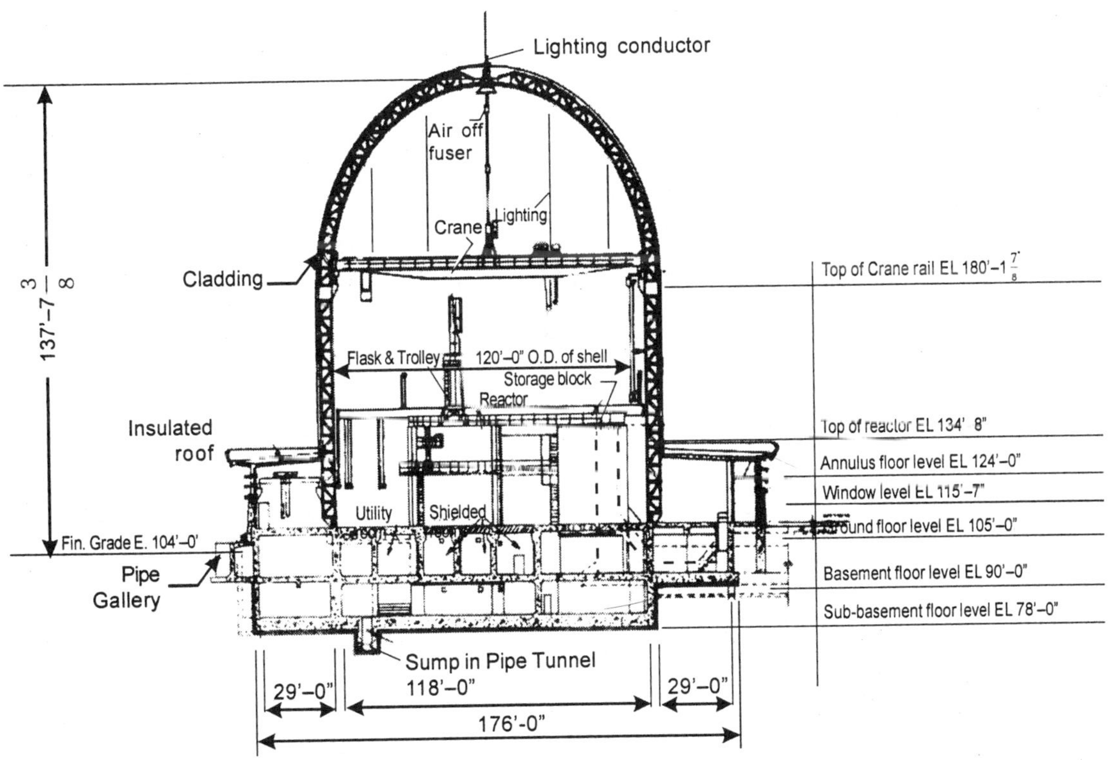

Fig. 14.6 CIR clading reactor hall and annulus – cross section.

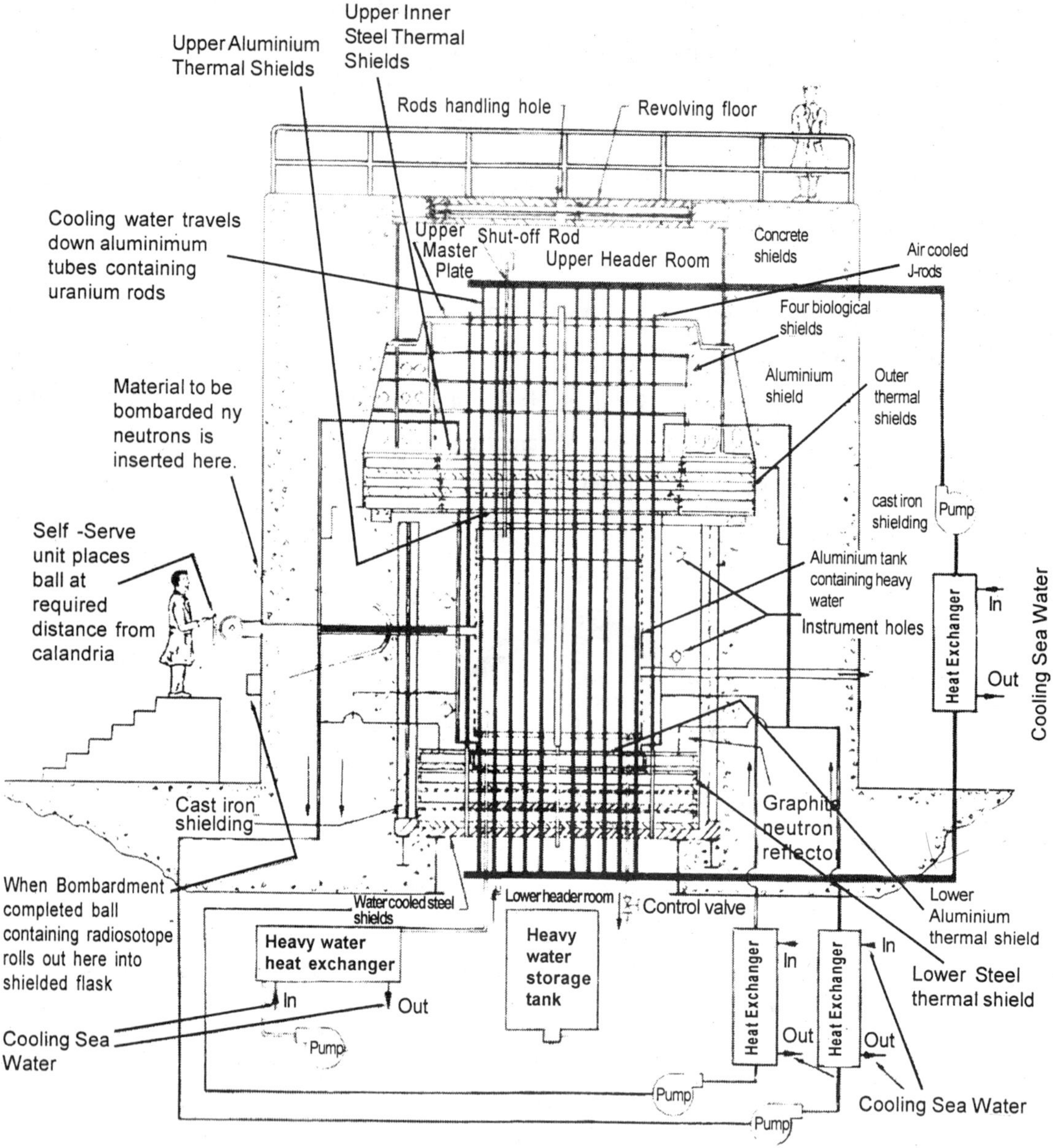

Fig. 14.7 *CIR* A schematic diagram.

Reactor is the name given to the container in which the fission of the nuclear fuel atoms takes place. It is housed in a pressure tight shell called 'rotunda'. The shell is fabricated by welding thick steel sheet with an operating pressure tolerance of 300%. The rotunda, the fuel elements (Uranium), moderator, reflector, thermal and biological shields are housed in a large structure called Calandria. Calandria is essentially the reactor structure and is made of aluminium.

Calandria also contains heavy water which acts as the moderator. Its purpose is to slow-down the fast neutrons emitted by Uranium 235 atoms undergoing fission. Moderation is done to that extent so that the reaction chain is just maintained. The neutrons liberated due to the fission travel with speeds of the order of 15000 km/s. These high speeds are brought down to about 1.5 km/s. by moderation.

Power in a reactor is a direct measure of the number of Uranium atoms splitting per second and it appears as heat. This heat is removed from the core to prevent unduly high temperatures developing near the actual working components. The reactor power (output) is controlled by varying the level of heavy water in the calandria. The reactor is shut down by inserting neutron absorbing shut off rods into the reactor rapidly. Simultaneously, the heavy water is also dumped into the heavy water storage tanks underneath.

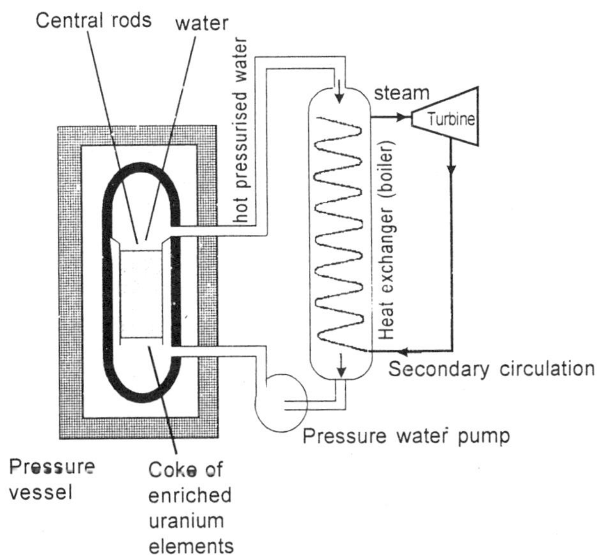

Fig. 14.8 Pressurised water reactors

The heat released on account of fission is taken up by the cooling water, which boils to steam. Steam is directed to the steam turbines for power generation (Fig. 14.9). Schematically show the steam generation and its feeding to the turbine in the case of pressurised water reactor and boiling water reactor. The heat output from the reactor is by insertion or withdrawl of neutron absorbing control rods. The neutron flux in the control rods determines the rate of fission chain reaction. Normal measurements are made of the temperatures of the fuel elements, the moderator, the coolant, and of the steam besides the rate of flow of the coolant.

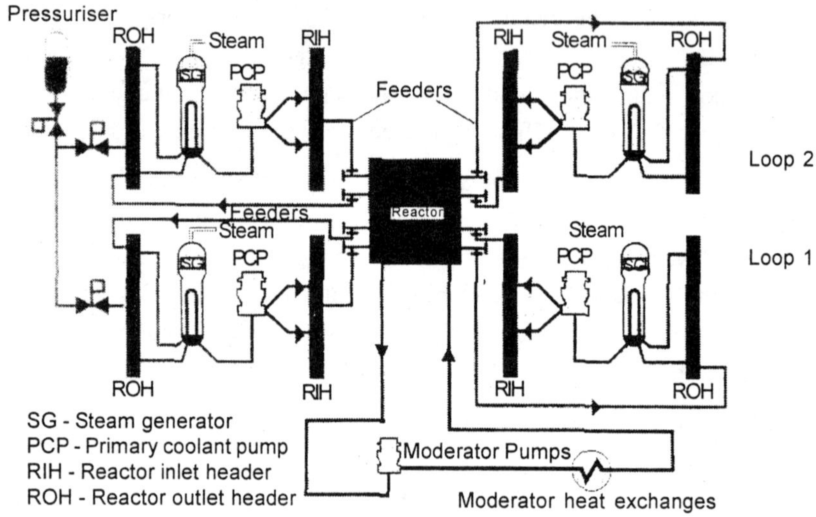

Fig. 14.9 Simplified flow diagram of PHWR.

Nuclear Waste

The safe storage and disposal of nuclear waste is a big challenge. Most important waste from nuclear power plants is spent as fuel. A large nuclear reactor produces about 3 cu. meters of spent fuel per year, that is, about 25-30 tons. It consists of unconverted uranium and significant qualities of actinides plutonium curium. About 3% of these are fission products and are responsible for the long-term radioactivity.

Spent fuel is highly radioactive and needs to be handled with great care. Though spent fuel becomes less radioactive after 40 years, the radio-active radiation flux is 99.99% low, yet its radiation is dangerous.

Spent fuel rods are stored in shielded basins of water called spent fuel pools, which are generally located on site. Water provides a shielding from radioactivity besides cooling the still decaying fission products. After a few decades some on-site storage involves moving the now cooler, less radioactive fuel to a dry-storage facility or dry cask storage, where the fuel is stored in steel and concrete containers until its radioactivity decreases naturally ("decays") to levels safe enough for other processing. This interim stage spans years or decades, depending on the type of fuel. "Today we stock containers of waste because currently scientists don't know how to reduce or eliminate the toxicity, but may be in 100 years, they may be able to do".

Reprocessing

Reprocessing can potentially recover up to 95% of the remaining uranium and plutonium in spent nuclear fuel, putting it into new mixed oxide fuel. This would produce a reduction in long term radioactivity within the remaining waste, since these are largely short-lived fission products, and reduces its volume by over 90%. Reprocessing of civilian fuel from power reactors is currently done on a large scale in Britian, France and (formerly) Russia, will be in China and perhaps in India, and is being done on an expanding scale in Japan. The full potential of reprocessing has not been achieved because it requires breeder reactors, which are not yet commercially available.

Reliability

Sun, wind, tides and waves cannot be controlled to provide directly either continuous base-load power, or peak-load power when it is needed. In practical terms they are therefore limited to some 10-20% of the capacity of an electricity grid, and cannot directly be applied as economic substitutes for coal or nuclear power, however important they may become in particular areas with favourable conditions.

Safety

The topic of nuclar safety covers

- the research and testing of the possible incidents/events at a nuclear power plant,
- what equipment and actions are designed to prevent those incidents/events from having serious consequences,
- the calculation of the probabilities of multiple systems and/or actions failing thus allowing serious consequences,
- the evaluation of the worst-possible timing and scope of those consequences (the worst-possible (in extreme) cases being a release of radiation),
- the actions taken to protect the public during a release of radiation,
- the training and rehearsals performed to ensure readiness in case an incident/event accident occurs.

15 Other Energy Resources

Presently, 80 percent of the world energy demand is met by the fossil fuels. According to reliable estimates, the production of world petroleum production will peak sometime during 1991-2020 and will start to decline. The position of natural gas is a bit better. The lower line shows coal production, if it is used as solid fuel. The curve in the middle is the expected production of fluid fuels, petroleum and natural gas. It can be seen that the world fluid fuel production will reach its peak around the year 2010 and then start to decline. The top curve gives the total fossil fuel estimates if synthetic gas and gasolene are produced from coal. In this case, the production rises until the year 2030 and then it starts to decrease.

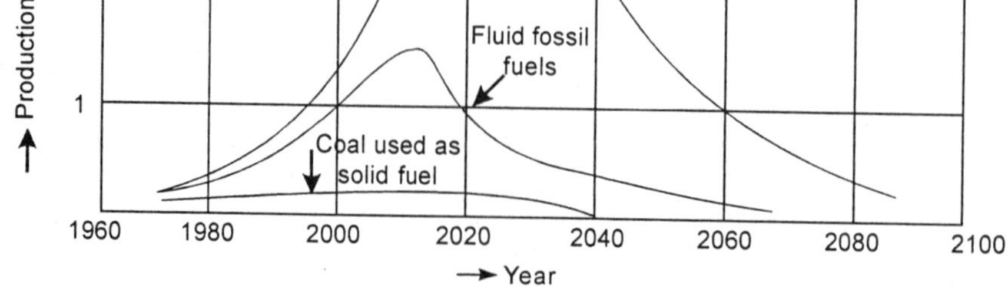

Fig. 15.1 Expected availability of fossil fuels.

As all the fossil fuels, whether solid, liquid or gaseous, contain combustible substances like carbon, hydrogen, nitrogen and sulphur and the products of combustion will be their oxides. Thus, the exhausts from coal-fired furnaces or automobiles or power stations contain CO_2, CO, SO_2, NO_X and of course H_2O. Water is of no consequence in terms of the harmful effects to the atmosphere. The oxides of carbon, sulphur and nitrogen however will accumulate in the atmosphere. Scientific data given by environmentalists has put this figure at 25 billion tons for the year 1989. This gigantic volume as already sent signals of doom on the humanity, wild life and acqueous life. Rain water which was containing acids, called acids rains, are reported from many parts of the world. Some lakes in United States, Canada and Sweden having experienced acid rains, are now devoid of fish and fauna. Studies indicate that the acid levels in the upper 60 meter layer of the oceans will continuously, increase to such an extent that by the year 2035, even the oceans will not be a hospitable environment for the fish and marine plants. Herein, the point should not be missed – acid rains do not fall only on lakes and oceans. The acid rains (fall or) attack on farms and buildings will ultimately lead to damage to crops on one hand and corrosion to buildings, on the other. Historical monuments suffering such an attack will be horrifying – they may not be amenable for even repair.

The cost of the damage as it is put - cost for repair, redress etc., due to the pollution hazard was calculated by an environmentalist in 1972 as $ 1.00 per gallon of gasolene consumed. Today, it may amount to $ 5.00 per gallon - roughly Rs. 45/- per litre of gasolene used by the mankind.

In addition to the above phenomenon of the dangers due to the products of combustion of gasolene, the myriad chemicals manufactured by the chemical industry from petroleum contain carbon, chlorine, fluorine etc., commonly referred to as Chlorofluorocarbons (CFCs). These chemicals, after use, escape into the atmosphere. They accumulate in the upper stratosphere and finally react with the ozone layer that protects the earth from the ultraviolet radiation from Sun. In this damage causing phenomenon, chlorine is the worst culprit. Already gaping holes of the size of united states and depth of Mount Everest are observed on the ozone layers over arctic and antarctic. The Montreal Protocol – the first international pact signed in 1987 by 92 Countries, declared to protect the ozone layer. In the absence of ozone layer or permanent damage to it, the ultraviolet radiation reaching the earth will cause skin cancer, cataracts and infectious diseases, besides the regular global warming.

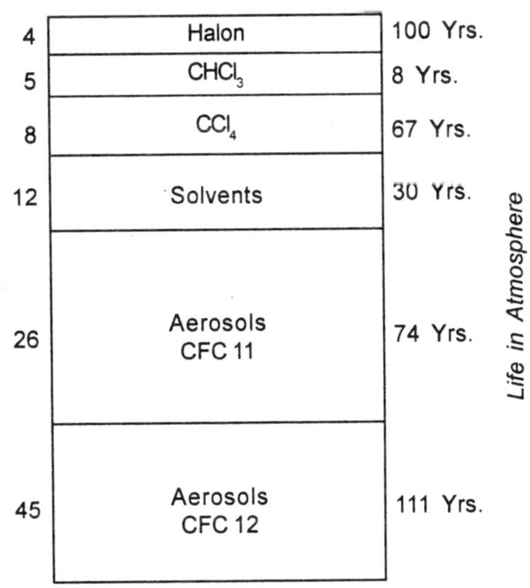

Fig. 15.2 Ozone depletion in the stratoshere.

The CFCs accumulation in the upper atmosphere is caused mostly by the emissions from the advanced countries. Fig. (15.3) pictorially depicts the chemicals effecting the ozone layers, their life in the upper atmospheres, Fig. 15.3 depicts the contribution of different regions of the world. It is obvious from the figures that the major culprits to this pollution are the so-called developed countries. The destruction of the environment as described above, in a nutshell, destroys the greenery on the earth and hence termed as 'Green House' effect.

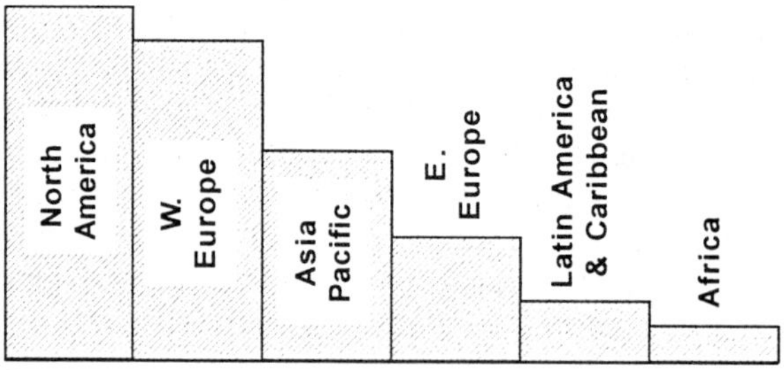

Fig. 15.3 Worldwide pollution contributors.

It is however, a matter of solace for the mankind that the developed nations numbering eleven, were forced to agree to progressively cut their production of chemicals of the family of Hydrochloroflurocarbons by 50% by 1997 and totally eliminate them by the turn of the century. Not only it was done, but the so-called developed countries are, even today, fighting against the implementation of the pact. A fund was also set up under the auspices of the U.N. to finance the elimination of the CFCs in the third world as well as technologies for alternatives.

Thus, the likely depletion of the fossil fuels, petroleum, natural gas and coal during the next century is a boon to the humanity. But the planet needs energy for its people to keep themselves happy comfortable and industrial. The Calorific values of petrol (gasolene) and ethyl alcohol compare well. Ethyl alcohol is a ready substitute for petrol. Brazil had switched to ethyl alcohol automobiles. There, the cultivation of sugarcane, is in fact, primarily for the manufacture of ethyl alcohol from molasses and the sugar is treated as by product. Sugarcane is a 10 month crop and thus the supply of motor fuel will be by agriculture.

Other forms of energy are also available in plenty for harnessing as,

1. Solar energy,
2. Wind energy,
3. Geo-thermal energy,
4. Ocean thermal energy,
5. Energy from organic wastes,
6. Hydrogen energy, and
7. Nuclear energy.

All the seven forms listed above, are nature's boon and inexhaustible. Hydrogen energy is recycling in nature – water is the source and the product formed after use of hydrogen as fuel. Above all no pollution. These different forms of energy sources and their utilisation are discussed briefly hereunder.

Table 15.1 Estimated potential and installed capacity of major renewable energy technologies in India.

Technology	Potential	Cumulative installation up to	
		March 1993	**April 2000***
Family-size biogas plants	12 million	1.76 million	3.02 million
Improved cookstoves	120 million	14.5 million	32 million
Solar	20 MW/km^2		
Solar thermal			
Solar hot water systems (m^2)		0.25 million	0.5 million
Solar cookers		0.29 million	0.485 million
Solar Photovoltaics			
Water pumps		756	3371
Power units		410 kW_p	1920 kW_p
Community lights and street lights		29,972	40,000
Home systems		14,594	1,00,000
Lanterns		—	2,50,000
Biomass	17000 MW		
Biomass Gasifier		—	34.36 MW
Bagasse cogeneration	3500 MW	—	222 MW
Windfarms	20000 MW	53 MW	1167 MW
Mini-Micro hydel	10000 MW	93 MW	217 MW
Waste to energy	1700 MW_e	—	15.21 MW_e

* provisional

Source : **Ministry of Non-Conventional Energy Sources,** Government of India

Importance to India

The average solar energy received in our country (India) is 0.75 kw per square meter of the total area of 3.29 million sq. km., nearly 40% is arid and semi-arid. Thus the solar intensity in these regions is above average for more than 3/4th of the year. Thus, we have an enormous potential for harnessing solar energy taking into account 20% power conversion efficiency and assuming a 0.1 per cent surface area utilisation – a staggering 5×10^4 megawatts of additional power. This is roughly equal to the present day power generation in the Country.

Wind energy

As we all know, wind blows throughout the world, the velocities of wind vary considerably from place to place and at the same place from time to time. Wind blows on the surface of the earth due to the earth receiving heat unevenly from sun. The poles receive less heat than the equator. Also, dry land heats up (and cools down) more quickly than the seas. This differential heating drives a global atmospheric convection system reaching from the earth's surface to the stratosphere, which acts as a virtual ceiling. Most of the energy stored in these wind movements can be found at high altitudes where continuous wind speeds of over 160 km/h (100 mph) occur. These can be harnessed to produce electric power by running turbines. An estimated 72 TW (Tera Watts) of wind energy potential is available.

Wind Power Generation

The amount of power transferred to a wind turbine is directly proportional to the density of the air, the area swept out by the rotor, and the cube of the wind speed.

The usable power *P* available in the wind is given by

$$P = \frac{1}{2}\alpha\rho\pi r^2 v^3,$$

where P = power in watts, α = an efficiency factor determined by the design of the turbine, ρ = mass density of air in kilograms per cubic meter, r = radius of the wind turbine in meters, and v = velocity of the air in meters per second.

As the wind turbine extracts energy from the air flow, the air is slowed down, which causes it to spread out. Albert Betz, a German physicist, determined in 1919 that a wind turbine can extract at most 59% of the energy that would otherwise flow through the turbine's cross section, that is α can never be higher than 0.59 in the above equation. The Betz limit applies regardless of the design of the turbine. An idea can be had from the curve in Fig. 15.4.

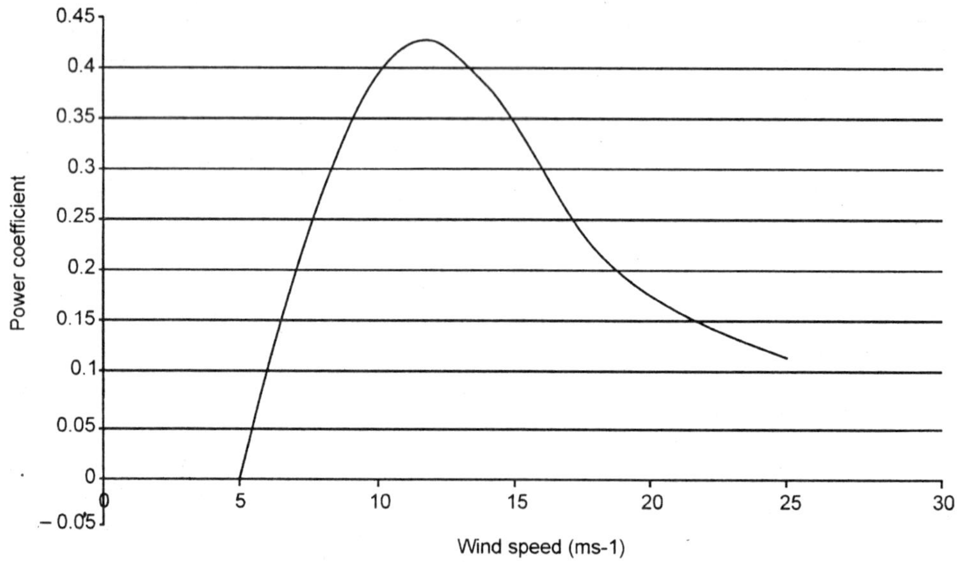

Fig. 15.4 Wind Turbine Power Coefficient.

This equation shows the effects of the mass rate of flow of air travelling through the turbine, and the energy of each unit mass of air flow due to its velocity. As an example, on a cool 15 °C (59 °F) day at sea level, air density is 1.225 kilograms per cubic metre. An 8 m/s (28.8 km/h or 18 mi/h) breeze blowing through a 100 meter diameter rotor would move almost 77, 000 kilograms of air per second through the swept area. The total power of the example breeze through a 100 meter diameter rotor would be about 2.5 megawatts. Betz' law states that no more than 1.5 megawatts could be extracted.

Induction generators, often used in power projects require reactive power for excitation. Substations used in wind power collection systems include substantial capacitor banks for power factor correction. Different types of wind turbine generators behave differently during transmission grid disturbances. Induction generators cannot support the system voltage during faults. Wind turbines with solid-state converters between the turbine generator and collector system have generally better properties for grid interconnection.

A number of such wind machines as they were commonly known as, are installed as a battery and power generated. The U.S. is generating electricity by wind power in some states like California since 1920. Large fans rotating due to winds on the farm side and their rotation being coupled to agricultural harvesting was practiced in Europe since the beginning of last century. In fact, that was the beginning of wind power utilisation. Then they found their way to the U.S. However wind energy harvesting for power took a set-back in the fifties and sixties due to the availability of cheap oil. But since the seventies, when the oil prices have started to rise in the international market, wind energy utilisation started to take strides again. Today, many countries have installed wind machines. Though fluctuating in generation, wind power is ideal for coastal and hilly regions.

Interest in wind power is picking up in our country also. Many technical institutions like Engineering colleges and polytechnics have experimental wind mills. But the interest, instead of academic, should be from realistic, necessity-oriented to make the schemes worthwhile.

Another aspect of wind energy utilisation is transport by waterways. Inland transport by rivers and canals is long forgotten due to the speed of transportation using lorries. We should go back to the slower mode of goods transport like waterways not only to save the oil but to minimise air pollution. The tide in the rivers and canals is due to the wind. Many transport boats can be run by hoisting the sail especially when the journey is in the wind direction. Running a boat or any water-borne carrier for transportation will eliminate the road-tyre friction which itself accounts for half the energy spent in road transportation. Barring essential commodities and perishables, all the other goods nowadays transported by lorries and tucks can be transported by water ways. The photograph (Fig. 15.5) shows a part of a wind machine battery.

California in U.S. is an outstanding example of harvesting wind power. The state whose industrial production ranks with the world's leading nations, has modernised their wind power to power generation techniques using latest high-tech. designs to drive their turbines. According to the statistics available, there were 10,023 turbines installed in California wind projects and 1,024 megawatts installed wind capacity in 1985. Capacity is defined as the total of usable wind and machines available to harvest it. California wind machines authority reported that their electricity production during the last three months of the year 1986 was 450 million kilowatts (with a 12% capacity ratio).

Electrical generation using wind power is not constant and regular. Hence wind power harnessing equipment should be installed alongwith thermal, nuclear or hydroelectric facility when the conditions for wind harvesting are favourable, the other facility can be shut down or run at a lower production capacity so that the costly inputs are saved. Uninterrupted supply can be maintained by ingeneous operation of the various facilities depending on the conditions and load requirement.

Fig. 15.5 A section of the wind machine battery.

For a country like India whose coast-line is around 2000 km harnessing of wind energy should be quite an interesting proposition. Present day costs and interrupted generation should not deter us from going in for wind energy. The issues like imports of oil, paying in foreign exchange and atmospheric pollution should be more deterrent factors in regard to oil.

Wind power installations world-wide have crossed 24.7 GW, producing over 14 TWH of energy annually. The World Energy Council has estimated that, by 2010 A.D., the world wind power capacity can increase to 53 GW under the current policy scenario, and even 89 GW under an ecologically deriven scenario. Wind power potential in our country is estimated to generate 45,195 MW. The details of wind power planning potential etc., of different states in our country is given Table 15.2, 15.3, 15.4.

Table 15.2 Wind Potential and State Government Approval.

Sl. No.	State	Gross Potential (MW) (a)	Technical Potential (MW) (b)	Installed Capacity (MW) (c)
1.	Andhra Pradesh	8275	1290	92.6
2.	Gujarat	9675	1450	166.9
3.	Karnataka	6620	900	124.2
4.	Kerala	875	500	2.0
5.	Madhya Pradesh	5500	75	22.6
6.	Maharashtra	3650	2500	401.2
7.	Orissa	1700	400	2
8.	Rajasthan	5400	500	61.7
9.	Tamilnadu	3050	1220	99.03
10.	West Bengal	450	450	1.1
11.	Other States	-	-	1.6
	Total	45195 MW	9285	974.93

Source : M N E S

(a) Assuming 0.5% of land availability for Wind Power generation in potential areas.

(b) As on 31.03.98, assuming 20% grid penetration

(c) As on 31.03.2003

Table 15.3 Possible generation per MW (in millions units).

Tamil Nadu	1.6 - 2.0
Maharashtra	1.4 - 1.6
Karnataka	1.4 - 2.0
Gujarat	1.2 - 1.4
Andhra Pradesh	1.2 - 1.6
Madhya Pradesh	1.2 - 1.4

Table 15.4

Items	Wheeling	Banking	Buy-back	Third party-sales	Capital Subsidy	Other Incentives
Andhra Pradesh	2% of energy	12 months (5% Escalation 95 - 96) Presently Rs. 3.32	Rs. 2.25/kwh	NOT Allowed	NOT available NEDCAP	Van Drawal 0.10 P/unit To give 10 lakhs/MW to Lakhs/mW to AP Transco, 1 lakh/to NEDCAP
Tamilnadu	5% of energy	5% for 12 months	Rs. 2.70/kwh (No Escalation)	Not Allowed	NIL	No generation tax.
Karnataka	30% of energy	2% every month for 12 months	Rs. 3.10 / kwh (2% Esc. from 01/09/2003)			Allowed to HT consumers same as for other industries. No generatin tax for 5 years Van drawal 0.40p/unit
Kerala	2% of energy	6 months	to be agreed mutually	-	15% (max Rs. 5 lakhs)	-
Uttar Pradesh	2% of energy	12 months	Rs. 2.25/kwh (5% Esc. 95-96)	Allowed	same as for other industries	-
West Bengal	2% of energy	6 months	to be decided on case to case basis	Not Allowed	-	-
Gujarat	2% of energy	6 months	Rs. 1.75/kwh	Not Allowed	-	
Madhya Pradesh	2% of energy	2% for 12 Months	Present Rs. 3.16p/ kwh	Allowed	same as for other industries	-
Maharashtra	2% of energy < 200 kms	2% for 12 months	Rs. 2.25/kwh (5% Esc.94-95)	Allowed	30% (max Rs. 20 lakhs per project)	Sales tax (Exemption for 6 years subject to a minimum PLF of 20%)
Rajashthan	2% of Energy	2% for 12 months	present Rs. 3.32/kwh	Allowed	-	-

Geo-thermal energy

The temperature inside the earth will be higher than on the surface. There are some places where the temperatures are very hot when depths of a few thousand feet are reached. Drilling is done at such places and to such hot depths. When water is sent inside it boils and the boiling water is taken out. This water can be employed to charge the boilers – the steam generated therefrom is used to drive turbines and produce electricity.

Ocean-thermal energy

Similarly, ocean depths have very hot strata of water and pipes lowered to that depth will be able to take out the water. The potential is tremendous – but the ocean thermal energy is mostly harnessed near the equitorial regions of the ocean bed.

Bio-mass energy

In countries like China and India whose population is the largest and second largest in the world, the treatment of human wastes is very pertinent and tangible proposition for the production of gas rich in methane. The animal population in India is the largest in the world. Dung charged generators in which the gases collect are designed and installed by the Khadi and Village Industries commission, throughout the country. The generator shown in Fig. 15.6 is essentially two bottom-less cylinders, inverted into one another. Dung is charges into the bottom container and the gasses released collect at the top. Suitable arrangement is made to take out the gas through pipeline. Arrangements are also made in the design to facilitate charging of dung and also removal of decomposed dung – to be used as manure.

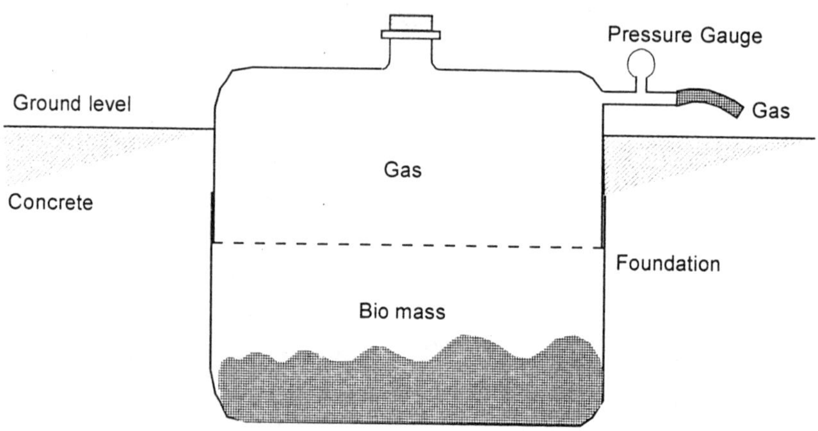

Fig. 15.6 Bio-gas generator.

The utilisation of bio-gas, from septic tanks of the homes is still easy to instal. Outlet pipe is fitted at the top; in place of the vent pipe and the organic gases taken out.

In addition to the above, treatment of sewage wastes in municipalities (townships) and cities needs a special mention. Nowadays, many towns and villages release their effluents into a nearby river, canal, lake or into the open. This practice is a health hazard, and recently many towns are installing sewage treatment plants to neutralize the causticity or acidity of the effluents before releasing them into open. Much work is done to process the sewage wastes and generate power out of the gases. The treatment is ideally suited for human welfare as well as economy. The solids are separated from sewage by allowing it to settle, Bacteria is inoculated in to the organic solid slurry. A 7-10 day cycle produces methane gas which is collected and utilised for power generation. It is reported that in Germany, 95% of sewage is treated and the power generated from the gases produced is not only sufficient to run the sewage treatment plant but is enough for street lighting.

The tremendous increase in the oil prices has forced a lot of research into the production of alternate fuels. Agricultural wastes are fermented and alcohol is distilled out – a viable and pollution free fuel. The large scale production economies are yet to be established, however. All said and done, it can be said that any organic matter discarded hitherto as waste, can be treated suitably and alcohol or methane gas coming in the process can be collected and utilised as a fuel.

Hydrogen energy

We have studied the different non-conventional energy forms. Each suffers from one drawback or the other. Eg: Solar energy cannot be produced throughout the day and on all the 365 days of the year. Wind power can be only harnessed intermittently. Thus, we need an intermediary energy and the user. The energy form must be storable, transportable, economic to produce; if possible reusable and pollution – free. All these pre-requisites are met by hydrogen. It is plentiful in the form of water. It is the cheapest synthetic fuel to manufacture per unit of energy stored in it. At the user end, it can be converted to many energy forms needed, more efficiently than others. It does not pollute and is recyclable.

In the system conceived*, hydrogen would be produced using whatever non-conventional primary energy source is available. It is then stored and / or transported to energy consumption centres. It can be used in every application where a fossil fuel is being used today. In addition to being permanent and environmentally most compatible, the hydrogen system has another advantage – Each Country will be able to produce its own energy carrier (H_2). The economic development will be faster due to the enormous quantity of funds saved which were hitherto being spent on import of fissil fuels.

Table 15.5 gives a comparison of hydrogen gasolene and natural gas. For a given amount of energy, hydrogen weighs about one third of the fossil fuels. But it is bulkier. For a given amount of energy hydrogen occupies 3.8 times the volume occupied by gasolene and in gaseous form 3.6 times the volume of natural gas. However, this volume penalty is 20-50% less. Since hydrogen can be converted onto other forms of energy at the user end more efficiently than fossil fuels. Its high flame speed and wide flammable limits make hydrogen a very good fuel for internal combustion engines, gas turbines and jet engines. Further high ignition temperature and low flame luminosity make it more safer fuel than others. It is also non-poisonous and recyclable.

* pionered by Dr. Nejat Veziroglu, Director, Clean Energy Research Institute, Coral Gables. Fl. U.S.A

Table 15.5 Properties of Gasolene, Natural gas and Hydrogen.

Property	Gasolene	Natural Gas	Hydrogen
Density (gr/cm^3)	0.73	0.78×10^{-3}	0.84×10^{-4} (gas) 0.71 10^{-1} (liq)
Boiling Point (°C) Lower Heating Value : Gravimetric (kJ/kg) Volumetric (kJ/m^3)	38/204 4.45×10^4 32.0×10^6	-156 4.80×10^4 37.3×10^3	-253 (20°K) 12.50×10^4 10.40×10^3(gas) 8.52×10^6 (liq)
Stoichiometric Composition In Air (Volume %)	1.76	9.43	29.3
Flammable limits (% in Air)	1.4-7.6	5 – 16	4 – 75
Flame Speed (m/sec) Flame Temperature in Air (°C)	0.40 2197	0.41 1875	3.45 2045
Ignition Temp. (°C) Flame Luminosity	257 High	540 Medium	585 low.

Production of hydrogen

Various methods of hydrogen production are available, the most important being electrolytic and thermochemical. Thousands of research papers are tuned out to perfect the process details like the electrodes, voltages, bath concentration etc. Also a lot of work is done in regard to the storage of hydrogen and development of 'hydrogen cells'. The reader is advised to refer to the references below for further details of hydrogen production.

Finally, on a techno-philosophical plane, it looks that the words of Jules Verne, said more than a century back, will come good. In his book the Mysterious Island, he speaks through a character, thus – ".... water decomposed into its primitive elements . . . and decomposed doubtless, by electricity, which will then have become a powerful and manageable force . . . . I believe that water will one day be employed as fuel, that hydrogen and oxygen which constitute it, used singly or together, will furnish an inexhaustible source of heat and light, of an intensity of which coal is not capable. Some day, the coalrooms of steamers and the tenders of Locomotives will, instead of coal, be stored with these two condensed gases, which will burn in the furnaces with enormous calorific power. I believe, that when the deposits of coal are exhausted, we shall heat and warm ourselves with water. Water will be the coal of the future."

Solar energy

The amount of solar energy reaching the earth in one minute exceeds the global energy demand for a year. The photo-voltaic effect of sun light is the basic principle involved in harnessing the solar energy. Sun rays bring warmth and heat to the earth. The thermocouple has a junction of dissimilar metals and their ends, when connected through a (milli) voltmeter, records some voltage. If a number of such thermocouples are connected in series, substantial voltages can be generated. Such an arrangement has came to be known as a 'Solar Cell'.

The conventional thermocouples like copper-constantin, iron – constantin and platinum-platinum-rhodium, are replaced by silicon and such cheaper metals. Not only cheap but they are photo voltaically more efficient. Year by year, more voltage efficient silicon cells are developed. The latest available amorphous silicon cell has an electrical efficiency of 17.5% (the percentage of volts of electrical energy produced to the heat-energy incident upon it). Cells made of crystalline silicon are made to fit onto the spacecrafts. These cells have an electrical conversion efficiency of 12%. Laboratory trials on the production of amorphous silicon cells were successful and 17.5% conversion efficiencies were reported.

Sputtering and photo induced chemical vapour deposition methods which were hitherto employed in the production of amorphous silicon are given a go-bye. Plasma enhanced vapour deposition of silicon is the latest method. In this method, silane gas is passed at a controlled rate between two electrode plates, one grounded and the other carrying a radio frequency potential. The field between the electrodes creates a plasma. The silane molecules are excited and free radicals are created. The resulting silicon is deposited onto a substrate. The low density of the localised states in hydrogenated amorphous silicon produces desirable device properties including a long minority-carrier diffusion length- the distance a 'hole', in this case will diffuse before combining with an electron in the solid.

Amorphous silicon alloys have low minority carrier mobilities (the order of 10^3 cm^2 S^{-1} V^{-1}) that produce relatively small minority-carrier diffusion lengths of 0.5 - 1.5 micrometers. This contrasts with the large mobilities (greater that 500 cm^2 S^{-1} V^{-1}) and long diffusion lengths of 50 micrometers or so found in crystalline silicon. Most sunlight is absorbed after passing through 1 micrometer of hydrogenated amorphous silicon. It requires about 50 micrometers of crystalline silicon. Therefore amorphous silicon, unlike crystalline silicon (Fig. 15.6), is more advantageous for use in producing thin film solar cells.

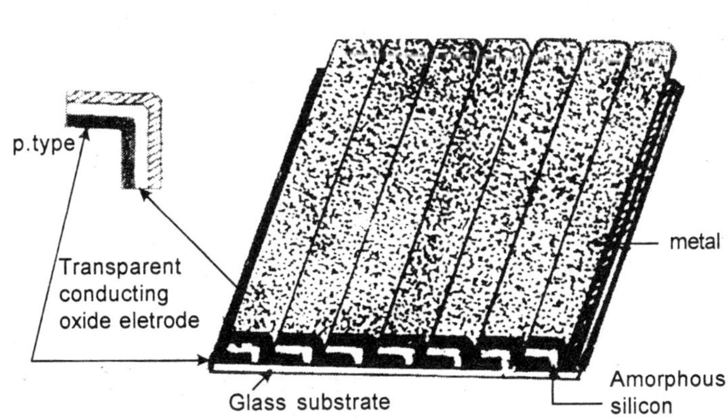

Fig. 15.6 Amorphous silicon cell.

Another benefit of hydrogenated amorphous silicon is that it can be deposited over a large area substrates, 40 cm wide and many meters long can be coated. The sizes of crystalline silicon devices are limited to the diameter of available crystal wafers, now commonly 12.5 cms. This, together with its relatively slow operation resulting from low carrier mobility, recommends hydrogenated amorphous silicon for any large area application where high speed of operation is not of paramount importance.

Design considerations

Definitions

Band gap

In a crystalline semiconductor, a range of energies that no electron or hole in a material can possess; the term has been carried over to amorphous semiconductors, even though localised states do exist in the gap, and for the that reason "mobility gap" is a more accurate term.

Dangling bond

A broken atomic bond in amorphous silicon, which can provide a centre for a localised state.

Density of localised states

The number of localised states in a particular energy range – an important determinant of an amorphous semiconductor's characteristics.

Extended state

An energy state extending throughout a solid material, allowing an electron or hole occupying it to travel freely throughout the solid.

Fill factor

The material - dependent factor that, when multiplied by the product of the open-circuit voltage and short-circuit current, gives the maximum power output of a photovoltaic cell, typically about 0.6 for commercial amorphous cells.

Localised state

An energy state associated with a particular location in solid material; an electron or hole occupying such a state is bound to a particular region in the solid.

Minority-carrier diffusion length

The average distance a minority carrier, usually a hole, travels in a solid before combining with a majority carrier, usually an electron.

The conversion efficiency of a practical solar cell is limited by intrinsic and extrinsic losses. Extrinsic losses include those caused by reflection of incoming light from the glass front plate of the cell, and the series resistance of contacts. The major intrinsic loss mechanism is incomplete extraction of the photogenerated carriers, primarily caused when photogenerated electron-hole pairs recombine at defect centres in the device. Another intrinsic loss mechanism is the inability of a cell with a specific optical band gap to absorb most photons in the broad solar spectrum. Photons with energies less than that of the band gap are not absorbed by the material, while those with higher energies lose their extra energy as heat.

Present calculations of the upper limit to the open circuit voltage range between 0.9 and 1.0 V. which can be improved to about 1.2 V if the band tails can be sharper – entirely possible with better material quality. This would improve the conversion efficiency by about 30 per cent - a break through. Maximum short-circuit current density for 1.7 electron volt- band - gap amorphous silicon is easily calculated as 21 milliamperes per square centimeter from the absorption coefficient and the known solar spectrum. Actual devices are in the range of the 15 to 18 mA/cm^2

Fill factor is difficult to calculate. Roughly, it depends on the sum of the depletion width and the minority-carrier diffusion length. For diffusion lengths of the order of the cell thickness (about 6000 to 8000 angstroms), the fill factor would be about 0.8, current cells have been measured in the laboratory at up to 0.74. Therefore the upper limit to the conversion efficiency of a single-junction cell is about 18%. This contrasts with efficiencies for the most widely sold amorphous cells of six per cent. And 11 to 14 percent for typical crystalline wafers. However, the effective efficiency for commercial crystalline modules is only about 70% of this figure because of the module area left uncovered by silicon when circular wafers are placed next to each other.

A solar cell requires a built-in electric field, maintained by a rectifying junction, to separate the electron-hole pairs created by incident illumination, thereby allowing them to be collected by the external contacts. In crystalline silicon the field is created at the junction of p^+ and n^+ layers. Because p^+ and n^+ layers in amorphous-silicon based materials have high concentration of defects, an efficient p^+, n^+ rectifying junction is not possible. Instead, an intrinsic layer (i) is inserted between the p^+ and n^+ layers, and the required field occurs at the p+ and the n+ –i junctions.

Typical hydrogenated amorphous silicon p+ - i - n+ solar cell fabrication begins with deposition of a wide - band - gap p+ layer. About 100 angstroms thick onto a textured transparent conducting tin-oxide film. This is followed by an i-layer 5000 to 7000 A° thick and a thin (100 A°) n+ layer. The cell is then completed with a reflective coating made of a metal like aluminium or silver. By using a textured transparent conducting oxide substrate and a reflector, the maximum possible light can be trapped in this type of thin solar cell.

Conversion efficiency would be significantly improved by a multijunction or tandem cell approach. Here the cells are connected in series and stacked on top of each other with the configuration $p^+ - i_1 - n^+ - p^+ - i_2 - n^+$. The material with the wider band gap (i_1) faces the incident illumination. The low-energy photons are directed to cells fabricated from narrow band-gap material (i_2) and the high-energy photons are directed to wide-band-gap cells (i_1). The low-energy photons pass through the cells until they reach one that can convert them to useful power. The thickness and values of the different semiconductor band gaps are arranged so the currents generated from the constituent cells are the same.

Most work on amorphous multi junction stacks is based on hydrogenated amorphous silicon alloy with a band gap of 1.7 electron volts, because of all existing amorphous materials, it offers the highest conversion efficiency in solar cells. The strategy is to make new amorous semiconductors with different band gaps by alloying process introduces additional disorder that often reduces the conversion efficiencies of the individual junctions. Laboratories in the U.S. and Japan have reported conversion efficiencies as high as 15 percent using the tandem cell approach. Efficiencies of the same order could be attained within the next few years if new amorphous alloys with tails as sharp as standard hydrogenated amorphous silicon are developed.

Stability of conversion efficiency is a greater problem with amorphous solar cells than crystalline cells. Hydrogenated solar cells do lose their conversion efficiency, probably because of excess charge carriers. However, research has established that firstly the tendency to lose efficiency is self limiting and secondly, the efficiency of the cell is restored by annealing at 150 °C just for a few minutes. Processes are established to maintain the loss of efficiency within 10% over a life span of 20 years

References

1. Ohta, T., Solar-Hydrogen Energy Systems, Pergamon Press, 1979.
2. Bockris, J. O'M., Energy Options: Real Economics and the Solar-Hydrogen System, Australia and New Zealand Book CO., 1980.
3. Williams, L.O., Hydrogen power : An Introduction to Hydrogen Energy and its Applications, Pergamon Press, 1980.

Information supplied by BARC., Mumbai.

UNIT II

Furnaces

16 Furnaces

Furnace is a term used to identify or define a closed space here heat is applied to a body in order to raise its temperature. The source of heat may be a fuel or electricity. Commonly, metals and alloys and sometimes non-metals are heated in furnaces. The purpose of heating defines the temperature of heating and the heating rate.

Increase in temperature softens the metals. They become amenable to deformation. This softening occurs with or without a change in the metallic structure. Heating to lower temperatures (below the critical temperature) of the metal softens it by relieving the internal stresses. On the other hand, metals heated to temperatures above the critical temperatures leads to changes in crystal structures and re-crystallization like annealing. Further, some metals and alloys are melted, ceramic products vitrified, coals coked, metals like zinc are vaporized (distilled) and many other processes are performed in furnaces.

Furnaces are classified as follows :

1. Ovens
2. Metal heating furnaces
3. Heat treating furnaces
4. Sintering furnaces
5. Coke ovens
6. Kilns
7. Melting furnaces
8. Extraction furnaces

Heat treating furnaces are again classified depending upon the type of heat treatment to be performed, e.g., normalizing, hardening, annealing, malleablising etc.

Another method of classification is based on the heating process, intermittent or continuous. Intermittent operating furnaces are called batch type furnaces. Still further classifications are made like movable hearth, vertical or horizontal and so on.

In addition to fuel fired furnaces, the electric furnaces are classified depending upon the principle, upon which heat is generated by electricity,

1. Resistance – muffle furnace
2. Arc – direct arc and indirect arc and
3. Induction furnaces

Thus, there are more then a dozen types of nomenclatures for the furnaces.

Furnaces used in metal extractions

Iron is the most voluminous metal extracted. Blast furnace is the common and in fact the only furnace used in the extraction of iron. Coke is the fuel employed. Iron ore and coke are charged from the top of the blast furnace, often times as tall as 40 meters and preheated air is sent into the furnace from the bottom.

The fuel descending from the top is burnt by the oxygen from the ascending air. The burning action is by counter current method. Various chemical reactions occur or and made to occur, ultimately yield pig iron. It is tapped from the bottom of the furnace and contains carbon up to 4.00%. This pig iron is further refined in open hearth furnaces, L.D. or Kaldo converters or electric arc furnaces to make steels of the required carbon percentages. These converters are also tall vessels about 20-25 meters high. No external fuel is burnt in them and composition refinement if iron is achieved by blowing oxygen into them by a lance. Though a misnomer, they are also called vertical furnaces just because of their height.

Blast furnace operation and chemistry are detailed in metallurgical literature. We are concerned here with the shape of the furnace. It is a tall structure of 40 meters, with a diameter of 1-1.5 meters. As said above such furnaces whose heights are many times larger than their diameters are called 'vertical furnaces'.

Besides, iron blast furnaces relatively smaller ones of are used in the extraction of copper also. The copper ore roasters are also tall structures and fall under vertical furnace class.

Copper ore contains lots of excess sulphide in the form iron sulphide which should be removed and brought down to the required levels. The sulphides are 'burnt'– sulphides are oxidised by employing hot air. The copper ore roaster is a multiple hearth furnace with circular hearths mounted to a vertical shaft which revolves slowly. About six to eight hearths are employed in each roaster. Alternate hearths taper from the centre to periphery where opening is provided for the ore to fall on the next lower hearth which is tapered towards the central portion. (The other hearths in between them taper from their peripheries towards the centre and fall onto the next hearth from the openings provided at the centre).

Rakes are fitted above each hearth so that the ore is continuously turned over. This process exposes fresh surfaces of the ore, to the oxygen (of the air). Arrangement is made for the ore to fall from one hearth to the other, just below. Hot air is admitted into the roaster from below and sulphur dioxide gas escapes from the top. A sketch of Hereshoff's roaster is shown in the Fig. 16.1. This roaster can be classed under vertical furnaces, for it is tall enough to come under this category about 5 meters high, oxidation of sulphide is an exothermic reaction. No fuel is needed to be supplied into the roaster the process is called pyritic roasting.

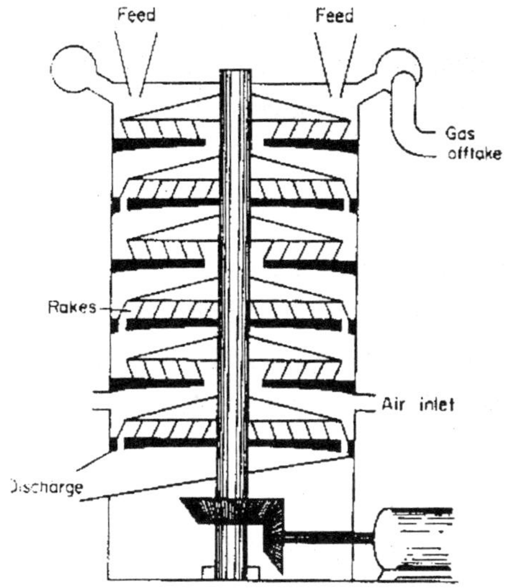

Fig. 16.1 Multiple hearth wedge type furnace for roasting sulphide ores pyritically. This combines features of hearth and stack furnaces. The rakes turn over the charge and trasport it through the furnace against the flow of hot gas.

Reheating furnaces

Vertical furnaces are employed in heat treatment also besides extraction. Lengthly objects like automobile leaf springs are normalized in vertical furnaces. Vertical furnaces are also used for the annealing of steel strip (Fig. 16.2).

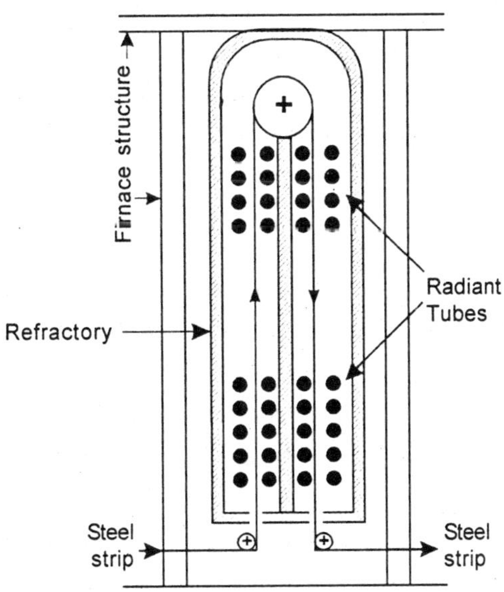

Fig. 16.2 Tower type furnace.

From the discussion we had so far, we can define a vertical furnace as the one in which the charge moves in a vertical direction, either from top to bottom. (mostly in cases of extraction furnaces) or bottom to top (in other cases). Of course, the movement of the charge is governed by the convenience of operation and the consequential design.

Continuous furnace

As the name refers to, the furnaces which are used continuously i.e. not being put off for the charging or unloading of the charge are called continuous furnaces. Herein, the steel is fed into the furnace from one end and withdrawn from the other. The heating capacity of the continuous furnaces is usually more than that of batch furnaces of a similar capacity. The furnaces are fired from the bottom, top or even sides.

The furnace is a long construction with provision for burners as said above. The hearth may be solid or will have provision for the charge to travel. Rollers, skids or chains may be fitted in the case of the so-called moving hearth. The length of the furnace is also divided into preheating, heating and soaking zones. Soaking zone provided when the furnace is used to heat thicker stock in order to effect temperature homogenization. The lengths of the aforesaid zones and temperature homogenisation, are determined by the heating stock thickness. Generally the length of the soaking zone will be about 1/3 to 1/6 of the high temperature zone.

It should be clearly understood that the soaking zone is a very important part of the furnace. The higher the rate of heating, the grater will be the temperature gradient from the surface to the centre in the stock unless its conductivity is very high and emissivity very low. The corners of the billets tend to melt down and scale also. The mixture builds up on the hearth (if solid) or falls down between the rollers and forms a solid which has to be removed periodically. These troubles are better avoided by keeping the furnace temperature below 1250 ^{0}C and providing a sufficient soaking zone. The heating capacity of the furnaces can be greatly increased by fitting burners on the sides, after the front firing burners.

Capacity of a continuous furnace

The capacities calculated for heating of steel in a continuous furnace take into account its weeklong performance. Any unforeseen interruptions like underperformance of the rolling mill or forge shop leading to not withdrawing the stock from the furnace is not reduced! The curves given in Fig. 16.3 furnish information on the rates at which heat is transferred to the exposed surfaces of the steel in a continuous furnace. Curves 1 and 2 are for pusher type furnaces (where the stock after heating, is pushed out) and 3 and 4 for an axial type continuous furnace where the stock exists in the furnaces on an endless chain. The furnaces are provided with water–cooled rollers on which the stock travels. Heat is applied from the top as well as bottom.

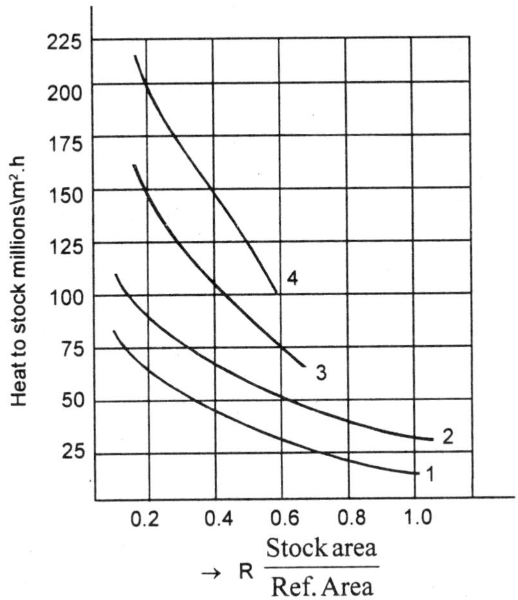

Fig. 16.3 Heat Transfer in a continuous furnace.

Let us examine how the heat is imparted to the stock in the furnace. We should know that the solid material that is heated in industrial furnaces is not necessarily continuous. Very often, the charge consists of separate pieces piled to various heights in the furnace. Heat flows from each solid piece to its neighbour by small contact surfaces or through gas filled spaces. These gas filled spaces possess very poor thermal conductivity. Heat flow in such a charge is bettered by the circulation of hot gases through the piled material.

Transmission of heat to the surface of the charge

Theoretically heat is transmitted by conduction, convection or radiation. In furnaces, this occurs by all the three processes. We will discuss only the essentials of heat transfer so that it will be helpful to the designers and furnace operators.

Conduction

The molecules of hot and cold materials do not change their relative positions when the two bodies are in contact. Heat transfer, occurring solely by conduction is rare in industrial furnaces. It occurs only when cold material (charge) is laid on a hot hearth. It also occurs when a cold metal is submerged in a salt bath or a bath of molten metal.

When two solids of different temperatures come into contact with each other (not separated by air or any other fluid) the contacting surfaces immediately assume an intermediate temperature. The temperature gradients at the contacting surfaces are inversely propositional to the conductivities of the two solids. The amount of heat transfer in unit time depends upon the temperature difference between the two solids as well as diffusivity and shape of the two contacting solids (Fig. 16.4).

When a piece of cold metal is dropped into a salt bath or molten metal bath, salt or the bath metal freezes on the surface of the metal piece and heat transfer takes place by conduction only. But after a very short time the salt jacket gets melted and from then on, heat transfer takes place by both conduction and convection. It should be noted that experimental determination of heat transfer coefficients in the heating of metal in liquids is extremely difficult.

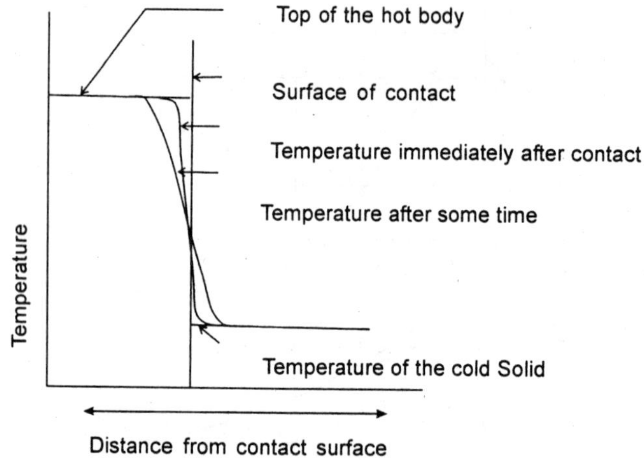

Fig. 16.4 Heat transfer by conduction.

Convection

A layer of fluid is held at the surface of each solid due to molecular and mass attraction. Heat is transferred to the solid through this stagnant layer by conduction. If a stream of gaseous fluid flows parallel to the surface of the solid (see Fig. 16.5), the vibrating particles of the stationary fluids at the surface of the solid and the passing gaseous fluid enter into a tangle. The thickness of the stagnant (poor conducting) boundary layer is reduced. Consequently the heat transfer is increased.

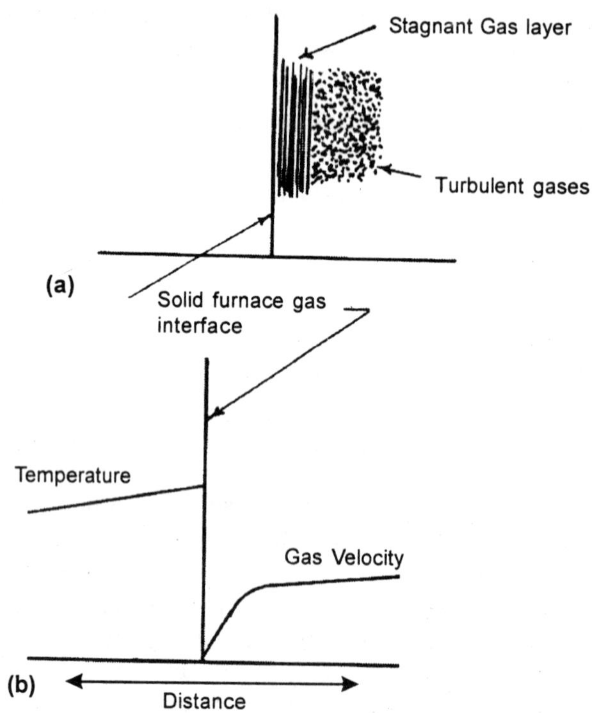

Fig. 16.5 Heat transfer by convection.

It is established that the transfer of heat per unit area in unit time is a function of mass velocity. For gaseous flow along plane walls, the equation is,

$$\frac{Q}{A} = 7.28\ q\ c^{0.78}\ (T_1 - T_2)\ t$$

where

Q	= Heat quantity
A	= Area
q	= Density
c	= Velocity of the fluid
$(T_1\text{-}T_2)$	= Difference in temperature
t	= Time in hours

Gas velocities and temperatures vary from place to place in the furnace. Sometimes the gas stream passes along the roof of the furnace without even contacting the heating stock. In many furnaces, the charge consists of individual pieces loaded in trays. Such a charge has no plane surface. The surface of the charge can be treated as an aggregate of cylindrical or spherical surfaces. Gases impinging upon them follow different laws of heat transfer. To give a general idea of the influence of mass velocity upon heat transfer, the above equation is replaced by a reasonably simple (and close to the actual values) one in the form,

$$Q = A\ (1 + 2.7q\ c)\ (T_1 - T_2)$$

where,

Q = heat quantity

q = density of the charge

c = furnace gas velocity

$(T_1 - T_2)$ = furnace gas temperature and charge temperature difference

t = time of heating in hours

Conduction and convection processes are predominant only in low temperature heat transfer up to 600-650 °C i.e., tempering, reheating furnaces and ovens. High velocities of furnace gas circulation are maintained to attain a maximum heat transfer.

Radiation between Solids

It is proved that heat transfer by radiation at 600 °C is about a tenth of the heat transfer by radiation at 1250 °C. Two solid bodies radiate heat. The net heat transfer between two solid bodies by radiation follows the fourth power law,

$$\frac{Q}{A} = \text{Coefficient } T^4$$

where

Q = Calories per square centimeter

T = Abs. Temperature (kelvin)

The value of coefficient in the above equation is 0.173. This is the Boltzmann constant of heat radiation. The emissivities of materials commonly encountered in industrial furnaces are given in Fig. 16.6 emissivity is equal to absorptivity. It is the heat absorbed by a body expressed as a fraction of the greatest possible heat absorption in unit time per unit area. The figure 0.173 is called the black body coefficient.

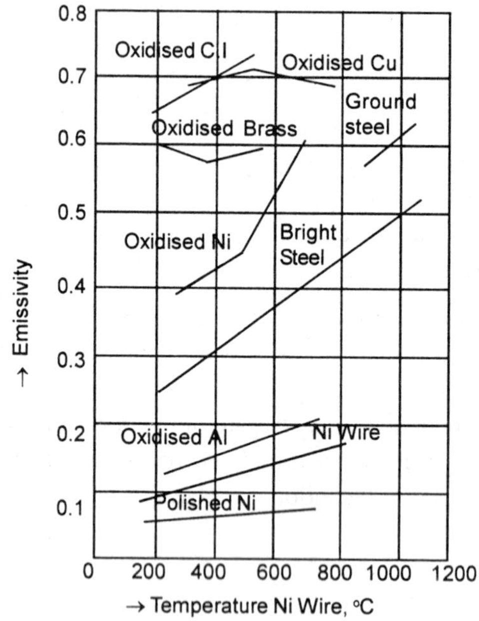

Fig. 16.6 Emissivities of some metals.

The above equation expresses the heat which a solid body radiates. Heat actually transferred to the surroundings is the difference between the heat emitted and the heat received. This difference, which actually is the black body radiation, is given by,

$$Q = 0.173\ A\left[\left(\frac{T_1}{100}\right)^4 - \left(\frac{T_2}{100}\right)^4\right]$$

where,

Q = Cals per hour

A = Area surrounding the body, m^2

T_1 = Hot body

T_2 = Cold body

It should be noted here neither the bodies heated in the furnace not the furnace walls (from where the heat radiation occurs) are black bodies. If both the heat exchanging bodies have the same emissivity, the coefficient 0.173 is multiplied by the emissivity. If the emissivities are different, the coefficient is composite and the equation for the two parallel plates becomes

$$Q = \frac{A^{0.173t}}{\frac{1}{e_1}\frac{A_1}{A_2}\left(\frac{1}{e_2} - 1\right)}\left(\frac{T_1}{100}\right)^4 - \left(\frac{T_2}{100}\right)^4$$

where,

$Q =$ quantity of heat exchanged cals.

$A_1 =$ smaller area, m^2

$A_2 =$ bigger area, m^2

$t =$ times hrs

e_1 and $e_2 =$ emissivities of A_1 and A_2

and T_1 and T_2 = Abs. temps of hotter and colder bodies

Simplifying

$$T_1^4 - T_2^4 = (T_1 - T_2)(T_1^3 + T_1^2 T_2 + T_1 T_2^2 + T_2^3)$$

If T_1 and T_2 difference is not much, the difference of their fourth powers approximately equals

$$4(T_1 - T_2)\left(\frac{T_1 + T_2}{2}\right)^3$$

From this expression it can be seen that the rate of heat transfer is extremely high at higher temperatures even if the temperature difference is very small. A degree of temperature difference at 1200 °C causes five times as much transfer of heat as one degree temperature difference causes at 550 °C.

All said and done, the above radiation equation is valid for radiations through vacuum or transparent gases which do not absorb heat.

Radiation between Clear Gases and Solids

While studying the radiation from gases to the solids, a clear distinction should be made between clear gases and luminous flames. Radiation from clear gases does not follow the fourth power law. It is found that only the clear gases which radiate appreciably are the tri-atomic gases like H_2O, CO_2 and SO_2. However, it is found that CO, though diatomic, gives off some radiation. Many diatomic gases like O_2, N_2 and H_2 have negligible radiating power.

The reason for the radiation from the gases not following the fourth power law is that it occurs only in certain wave lenghts.

Radiation between Luminous Flames and Solids

Flames are always luminous. If a flame is cooled so that it no longer remains luminous, it becomes smoke. Luminosity of a flame is caused by the glowing smoke particles. Of course, the glowing ash particles also contribute to the luminosity of the flame emanating from the burning solid fuels. Emissivity of a flame is governed by the number and size of the solid particles in it. Emissivity varies between the emissivity of clear gases and a high value of 0.95. It is found that it will be high in a short section of flame travel only. The relation between the emissivity and the distance from the tip of the burner is shown in Fig. 16.7.

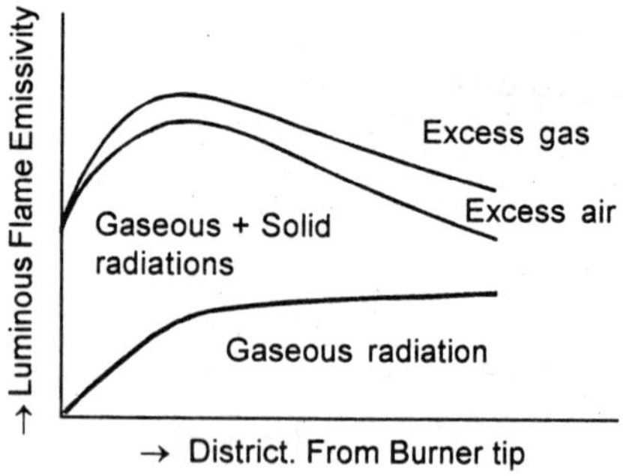

Fig. 16.7 Variation of emissivity with distance from the tip of the burner.

High emissivity exists only up to a short distance from the burner tip. The hydrocarbons in the fuel air mixture need time to crack and bring the resulting smoke particles up to the temperature of the burning gases. As the flame travels along, formation of new smoke particles and combustion of the previously formed particles balances. A short distance beyond that point, no new smoke particles are formed; the existing particles are burnt and finally a point is reached when the flame extinguishes. It is ideal that this extinguishing occurs when the products of combustion pass into the flue.

Flame radiation is a function of many variables,

1. Composition of the fuel
2. Fuel air ratio
3. Fuel air temperatures and rate of their mixing
4. Thickness of the flame and,
5. Distance from the burner.

Fig. 16.8 shows the above variables in a graphic form. The flame emissivity is plotted against C/H ratio of the fuel. For all practical purposes, the average emissivity may be taken as half the value shown in the graph.

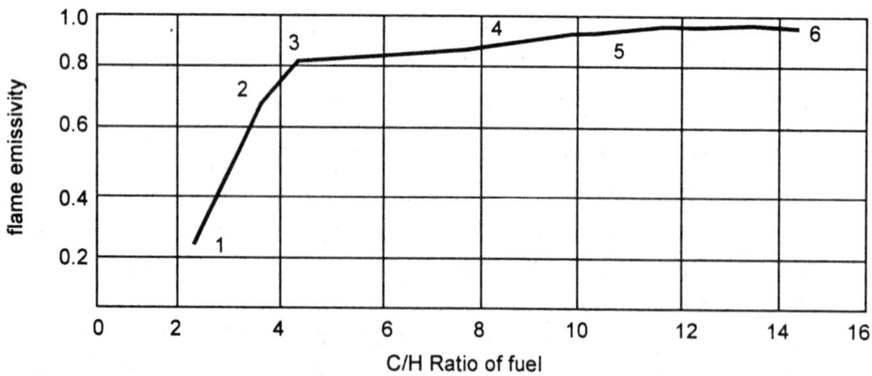

Fig. 16.8 Variation of flame emissivity with the C/H ratio in fuel.

A high emissivity flame radiates almost like a solid. Heat flow in a furnace is diagrammatically illustrated in Fig. 16.9. It can be seen that the surface elements like the furnace walls and the charge are convection heated 3 and 6. A molecule of gas-air mix, in other words, furnace gas radiates heat in almost all directions 2-8. Thus each of the particles of combustion and the elements of surfaces of walls and charge radiate heat in all directions. So it is extremely difficult to calculate the heat transfer in a fuel – fired furnace due to the large number of variables – temperature, composition, velocity of the gases, thickness of the layer of gases between the furnace walls and the charge, the ratio of wall surface exposed to the charge to the charge surface and their emissivities.

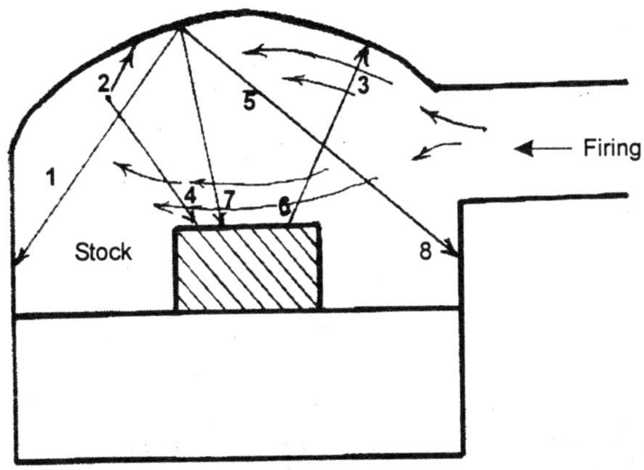

Fig. 16.9 Heat radiation in a furnace.

Due to the above it is advisable to compute heat transfer in a simple case and proceed to extend it to more and more complicated cases. The calculations are not difficult but very long and laborious. The best way suggested is to experiment with prototypes and proceed therefrom, of course with the backing of the operator's experience.

17 Heating Capacity of Furnaces

The heating capacity of a furnace is usually expressed by the weight of the metal that can be heated in unit time to a given temperature at the coldest spot of the charge, without overheating the rest of the charge. The cost of a furnace is proportional to its size. Heating capacity per unit volume is also important. Thus, heating capacity is expressed in two ways,

Weight heated / hour × furnace volume

or Weight heated / hour × furnace hearth area

When a large tank is to be annealed, the furnace volume should be sufficiently large to not only house the tank but also to provide space for the circulation of the combustion gases. On the other hand, in annealing a long gun barrel suspended in a cylindrical annealing furnace, the capacity per unit of hearth area is very big. In the later case, it is common to call the furnace area as the area. Thus, it is more useful and common to call the hourly weight (of stock heated) per square meter of the hearth than that of the hourly weight per cubic meter of the volume of the furnace.

Heating capacity in whatever way is considered, depends upon the following variables :

(a) rate of heat release

(b) rate of heat transfer to the charge

(c) rate of heat conduction to the coldest portion of the charge

(a) ***Effect of heat release :***

A large number of electrically heated furnaces are fitted with heating elements that are embedded in the furnace walls and roof. The rate at which heat is released per square meter (element included) of wall depends upon many factors, most important of them being the service life of the element. This, in turn, is governed by the element material, their spacing and furnace atmosphere. Under normal functioning, the heat release is controlled by the current input.

Heating devices employed in fuel fired furnaces are discussed in detail under different fuels elsewhere in this book. In a nutshell, the heat release is directly proportional to the efficient combustion of the fuel used.

(b) ***Effect of heat transfer to the change :***

When adequate heat is released into the furnace at a sufficiently high temperature, the following factors effect the furnace capacity :

(a) Temperature of the furnace walls when cold stock is charged,

(b) Temperature to which the stock needs to be heated,

(c) Temperature of the products of combustion,

(d) Emissivity of the products of combustion,

(e) Emissivity of the furnace walls,

(f) Emissivity of the stock being heated,

(g) Ratio of the furnace wall surface area to the stock surface area,

(h) Thickness of the layer of products of combustion,

(i) Thermal conductivity of the stock (including voids),

(j) Desired temperature uniformity,

(k) Thickness of the heating stock,

(l) Furnace size (hearth area and volume),

(m) Velocity of the furnace gases and

(n) Circulation of the furnace gases.

Logically saying, heat transfer to the charge determines the heating capacity in the case of thin heating stock. However, temperature homogenization of the stock determines the heating capacity while heating thick stock of poor thermal conductivity.

In the case of thin stock of high thermal conductivity, the differential equation for heat transfer any time is,

$$\begin{aligned} dQ &= k \times A \times (T_g - T_a) \times dt \\ &= W \times C_p \times dT4 \end{aligned}$$

where,

dQ = Heat transmitted

k = Heat transmitted per sq.m.hr °C

A = Area of the stock sq. metres

T_g = Temperature of furnace gases

T_a = Temperature of stock

dt = Time hrs

W = Wt. of the stock kg

C_p = Sp. ht of stock. K. Cal/kg/C

dT = Temperature rise of the stock

When k and T_g remain constant during the heating, the above equation can be solved by integration to get the time of heating, thus,

$$t = \frac{WC_p}{kA} \log \frac{(T_g - T_i)}{(T_g - T_f)}$$

where,

T_i = initial temperature of the stock

T_f = final temperature of the stock

If we want to find the temperature of the stock at the end of some time, say t, the equation can be written as,

$$T_f = T_g - (T_g - T_i)e^{\frac{-kA_t}{WC_p}}$$

Because of the practical difficulty in measuring the temperature T_g, the temperature of the furnace wall is used in the equation in place of Tg. In such cases, the value of the constant k changes. This can be better approached if the total heating (temperature rise) is divided into smaller ranges and the average coefficient k for each range can be accurately substituted in the equation. The step wise or rangewise heating times can be summed up to get the total heating time. The variation in the value of k in each small temperature range is negligible.

Fig. 17.1 gives two curves of the above said computations. The step wise calculations and adding them up is also a bit cumbersome in the industry. So, another method is suggested. It involves in substituting an average value for k in the log equation. This method, though simpler, carries with it a certain degree of inaccuracy. To avoid the logarithmic equation altogether, yet another method (of equal approximation) is adopted which makes use of the equation,

Heat transfer $(T_f - T_s) \times k$

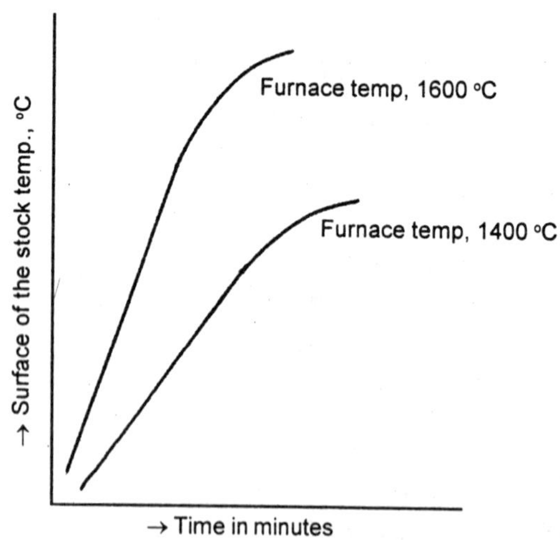

Fig. 17.1 Variation of the stock temperature, while heating at different temperatures.

In a batch type furnace, the temperatures of products of combustion and refractories should be so selected that the charge is not spoiled due to overheating if by any chance it stays in the furnace for an usually long time. Consequently, the temperature of the products of combustion is fixed to be about 5% - 8% higher that the required final surface temperature of the charge. Depending upon the selected excess temperature of products of combustion, the time required for heating is based on 92 -98% of the available temperature difference. In all the cases, the average temperature of the surface of the stock (with regard to time) is 71% of the temperature rise if the heat transfer occurs by convection only and is 65% if the heat is transferred by radiation only. Thus, a value of two thirds of the temperatures rise is suitable for all calculations. The relationship is graphically shown in Fig. 17.2.

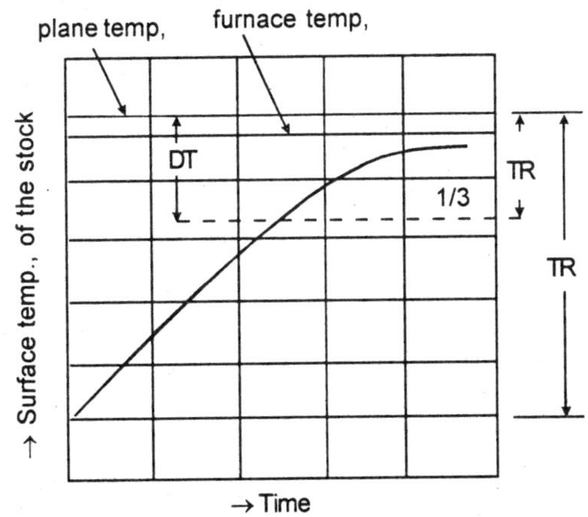

Fig. 17.2 Time -Temperature relationship during the heating of stock.

The average coefficient of heat transfer is dependent upon many variables of which the temperatures of the stock should be heated. So, it is more useful to plot the coefficient of the heat transfer as a function of the final temperature of the stock. The ratio R of the of the furnace is an important variable. Whenever the cold stock is placed in the furnace the temperature drops. If R is small, this temperature drop will be small. The heating time is also reduced. In addition, the emissivity of the stock also plays an important part. These three variables are combined and their influence on heating time is shown in Figure 17.3.

Effect of stock arrangement on the earth

In the case of a charge of solids on a furnace hearth say billets, space should be provided between them. The open space of the hearth between the billets which is atleast of the size of the billet width, receives heat from the gases, furnace walls and furnace roof. This heat is radiated onto the stock and heats it. Figure 17.4 illustrates the arrangement of a charge of billets on the hearth of a batch type furnace. In the case described, the heating surface of the billets is 50% more than that of the slab of half the thickness of the billet.

Stacking the charges as illustrated in Fig. 17.5 is common with the false notion that the three - high packing increases the heating capacity of the furnace (in kg per sq.m). It is observed that the three layers take three times more time to get heated up to the desired temperature than does a single layer. The pieces in the top layer marked 1. are heated directly by the radiation from the roof and combustion gases. The pieces marked 2. are heated by radiation from the pieces of the upper row.

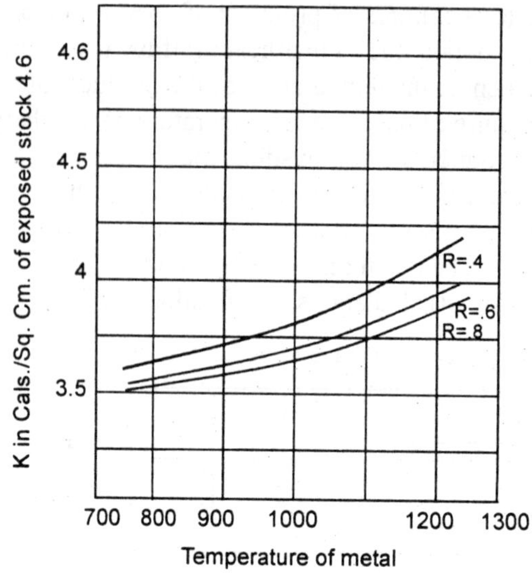

Fig. 17.3 Coefficient of heat transfer to stock surface.

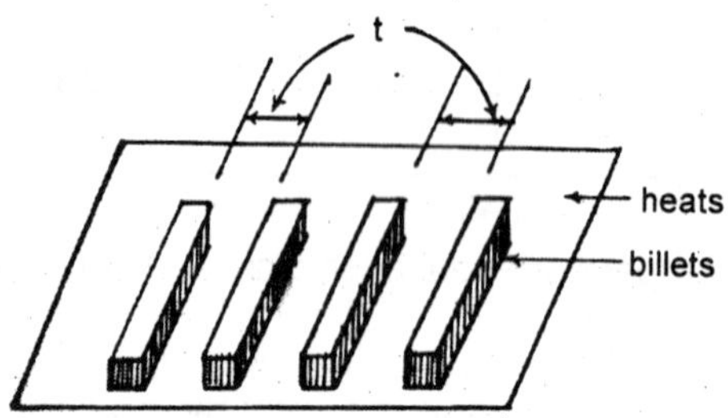

Fig. 17.4 Billets placed on a furnace hearth.

The only advantage, however, is this charging method saves time of charging and its periodicity if the withdrawal of pieces is done one-by-one from the top. It is followed in reheating furnaces with the hot forming processes.

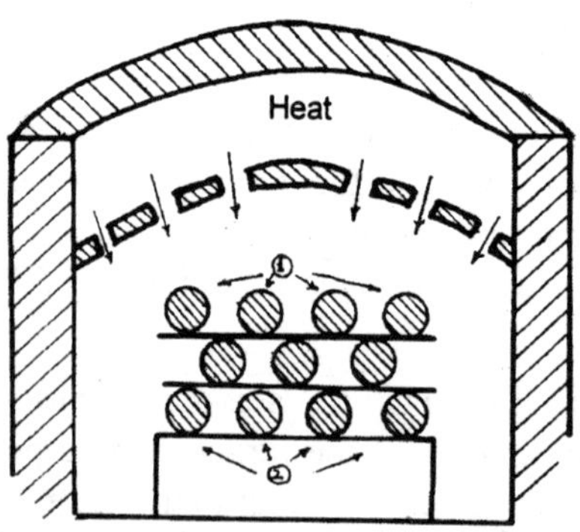

Fig. 17.5 Stacked charge in a furnace.

Effect of the thickness of the stock

Heating of metals is an old practice. Many a thumb rule are in use for evaluating the heating times depending upon the charge thickness. In a majority of steels, heat travels a thickness of 100 mm in 15 minutes. Another rule puts it as 20 minutes per a diameter 250 mm. These are followed for mild steel and in case of alloy steel, the times consumed are doubled. The times of heating commonly prescribed for annealing are one hour per a section of 250 mm if the stock receives heat from all directions and the stock size is relatively small compared to the size of the furnace. The temperature relationships are illustrated in Fig. 17.6. The temperature difference and the diameter of a cylindrical stock are the parameters in the illustration. The temperature curves are geometrically similar and the temperature difference is proportional to the diameter of the stock.

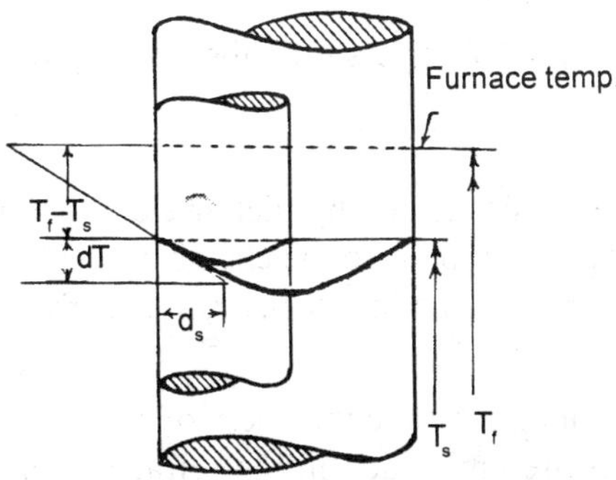

Fig. 17.6 Effect of size on temperature distribution.

In the heating of ingots and large stock and annealing, temperature homogenization is achieved only after a long time. This time is commonly known as soaking period. There is no hard and fast rule with respect to soaking period for thin stock say up to 75 mm diameter. But as the cylinder size increases the soaking period increases dramatically. For, example, the soaking time required for an ingot of 50 cm diameter, will be around 5 hours. Again the soaking time for large slabs will be more than for cylinders.

Even while going in for a rough and approximate calculation, the heating periods vary widely depending upon the varying shapes and sizes of the stock.

Vertical heating

Lenghtly objects are heated keeping them in vertical positions. Ingot heating in soaking pits is an outstanding example of heating. Calculation of heating capacity of soaking pits is impossible and meaningless. A common rule for heating time is one hour per each hour of pouring time – from pouring in the melting shop to charging in the soaking pit. For alloy steels, the heating time will be twice this. For an ingot heating furnace of two and half meters by ten meters size, the weight charged varied from 75 tons of alloy steel to 150 tons of plain carbon steel ingots. A mild steel ingot being removed from the soaking pit in Bhilai steel plant is shown in Fig. 17.7.

Fig. 17.7 Ingots from the soaking pit.

Muffle furnaces

Muffle is a chamber heated by any means i.e., by fuel or electricity which replaces the hearth in a conventional furnace. Any heat application is to the chamber which in turn passes it onto the charge inside it. The muffle is made of fireclay or alloy steel. From the aforesaid description it is useful only for heating to temperatures below 1000 °C.

The strength and heat constraints limit the thickness of the refractory muffle thickness to 20-30 mm. Electrical heating elements are embedded in the refractory or the whole casing is heated by furnace gases from all round. Heating stock in a muffle protects the stock from the furnace atmosphere and this is claimed as the top advantage in heating. A sketch of the muffle is shown in Fig. 17.8

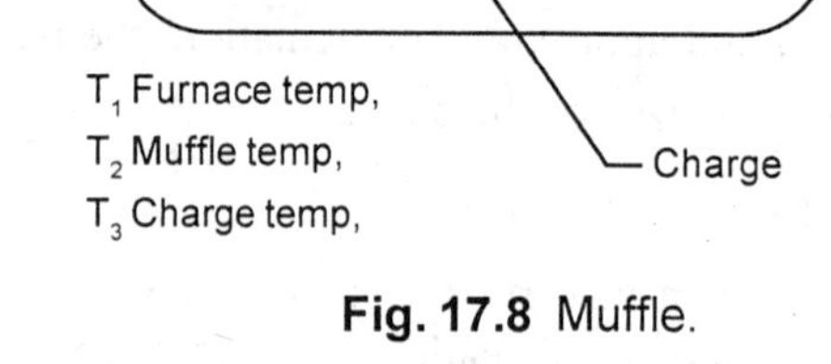

Fig. 17.8 Muffle.

As said above, the muffle walls are made of a refractory which possesses a high thermal conductivity and resistance to heat (refractivity). Fireclay and silicon carbide are in common use. Some muffles employ radiant tubes which are like flue-tube boilers in operation. These flue tubes get heat which in turn radiate it onto the charge. Radiant tubes are more commonly used in continuous furnaces. The heating capacities of the radiant tubes is limited by the heat that can be radiated from the tubes in unit time.

Reheating capacities in the temperature range* 800 - 1000 °*C

Heating capacities of these medium temperature furnaces can be determined as is done in the case of high temperatures furnaces. Although less heat is needed to be imparted to the furnace stock (weight wise), heating time is longer and heating capacity is lower owing to the fact that in these temperatures ranges, heat transfer by radiation is much less than at higher temperatures. Heat transfer coefficient (of 0.4, 0.6 etc) can be applied giving due consideration to the multipliers. This is only 40% of the value for a temperature range of 1000 - 1250 °C.

The temperature range is specifically considered because copper and its alloys are heated in this range. By comparison to steel, the heating time per an equal section equals the heating time of steel multiplied by

$$\frac{\text{Conductivity of steel} \times \text{Specific heat of the other metal}}{\text{Conductivity of the other metal} \times \text{specific heat of steel}}$$

The rate of heating of the interior of the metal expressed in cubic meters / hour is proportional to;

$$\frac{\text{Conductivity}}{\text{Specific heat} \times \text{density}}$$

It is proved by calculation and practically observed that copper equal to double the weight of steel can be heated per sq. mt hr. to the same temperature say 850-950 °C. Also, much smaller furnaces are enough for copper than those for steels.

Heat transfer and average heating capacity values from practice

The capacities of batch furnaces are limited owing to the danger of over heating of the stock. When the Hearth is properly filled, the ratio R (Stock surface/refractory surface) is of no consequence. The Table 17.1 gives some practical data regarding different heating processes.

Table 17.1

Material and purpose	Desired final temp. °C	Heat Capacity kg/sq.mt,hr
Steel :		
Hot working low C	1300	60
Hot working high C or alloy	1150 - 1200	40
Hot working Stainless steel	1250	40
Butt and lap welding	1475	90
Hardening	900	30
Drawing	550 - 575	25
Full annealing	800	5
Process anneal/tempering	660	15
Copper and Brass :		
Forming	850	100
Breakdown anneal		
Coils, sheet and tubes	725 - 750	70
Full anneal		
Coils tube and sheet	725 - 750	35
Aluminium :		
Forming ingots	550 - 575	65
Forming billets	550 - 575	35
Annealing coils	500	35

The heating capacity values given above are average values only.

Low temperature furnaces and ovens

So far we have discussed about furnaces which operate above 800 °C. At such temperatures, heat radiation is very active. Radiation at 1250 °C is five times as much as it is at 500 °C. The scenario is very different in furnaces and ovens operating below 750 °C. As seen above, if the heat transfer by radiation only is to be depended upon, the furnaces should be designed to be 6 times bigger in size for the same capacity of charge. But, fortunately, when radiation is insufficient, convection takes over. Furnace gases are also circulated inside the furnace by using fans. A balance has to be struck between the furnace size, cost of fuel and temperature uniformity in the charge. Emissivity of the charge plays an important role. The brighter the charge, the higher will be the travel of the charge.

Salt bath furnaces

Molten salts and metals are used to heat some objects, especially small in size. The stock is taken in baskets made up of wire mesh and lowered into the molten bath for the specified heating time and taken out. The stock attains the temperature of the molten bath. Herein it should be noted that heat is transferred by the liquid bath to the stock by conduction only. Convection may play a small role if the stock is shaken or agitated.

The salt baths and liquid metal baths have only a limited application. Their use is confined to low temperature heating only - limited by their melting point. An outstanding advantage of liquid bath furnaces is the metal keeping its originality - no scaling, oxidation and other types of chemical attack by furnace atmospheres.

Another constraint here is the size of the stock. Articles of a few hundred grams limited to a maximum of 750, can be successfully and conveniently handled in salt baths.

18 Furnace Design

All furnaces are built with metal and non-metallic parts which function in tandem. The non-metallic parts are made of heat-resisting products, commonly called refractories. Strength and durability of the furnace is of paramount importance as in any other structure or assembly but is really made complicated due to the heat factor. Many factors should be taken into account which effect durability (or service) of a furnace. They are listed here under :

1. Temperature of operation and fluctuation.
2. Effects of the various products of fuel combustion like the oxides, sulphur compounds and slag. Also the effects of oxygen and other gases on the furnace walls and hearth during service.
3. Explosions.
4. Mechanical injury by solids.
5. Effect of steam and water (mostly leakage)
6. Excessive loads on the roof and the side walls.
7. Vibrations, many times leading to damaging foundation.

Once we have a broad idea regarding the possible dangerous sources, we can proceed to evaluate the different materials used in the furnace and their capacity to successfully withstand the possible attack or otherwise. It is natural to select those materials for the construction of the furnace which can withstand the deleterious effects and yet economical. Cast iron and steel are the cheapest metallic materials which possess high strengths and cheap, are selected for use in furnace construction whereever possible. From the elaborate data available, cast irons are more stable than steels to withstand higher temperatures. Further, cast iron is preferable to steel in comparison for components in tension. Ductile cast iron is preferable to steel in comparison. For components in tension, ductile cast iron is preferred to ordinary cast iron.

When cast iron is used for making the hearth, it is suggested to break up the hearth into short sections and lock one end into refractory and leave sufficient gaps on the other end to provide for its growth at elevated temperatures. Though firebrick and iron have similar coefficients of thermal expansions, the hearth bars (in the case of continuous furnaces) assume more significance for, they absorb the heat first and that too quickly. This locking is diagrammatically shown in Fig. 18.1

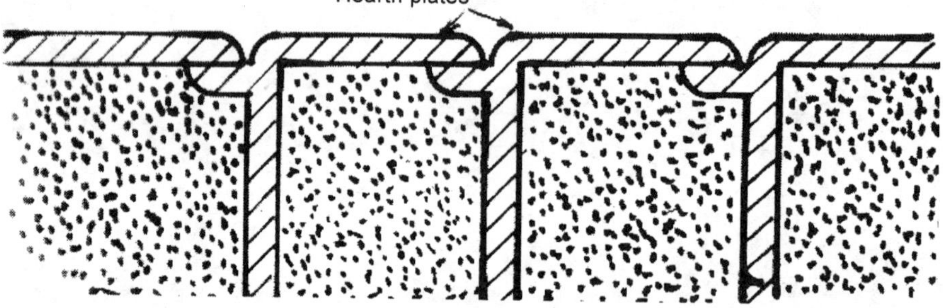

Fig. 18.1 Cast iron hearth plates anchored in brickwork.

Growth of cast iron is its expansion with temperature which does not vanish on cooling. It has considerable effect after repeated usage at temperatures up to 800 °C. It is found that ductile iron has a relatively small growth. Alloying elements like silicon or chromium greatly reduce the permanent growth.

Generally metals for continuous and successful service in furnaces operating above 750 - 800 °C should be resistant to oxidation and mild sulphur dioxide attack and possess good creep properties. Alloying with Ni, Cr, Mo, and W is found to impart these properties to the iron. Nickel chromium alloys are in good use for electrical resistors, carburising boxes, hearth plates and other miscellaneous heat-treating containers. High temperature alloys are coming up with every passing year owing to the space utility research. Creep strength is a prescribed stress which at a given time cannot create more than the stipulated elongation in the material. Commonly a creep of 1% is stipulated over a time period of 100,000 hrs at the desired temperature.

The three curves in Fig. 18.2, 18.3 and 18.4 illustrate the high temperature strengths (creep) of Nickel Chromium steels commonly used in electric furnaces. The present day creep resistant alloy market is very tight cost wise and over loaded, choice wise. Certain broad-based observations will give a clear idea regarding the usefulness of the commonly available alloys

When the fuel used is an oil or coke oven gas containing some sulphur, the alloys used in the furnace construction should have at least 24% chromium. When the operating the temperatures are 1000 °C and above a common composition is 26% chromium, 12% Nickel and 0.5% Carbon and the steel is austenitic in structure. When the sulphur problem is not there, the nickel percentage can be increased up to 20 to impart more strength. On the other hand, if the sulphur problem is severe, the chromium percentage may be increased up to 29 and nickel reduced to 9. This alloy, though not as strong as high nickel alloy, has a better resistance to sulphur attack.

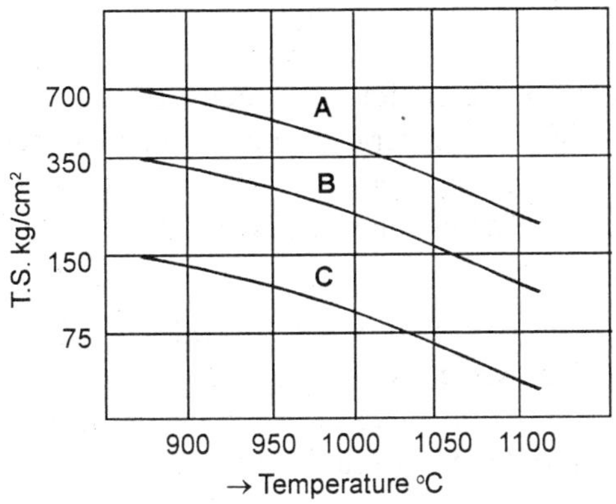

25% Cr, 35% Ni, 0.35% C } Austenitic steel

A. 100 Hrs Life stress
B. Creep stress
C. Recommended design stress

Fig. 18.2 Austenitic steel.

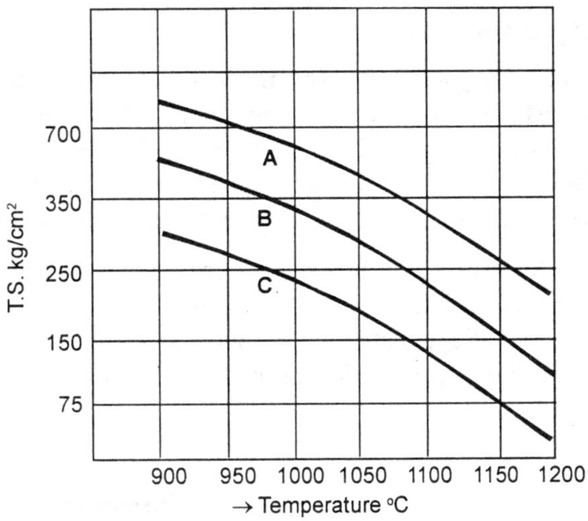

18% Cr, 38% Ni, 0.5% C } Austenitic steel

A. 100 Hrs Life stress
B. Creep stress
C. Recommended design stress

Fig. 18.3 Austenitic steel.

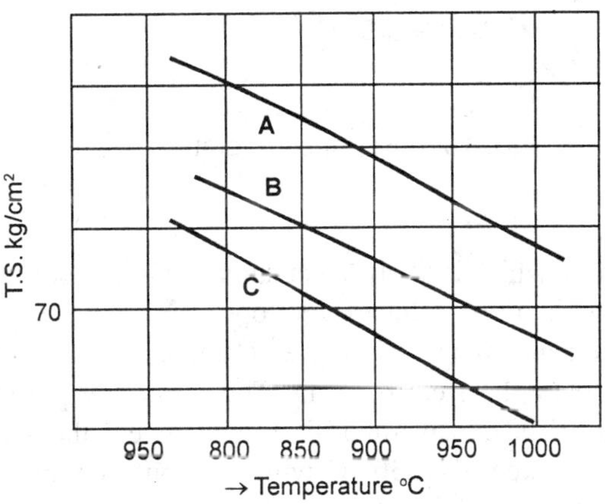

25% Cr, 9% Ni, 0.35% C } Austenitic steel

A. 100 Hrs Life stress
B. Creep stress
C. Recommended design stress

Fig. 18.4 Automatic steel.

Alloys with high nickel contents above 25% have a very good strength and also possess resistance to oxidation up to 1250 °C. Further, they have good resistance to thermal fatigue. The alloy finds its application to make retorts, calcining tubes and moving parts and parts subjected to bending loads. Temperature fluctuations of extreme type demand the use of alloys containing 60% Ni and 12% Cr of course, in the absence of sulphur threat.

Refractories

Of the many refractories available, fireclay stands out to be the refractory for use in industrial furnaces. It has good high temperature strength, resistance to furnace atmospheric conditions like furnace gases and slag. Light weight fire brick with over 40% porosity is used as insulating brick also. More about refractories is discussed under Refractories elsewhere in this volume. The only disadvantage with firebrick is its inability to withstand heating/cooling cycles.

Reverting to light weight firebricks, we should agree that there is no furnace in which this brick is not used. They form the first layer near the steel shell. Many varieties of these bricks are made to suit varied applications. The porosity and the pore structure (open or closed pores) are controlled while compacting and sintering. The use of insulated refractory lining in a furnace hood is illustrated in Fig. 18.5.

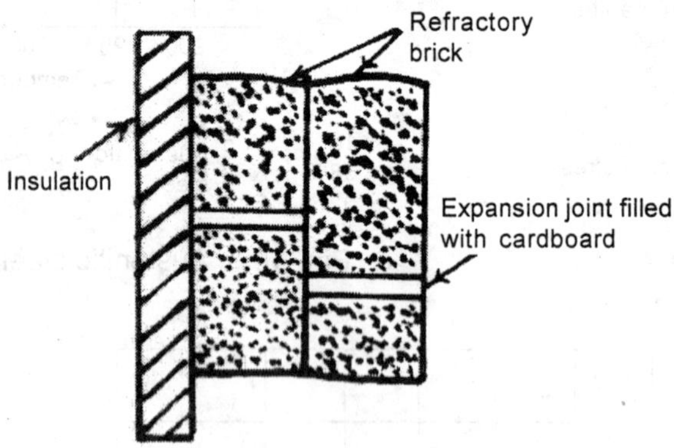

Fig. 18.5 Expansion joint.

Furnace roof

Most prominent portion in a furnace which is likely to get damaged is the roof. It should be emphasized again the basic law in theory of structures - whenever an opening is covered, the covering portion is made up of inter-balancing tension and compression layers. Refractories are very weak under tension, the tension stresses are taken up by the steel backing. The refractory portion of the roof will be experiencing wholly compression. The expansion of firebrick between the room temperature and the temperature of furnace operation taken as 1250 °C will be about 6cm/m. The inside of the arch expands while its outside retains its original size. Instability creeps into the whole roof with the surface facing the hearth becoming loose. Some portion may start to fall into the hearth. Thus, after some days of operation the roof thickness can be seen to decrease. This non-uniform thickness itself is a warning to the future collapse.

Suspended roofs are found to last longer and are preferred especially if the diameter of the furnace is more than 4 meters. Special shapes of bricks are suspended from steel girders to form a flat roof. Many types of suspensions are in vogue. However, the general construction consists of metallic hangers suspended from overhead beams. The lower ends of the hangers fit onto holes or slots in the roof tiles or grip projections of the tiles. Efforts are made to reduce the number of roof hangers by making larger roof tiles. Some designs use crossbars to carry the tiles with a few of them suspended from overhead beams.

There is a difference between sprung roofs and suspended roofs. In case of any leakage, a small leakage in a sprung roof through which the products of combustion escape does not cause much of a problem. Sulphur dioxide in the products of combustion corrodes the steel in the suspended roofs. This corrosion will be more if the steel is containing nickel. If the roof tiles are covered with thick insulation, the gases condense the moisture on the insulation resulting in the formation of sulphuric acid. This attacks the hangers very rapidly and the roof may cave in.

Insulation is another difficulty. Thick insulation raises the temperature of the uppermost portion of the tiles to almost the furnace temperature. Once the insulation is thick, it heats up the hangers elongating them due to the weight of the tiles they suppc That's why refractory hangers are introduced wherever thick insulation is employed.

Yet another difficulty is with the repair of the roof. Complicated designs of the roof make the repairer remove many tiles to reach the damaged tile at the bottom. But we should understand here, any advancement to overcome the practical difficulty will bring in its own new drawbacks. The experienced furnace man believes that service of the furnace is mostly governed by the quality of the materials used and the skill of operator.

Strength of hearths

Strength of the hearth and the foundation of the furnace are as important to the furnace as legs for a man to stand. Hearth performs the dual function of carrying the load of the charge as well as transmitting the heat to the charge. If the furnace is bottom fired, the hearth takes about 75% of the heat supplied and the balance goes to the charge; a wastage intolerable. So hearths with holes are designed so that some heat passes onto the charge directly. This also helps in lowering the heat under the hearth chamber so that its life will be more. Herein, another important point should not be missed - when the stock is heated on a perforated hearth, it should not rest on the hearth but should lie elevated using rails or some other rests. This helps in obtaining a uniform heat. In conditions when the stock has to rest directly on the hearth of an under fired furnace, it becomes imminent to make the hearth stronger and also of a refractory of good thermal conductivity. Silicon carbide stands out as a first choice because its thermal conductivity is 7 times to that of fireclay and strength 12 times, at furnace temperatures.

A hearth made of silicon carbide is also 10 times costlier than a fireclay hearth. Hence the practice still common is to go in for firebrick only and take necessary steps to meet the demands of the operation. A thumb rule for calculation of thickness of the hearth is,

Thickness of the hearth = D/6 or D/8

where,

- D is the smallest dimension of the hearth.
- 8 or 6 in the denominator of the aforesaid equation are governed by the temperature of operation of the furnace. 6 for temperatures up 1250 °C and and 8 for temperatures up to 850-900 °C.

Foundations

Furnace foundation distributes the non uniform furnace weight uniformly. The size of the concrete foundation, its reinforcements etc., are all available from data books, given the nature and type of the soil. Furnace capacity, operating temperature and the stock heated are the parameters that determine the furnace foundation. E.g., the foundation is provided with springs for furnaces situated near a steam forging hammer. Large furnaces which continuously operate at high temperatures are installed on foundation made after digging out the earth and filled with a metallurgical furnace slag.

Side walls, partitions and other vertical components

Hearths and roofs of furnaces are the other major regions where troubles may arise. Comparatively, the walls of heating and annealing furnaces causes less troubles. Basic precautions like providing expansion joint and avoiding unusually thick brick work (more than 30 cm) are important. If thick brick work is needed any times, it should be supported by steel hooks entangled to the steel angles (Fig. 18.6 and 18.7). Thus, the danger of the refractory falling onto the hearth is minimized. Generally, the sidewall in a furnace seldom falls because the thrust of the arch presses the skewback against the binding. Also the friction between the skewback and the top of the wall holds it in position.

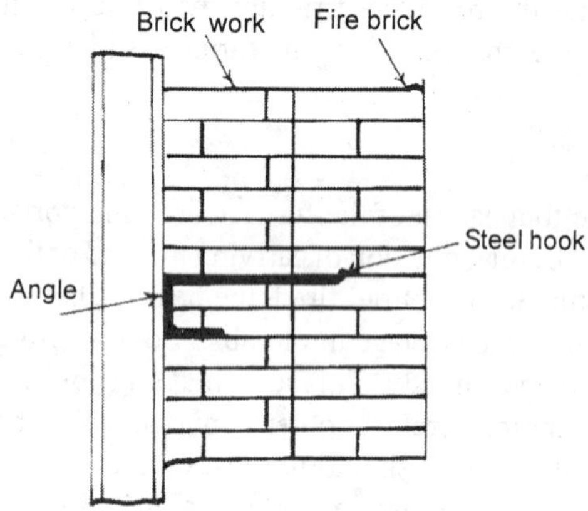

Fig. 18.6 Large furnace wall supported by hook.

Partition walls and bridge walls are heated from both sides. So they must be built of high grade materials, especially if the operating temperatures are in excess of 1300-1350 °C. The partition walls in ingot heating furnaces (soaking pits) are made with high grade firebrick or silica stone to a thickness of a meter give good service, if proper care is taken in heating and cooling the furnace.

Special partition walls over which flame or flue gases flow from one chamber to another in a furnace are called bridge walls. These are common in regenerative furnaces and in the direct fired furnaces where coal is the fuel. These experience the difficulty not only with the high temperature but the ash particles of the coal, and iron oxide particles impinge on them directly. Due to the severity of service conditions, the bridge walls are maintained every weekly holiday. Water-cooling helps the wall life. As it does not have any support laterally, the portion which is exposed to high temperatures should be sufficiently thick. It should be 2/3 thick as its height in furnaces where the temperature exceeds 1250-1300 °C. The bridge wall is constructed in such a way that it is wider at the bottom than at the top. Low temperature operating furnaces may have somewhat thinner bridge walls.

Protection of walls and roofs by mortar and cements

The brickwork of the wall is exposed to the furnace conditions which tend to be severe when the temperatures of operation are in the higher ranges of 1200 °C and above. Non uniform erosion occurs

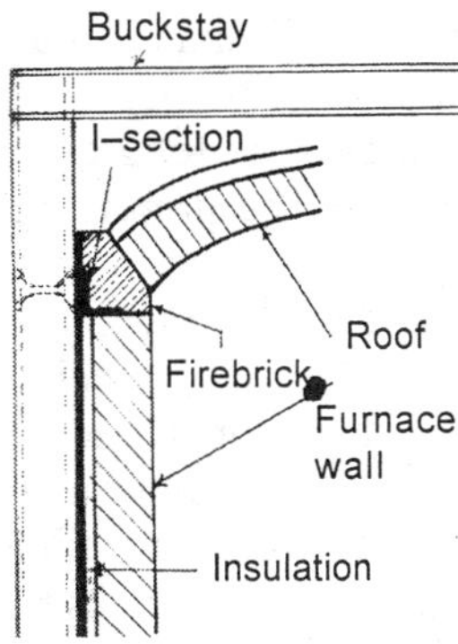

Fig. 18.7 Furnace wall.

in the bricks and immediate maintenance is called for to arrest further damage. Fireclay mortar is used for such repairs. Even when used in laying the furnace walls, these mortars and cements do not possess the same brick characteristics due to their 'raw' nature. Further, cheaper quality mortar may melt or spall when used especially in the bottom portions of the walls and furnace sides of the arches. Consequently, lining may assume the shape as depicted in Fig. 18.8 which is highly exaggerated for the purpose of greater understanding. Mortars of improved quality are available, one, hot –setting and the other-cold setting. Hot setting mortars do not bond until the place where they are used is heated to the prescribed temperature of setting. Then the brick work mortar joint becomes truly monolithic. The other mortar is a mixture of 10% salt, lime or Portland cement with high alumina clay, quartzite or chromite ore. Here, no fusion occurs as in the case of hot setting mortars. So, a sort of chemical combination should take place between the materials of the brick. Some time is necessary for this action and fusion temperature is lowered at the interface between bricks and the mortar, still withstanding the heat from the gases escaping out of the furnace.

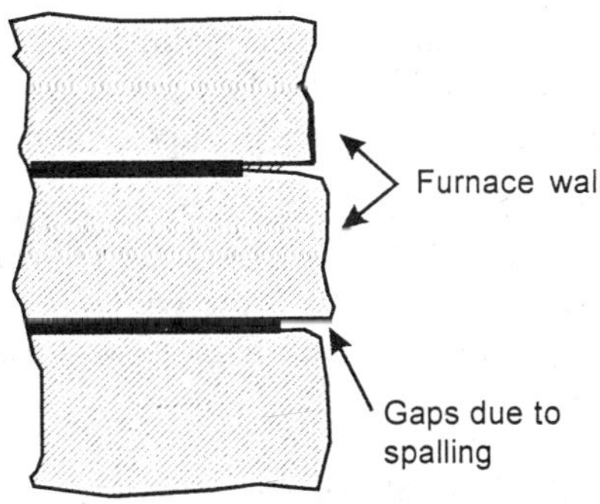

Fig. 18.8 Wall damage needing repair.

Doors

After hearth and roof, the most susceptible part in a furnace is its door. The door should be tight and close the furnace perfectly in order to insulate the furnace from outside. Doors are mainly of two types-lifting or sliding type and hinged or swinging type.

Operation of the doors consists of opening and closing. When the door is opened, the lining is cooled and when it is closed it is heated again. This temperature cycle induces spalling in many a refractory material. Some refractory cements withstand this temperature changes very well and they are used to blind the refractory brick in door frames. Doors consist of frames lined with refractories. The design and maintenance of doors is easy as long as furnace temperature does not exceed 1000 °C. Difficulties crop up when it exceeds. The firebrick lining in the door frame becomes loose and tends to drop out. Use of a good mortar will certainly minimize this danger. The bottom portion of the door generally gets the knock during the withdrawing of the heated stock. The workmen open the door only to the extent required. While the stock is being withdrawn in a hurry, there is every likelihood of it hitting the door lining. When the door is tried to be closed in a hurry to avoid heat loss, it is slammed agonist its seat. Few doors can withstand this rough treatment. A door of substantial durability is cast in cast iron poured around the firebrick laid in a mould and heated. Iron penetrates into the cracks, gaps and other openings and grips the bricks tightly. Such a door will become useless only on spalling or burning off of the refractory.

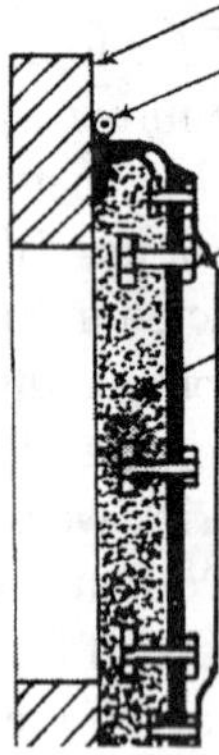

Fig. 18.9 Refractory held in position with bolts (door).

Vertically lifting doors counterbalanced by weights are in general use. These doors are of huge sizes, often exceeding 5-6 square meters. Water cooling is employed to enhance the life of the doors in some cases but not recommended as a standard practice. Electric or pneumatic operation of the lifting or sliding doors is also practiced depending upon the design.

Doors made up of halves are used in furnaces in the forge shops. Proper guiding of each half is difficult. Unless great care is taken, the two halves tend-to flap around and leave out space by hanging out of the positions. Flame discharges through the wide openings leading to the burning out of the doors, door frames and even the furnace fans. That is why use of split mechanism is discontinued.

Dampers

Damper is an obstruction to the flow of flue gases in order to control the pressure inside a furnace. As a common practice, dampers are made of high grade nodular cast iron for use at flue gas temperature up to 500-650 °C. For higher temperatures up to 800-900 °C, low alloy steel is preferred to nodular iron. For use at still higher temperatures say up to 1500 °C, bricks or tiles are out into water-cooled frame immediately below the cross beam. These are operated as well as held in place by 20 mm rods, welded to water cooled vertical members of the frame. These act as vertical slides made out of refractory fitted into a water cooled frame. The sliding action for opening and closing of the flue is achieved by the use of cables.

19 Electric Heating

All materials possess the property of electrical resistance. That is to oppose the flow of electricity through them. Electric resistance in some metals is very less and they conduct electricity freely and are called good conductors. Metals in general and noble metals - copper, silver and gold, in particular are good electrical conductors. Many metals offer some resistance and as a consequence they get heated up when current flows through them. The amount of heat generated in the material depends upon the current density and the specific resistance of the material. The materials which offer substantial resistance (R) to the flow of current are called resistors. These resistors are used for the production of heat by electricity.

The amount of heat H developed in an electrical circuit is given by Joule's law, which states,

$$H = \frac{I^2 RT}{1000} \text{ kwh} = 0.86\ I^2RT \text{ kilocals.}$$

where,

I = the current in amps.

T = time of current flow in hours.

R = resistance, ohms.

The mechanism of heat generation is simple. The resistor gets heated up due to the flow of current in it and the heat is passed on to the neighborhood. The neighborhood is the fireclay chamber which also gets heated up. The fireclay chamber is the muffle wherein the stock is kept for heating. Heat transfer in a furnace is described under the relevant chapter elsewhere. Sketches of muffles employing electrical resistors are given in Fig. (19.1)

Non-metallic resistors are used for temperatures above 1000 °C but have their own drawbacks. Graphite for example, is not amenable to shaping. Heating elements of graphite are shaped only by machining. Silicon carbide is another material for resistors. They are sold as rods or bars of specialized sizes and brand names. The rationale in the manufacture of these standard sizes lies in the making of what is called 'hot length' of the bar. The ends of the bar are made thicker so that they protrude outside through the furnace wall to facilitate electrical connections. These ends are metallised and offer much less resistance. So they remain relatively cool. The maximum operating temperature with silicon carbide elements is 1550 °C.

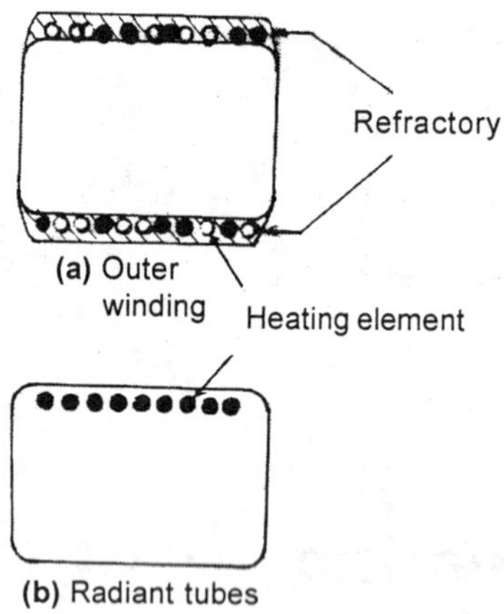

Fig. 19.1 Muffles with (a) outer winding (b) Radiant tubes.

Both the constituents of the bar, namely silicon and carbon, get oxidized above 900 °C. Silicon gets oxidized to silica which protects the rod. The oxidation of the skin of the element increases its life; the presence of hydrogen in the furnace acts otherwise, reducing the life of the rod. Another important point in achieving larger life of the resistor is maintaining the ideal spacing between them and the furnace wall. The distance between resistors, the ideal spacing, should be two diameters.

Liquid Resistors

Glass and molten salts conduct electricity. In their use, care should be taken to see that the molten bath is not solidified even on weekends or holidays. If it solidifies problems crop up in restarting because glass and many of the salts are bad conductors when solid. It is recommended to maintain a pool of liquid so that restarting is conveniently possible.

The two electrodes i.e. resistors are hung into the metal or salt maintaining an optimum distance between them. When the electrodes are close, the passing alternating current generates electrodynamic forces in the liquid causing agitation. This circulation helps in accomplishing a uniform bath temperature, preventing the liquid to be in contact with the electrodes for longer periods of time than necessary.

Use of metallic resistors is developed to achieve better service. The advantages of formability of metals and their high resistance have led to this. Metals used at first were molybdenum and molybdenum-silicon alloys. Yet, oxidation problems cropped up, above say 1500 °C where some salts melt. Again the research reverted back to platinum. Whatever metal or alloy is employed as a resistor, it has its own limitations. Selection of a proper (suitable) resistor rests with the metallurgist and the operator on the job.

Arc furnaces

When an arc is struck between two conductors, a large quantity of heat is generated at the arc. Arc temperature is 3600 °C, a temperature at which almost all the metals and alloys melt.

Welding of metals employs electric arc because of its developing high temperature. Use of an electric arc in the extraction and purification of many metals is common. An electric arc is struck between electrodes which are held just above the surface of the charge in a crucible which is covered from the top. The electrodes are inserted horizontally. The charge melts owing to the heat of the arc produced just above. The electrodes are made of platinum. Platinum, being a noble metal does not melt or oxidize easily and the electrodes remain intact. Other materials like copper alloys, graphite etc. will erode away - rather get consumed. Such furnaces in which the electrodes are consumed like that are called consumable electrode arc furnaces. Furnaces which employ electrodes of platinum as said above are called non-consumable electrode furnaces. Melting occurs due to the heat generated just above the charge. So, such furnaces are classified as indirect arc furnaces.

Arc can also be struck between an electrode entering the furnace from its dome (roof) and the charge which acts as negative. Such an arc furnace is nomenclatured as 'direct arc furnace'. In this furnace the arc is struck by the electrode directly with the charge (to be melted). So far we have discussed the basics of an arc furnace. Electric arc furnaces as described above are seldom made except for laboratory demonstrations. Today's electric arc furnaces use three phase power supply. A schematic diagram of three phase electric arc furnace is given in Fig. 19.2. A photograph of an arc furnace is given in Fig. 19.3. The furnace commonly known as Heroult's electric arc furnace is used for steel making or steel melting in foundries.

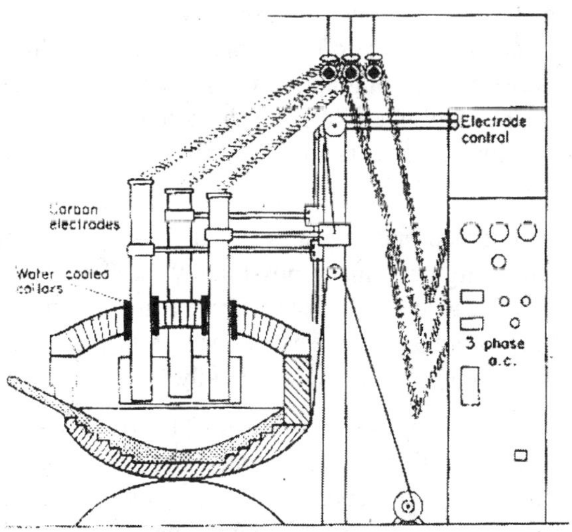

Fig. 19.2 Hall-Heroult type three phase direct arc melting furnace as used for steelmaking. Electrode positions are continuously adjusted. Charging may be via doors or through a removable roof. Furnace tilts for slagging and casting.

Fig. 19.3 Der Hochleistungs - Elektrolichtbogenofen.

The furnace may be of a small capacity 1-5 tons or of large a capacity up to 250 tons. The former are used in the foundries whereas furnaces of larger capacities are used in steel making.

It has a swinging roof having three holes through which the electrodes are lowered into the furnace. These holes are fitted with water cooled copper sleeves to minimize the heat damage to the roof linging. The electrodes are made up of graphite and self-baking type. They are known as Soderberg electrodes. Graphite paste, specially made to form the electrode is charged into the electrode dies which in its descent through the top of gets solidified (baked) on account of the high temperatures prevailing at the furnace roof.

Large furnaces are top charged and furnaces up to five tones capacity are generally charged though a charging door. Top charging is made possible by the furnace design of having a swinging roof. The electrodes are lifted upwards out of the furnace and the furnace dome swung sideways. The charge is made and thereafter the dome is replaced and the electrodes lowered for furnace operation. All these functions are performed automatically.

Electrical arc furnace steel making is similar of open hearth process. It has an added advantage greater control over the steel composition. The economics of steel production i.e cost per ton of steel produced is almost the same. The power consumption per ton of steel produced varies in the range of 600-850 KWH. Plain carbon steels, whose tap to tap time is 2.5 to 2.75 hours consume less while alloy steels like stainless steels consume higher units owing to longer tap to tap time (of about 4 hours). Converted into money, this works out to be similar to the cost of the fuel in the case of open hearth furnace.

Metal is tapped from the electric arc furnace by tilting it. The bottom cup of the furnace i.e., the body, is located on a rocker mechanism to enable it to be lowered up to 20^0 from the horizontal for tapping. Later, it is brought to the horizontal position and is ready for charging.

Furnace linings differ according to the acid or basic process of refining adopted. Tarred dolomite or chrome magnesite are the common basic linings. The roof of the furnace is lined with sillimanite or silica or high alumina fireclay. Roof does not come into contact with metal or slag. The selection of the refractory for the roof is made keeping in view its capacity to resist high temperatures and spalling.

Induction heating

Change of direction of current flow in a conductor causes a change in the electromagnetism around it. This can be utilized to produce an electric current in a suitably placed object. In this process, the object gets heated up. What we generally term as 'iron loss' in a generator, is utilized here in induction heating. The equipment for induction heating is basically very simple - a coil of wire wherein alternate current flows. This coil is called the induction coil and surrounds the object to be heated.

The conduction of alternating current is associated with what is commonly called 'skin effect'. It is found that when an alternating current passes through a wire, a lot of the current travels through the surface or through a very thin layer of the surface of the conductor. This is called skin effect. Steinmetz had developed an equation for this induction heating which is as follows:

$$P = \frac{5030}{\sqrt{F\mu}}\sqrt{r}$$

Where P = depth in cms for which the current penetrates when the magnetic flux is induced from the primary.

r = Resistivity of the charge Ohms / cm^2 / cm

F = frequency c/s and

μ = magnetic permeability of the charge (μ = 1 for iron at elevated temperatures). Thus, for a given material, if the frequency is increased from 50 to 2500 c/s, the depth of penetration is decreased approximately by 1/7th

In the construction of induction coils, this is taken advantage of and a copper pipe of 2 cm dia is used instead of a solid copper of 2 cm dia for the conduction in both of them is the same. The skin effect grows with frequency not only in the coil but also in the work load. At high frequencies, almost all the heating occurs in the skin of the work blank. The thickness to which the work blank gets heated up increases and of course, the rate of heating, as the frequency is decreased. It should be understood that the heat drop from the surface to the centre is exponential. The heat drop is more gradual in the case of lower frequencies.

Bars or billets of large sections can be heated by low frequency induction if the heating should be throughout the section say, for rolling or forging. High frequency however, is needed for case hardening heat treatment because only the skin has to be heated to a high temperature and quenched. The quenching medium employed in induction hardening is compressed air.

In induction heating of metallic work it should be thoroughly insulated from the induction coil. If the diameter of the blank is small (say less than 50 mm. for mild steel) air is sufficient to function as an insulator. The outside of the blank is extremely hot at the end of the heating cycle. It starts to dissipate the heat from its surface towards inside and also loses some heat to the atmosphere. Temperature equalization occurs in the blank owing to the first phenomenon. The diameter up to which air insulation is sufficient varies with the material of the bar. Different metals have different softening temperatures, conductivities and emissivities. Frequency too has an influence.

In the induction heating of bars and heavy sections air is sufficient as an insulator for electrical insulation between the induction coil and the work blank. However, this does not and can not provide heat insulation. Consequently too much heat is lost unless proper thermal insulation is provided. A refractory, like sillimanite which has resistance to high temperature, is rammed between the turns of the induction coil. The thickness of the refractory should be an optimum, say 12-14 mm. A thick insulation lowers the efficiency and power factor whereas a thin refractory does not in any way help heating the stock. A sectional diagram of an induction furnace is shown in Fig. 19.4 wherein the induction coils embedded in refractory can be seen.

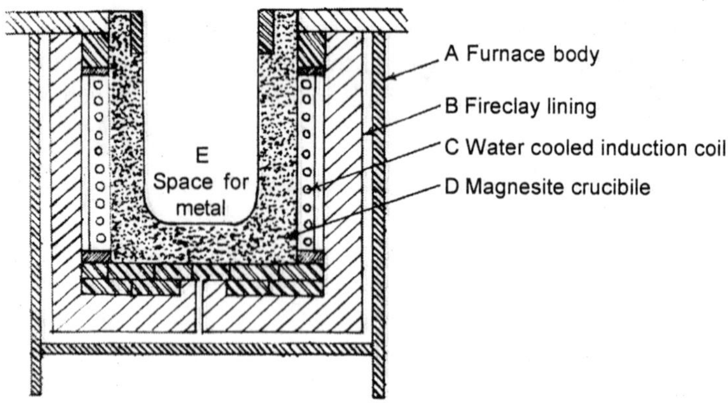

Fig. 19.4 Cross section of an induction furnace.

Electrical induction furnaces are progressively employed in foundries where the maintenance of the quality of the castings takes precedence over the cost of electric power. There is no contamination of the metal in induction melting. So far induction furnace have not been tried in composite iron and steel plants, may be due to the capacity and power restraints.

20 Heat Economics

Heat economics deals with the money spent in the process of heating a product in a furnace. It can be said that it is the cost of heating per ton of stock. It can be compared to the term 'Direct cost' in the cost accounting terminology. Other costs also accrue - like cost of salvaging the metal, partially damaged during heating and the losses resulting due to scrapping during the inspecting process. The latter two costs can be taken as the indirect costs, yet added up to the cost of heating.

In the furnace operation all the heat sent into the furnace is not utilized for raising the temperature of the stock only. Much of it is lost from the heat economy point of view, in the following ways.

1. Taken up by the cold furnace Fig. 20.1
2. Carried away by the flue gasses Fig. 20.2
3. Escapes through the roof, door and door gaps
4. Conduction and radiation through the refractories.

Heat loss in the forms 3 and 4 mentioned above are the necessary evils associated with furnace operation. They cannot be avoided but only minimized. Heat taken by a cold furnace (1 above) is a must, for the furnace should, after all, be heated to its temperature of operation. This accounts for nearly 40% of the heat input. Though this is a one time phenomenon, the quantity involved is substantial. An idea of this can be had form Fig. 20.1. Heat carried away by the products of combustion (3 above) will be in potential form i.e. as unburnt fuel or kinetic form as their sensible heat, including the latent heat of steam present. The sensible heat in flue gases in shown in Fig. 20.2. Flue gases contain excess air joining them due to suction through doors and joints. Economy in heat management of a furnace comprises of recovery of heat from these flue gases.

Two methods of waste heat recovery from the flue gases are in vogue. One is a continuous process of heat recovery using recuperators and the other, an intermittent process, by the use of regenerators. Recuperator is a chamber like device through which flue gases are passed. Heat in the flue gases is extracted by a stream of cold air. They are classified depending upon the directions of flue gases and air in them. The three types are illustrated in Fig. 20.3. Calculation of heat transfer in recuperators is a very approximate mathematical exercise. Variables like density and velocity of the flue gases and air, leakage and considerable variation in the value of heat transfer coefficient come into the equation; besides of course, the temperatures of flue gases and air. It is therefore advised to go in for a simple thumb rule formula which states,

Heat transferred = weight of flue gases × temperature drop × average specific heat flowing in unit time

= Heating surface × coefficient of heat transmission × mean temp. diff. between flue gases and air

= Weight of air flowing in unit time × rise in temperature of air × average sp. ht. of air

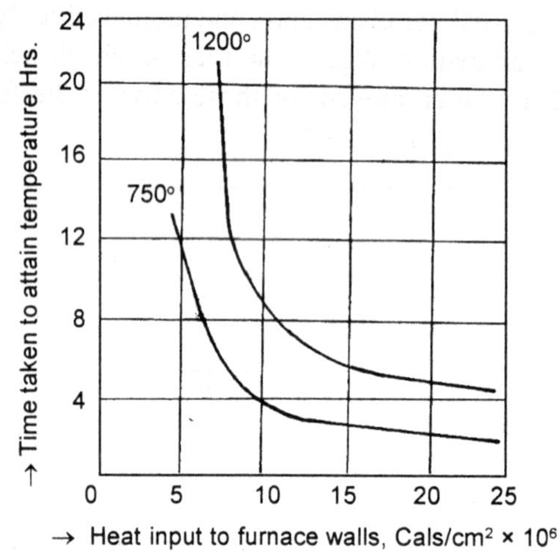

Fig. 20.1

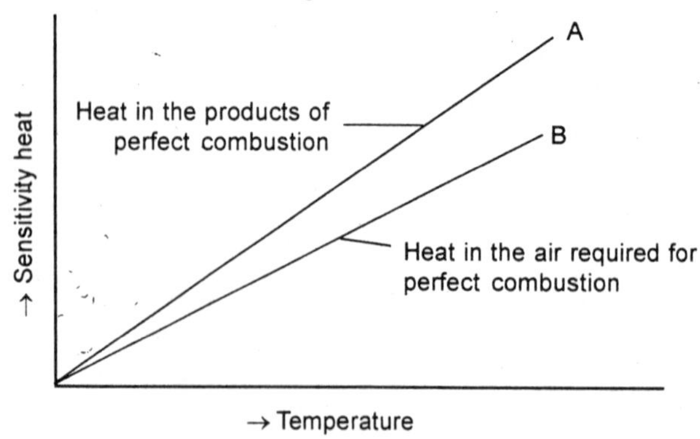

Fig. 20.2

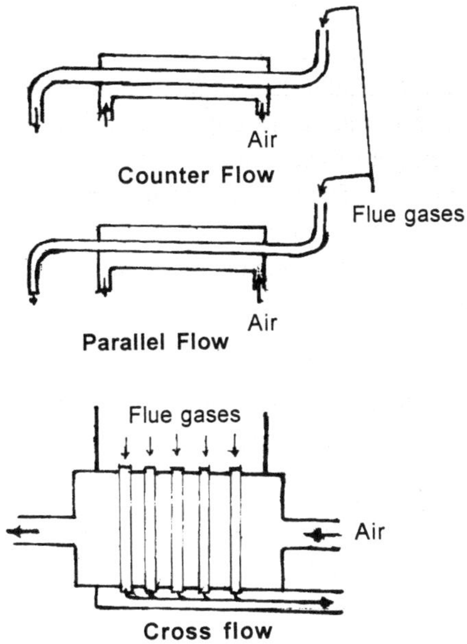

Fig. 20.3 Types of recuperators.

Thus $$W_g (T_2 - T_1) \text{ gas} = A \times k \times (T_g - T_a) = W_a \times (T_2 - T_1) \text{ air} \times C_a$$

The value of coefficient of heat transmission k is really handy. The units of the coefficient of heat transmission are in K. cals/ m² hr °C. This is the reciprocal of the summary resistance which ia made up as,

$$k = \frac{1}{R_a + R_g + R_w}$$

where

R_a = heat resistance from air to wall

R_g = heat resistance from flue gas to wall

R_w = heat resistance to heat flow in the wall (refractory)

It helps in the determination of the area of the heating surface in a recuperator.

As a general rule it is said that every degree of pre-heat of air manifests itself in the temperature rise by one degree in the furnace. Thus, if a furnace is fired with fuel and preheated air say at 300 °C, the furnace temperature also records a rise of 300 °C. This is not a straight line relationship. After a certain value of the temperature of preheat the furnace temperature gets stabilized. The advantage of preheating manifests itself in promoting a 100% burning to the fuel and high heat emission. The heating time of the stock is also reduced. Recuperators and regenerators themselves should be regarded as low temperature furnaces or ovens.

Copper pipes were employed in the early recuperators because copper is a good conductor. With the advent of high temperatures, increase of the cost of copper and the deleterious effects of the flue gas constituents rising, chequer tile work of fireclay was started to be used. Tile or chequer brick work helps in reducing the velocities of gases in the recuperators. This promotes good heat transfer. One difficulty with refractory lined recuperators is, however, is the gas and air velocities and thereby their quantities cannot be precisely controlled because the brick work starts to leak on some usage. The value of coefficient of heat transfer is taken as 2.5.

Pick-up is a common term used in the recuperator language. It is similar to the term efficiency in any other operation. Pick up is a fraction $\frac{(T_2 - T_1)\text{air}}{(T_{2a} - T_g)}$.

Commonly pick up is limited to 60%. This can be increased up to 75% as the fuel goes up. Herein one point cannot be overlooked i.e the recuperator size goes up as the pick up increases.

Radiation Recuperator

The property of thermal radiation is harnesses in the design of this appliance. Radiation recuperator is a tall cylindrical body made up of two concentric sheet metal shells. There is an annular space between the two shells. The air to be heated passes through this annulus. Hot flue gases enter the recuperator axially from the top (or bottom) Fig. 20.4. The total of the whole gas inlet (diameter) is much smaller compared to the diameter of the recuperator. The gas mixes with the cooler gas in the recuperator and temperature equalization takes place.

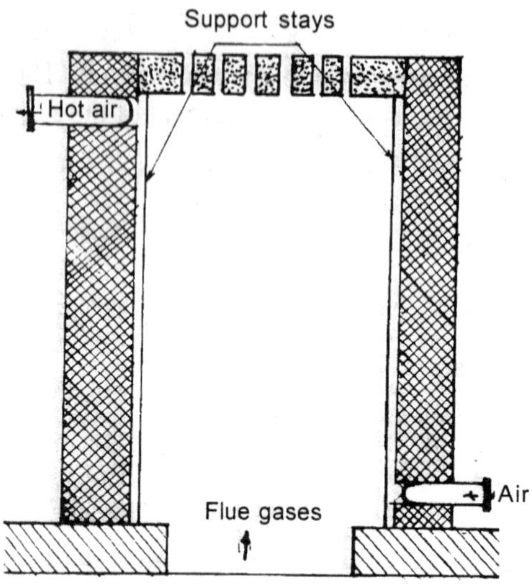

Fig. 20.4 Radiation recuperator.

Heat in the flue gases is radiated to the walls of the recuperators. The metal surface wall of the inner shell picks up the heat and conducts to the air which is flowing through the annulus. The outside of the recuperator is insulated to avoid any loss of heat into the atmosphere. The air gets heated up by the counter flow principle. The metal at the hot end is protected by the principle of small diameter gas stream and large diameter absorbing area. This description is of a simple design and forms the basis of a radiation recuperator. This is modified and progressively bettered. Modern recuperators, as tall as 20 m are working quite satisfactorily.

Regenerators

Regenerators are large constructions with chequer brick carefully laid so as to make continuous and zigzag ducts for gases to pass through. There will be more than one regenerator with a furnace. These regenerators are inter connected with changeover valves. These valves are operated either manually or with electric or electronic timers for putting on any of the regenerator to use i.e. on air or on gas. Putting on gas means, the flue gases are admitted into the regenerator. The hot gases while passing through the zigzag path of the firebrick lose their heat to the brickwok. After sometime, the gas supply to the regenerator is cut off and directed into another and the former regenerator is put 'on air', The cold air admitted into the heated chequer brick, gets heated up.

Almost all the furnaces operating at high temperature i.e. 1000 °C and above and the fuel fired are associated with regenerators. The pig iron blast furnace is supplemented with three regenerators which are called blast furnace stoves. The blast furnace gets heated air from one regenerator once in every 20 minutes. Every open hearth furnace used in steel making industry is fitted with two sets of regenerators.

Fig. 20.5 shows the changes in temperatures of a regenerator with time and space after the reversal of the direction of gas flow. It can be seen that the temperature falls sharply during the first few minutes after it is put on air.

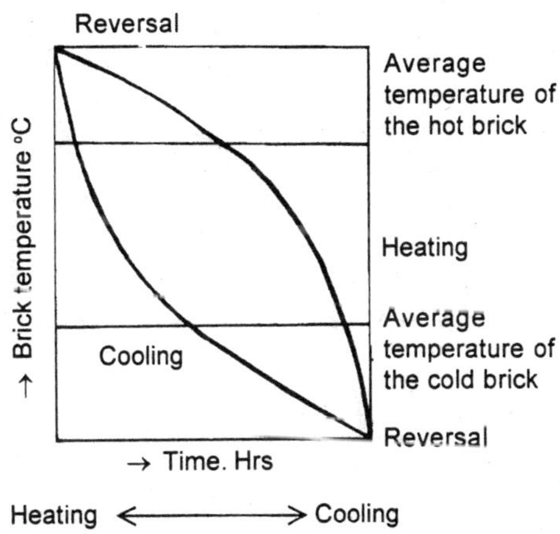

Fig. 20.5 Temperature changes in a radiation recuperator.

As seen above, the purpose of a regenerator or recuperator is to abstract the maximum possible heat from the gases escaping from the furnace. This heat is stored for a few minutes in a metal or refractory chequer work and again passed on to the (cold) air entering the regenerator. The sensible heat of the air is increased i.e. its temperature is increased in the regenerator. The air enters the furnace through the regenerator and the furnace temperature would be higher than when fired with cold air. This way, a fraction of the heat escaping out of the furnace with flue gases, is taken back and re-circulated. Effects of using preheated air is plotted against the fuel saved in Fig. 20.6 and the heat generated per unit weight of fuel is plotted against air pre heat in Fig. 20.7.

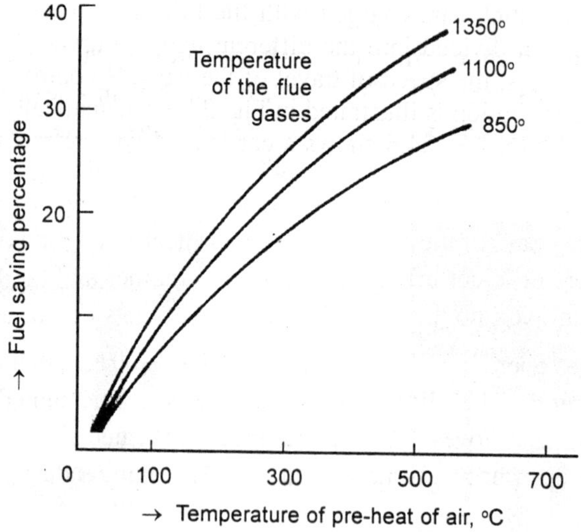

Fig. 20.6 Temperature of preheat of air.

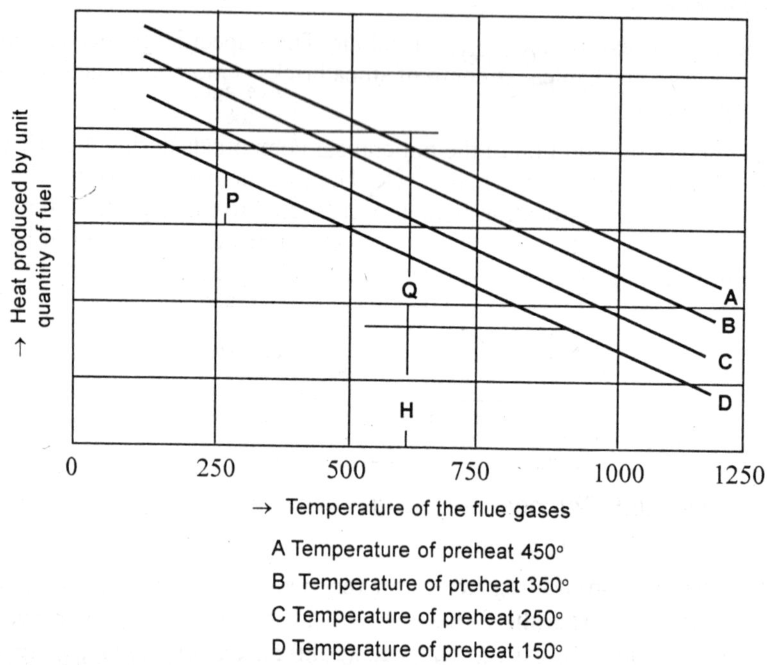

Fig. 20.7 Temperature of flue gases.

21 Furnace Atmospheres

We have seen and understood so far what a furnace and its main purpose . Study of furnaces is not complete without understandings what happens in them, besides transfer of heat to the charge. If a charge suffers metallurgical damage due to the conditions in the furnace, the whole process is a waste of time, fuel and above all, the material itself.

Extraction and refining furnaces deal with liquid metals. The processes involved may be oxidation or reduction of the charge, in a prescribed fashion. The conditions inside the furnace are tailored to suit the process. This is generally accomplished by making suitable furnace additions like adding iron ore, mill scale to steel in an open hearth or electric furnace to reduce the carbon content of the charge; adding ferro-alloys for de-oxidizing the excess iron oxidized and make up the final composition of steel. In the former case of one boil period, we say that an oxidizing atmosphere is maintained in the furnace. In the subsequent case of addition of coke or ferro-alloys it is said that a reducing atmosphere is maintained to recover the iron from the excessive oxidation – to prevent FeO from joining the slag and return to the metal as iron. The terminology has a reference to the metal/slag bath. On the other hand, when a metal or alloy is heated as a first step for further mechanical processing like rolling, forging, drawing etc. or a deformed metal or alloy is being reheated for improving mechanical properties like annealing, normalizing, etc. and for heat treatment processes mostly involving chemical change in its surface like carburizing, nitriding, cyaniding, in the reheating furnace occupies paramount importance. Furnace atmosphere cannot be oxidizing so as to promote scaling of steel which is being austenitised for hardening (quenching).

When steel is heated in a furnace, it is the temperature which effects the structural changes in it i.e. take it to an austenitic crystal structure by increasing temperature. The temperature in the furnace which consists of flue gases – water vapour, carbon dioxide, carbon monoxide and oxygen, play a leading role in maintaining the chemistry of the steel 'in tact'. The equilibrium of these gases at different temperatures is plotted in the Fig. 21.1. The presence of water vapour and carbon gases will be a must when the furnace is fuel-fired, as in 90% of the cases. Even when an electrically heated furnace is used, these gases will be present, but in very small quantities from the air in the furnace and oxidation of some carbon from the steel surface occurs.

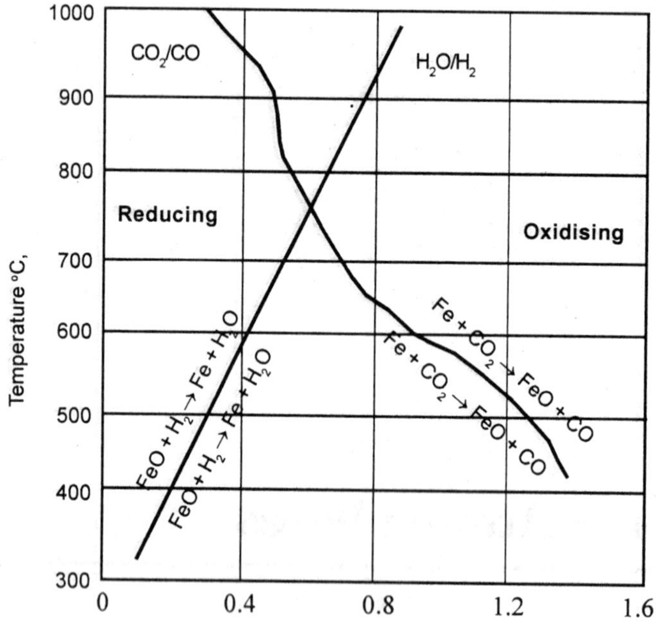

Fig. 21.1 Equilibrium between iron, carbon monoxide and water vapour.

Commonly our focus will be to avoid the surface decarburization and oxidation of steel in a furnace. Various methods of achieving this are adopted, as follows :

1. Supplying adequate amount of air to achieve just a complete combustion of the fuel. This prevents the presence of free oxygen in the furnace.
2. Perfect sealing of the furnace to avoid seepage of air into the furnace or maintaining a slightly more than atmospheric pressure inside.
3. To introduce reducing gases like higher hydrocarbons so that the gases inside, will always be of a reducing nature.

The equilibria $2CO \rightarrow CO_2 + C$ and $2H_2 + O_2 \rightarrow 2H_2O$ are studied and suitable temperature and pressures for the promoting of reduction reactions are best tried to be maintained.

Special atmosphere

The above discussion is aimed at preventing any loss to the surface composition of the steels. Case hardening process, involving a change in the composition of the surface of the steel warrants this. Case carburizing increases the percentage of carbon in the surface layers of steel to a certain depth. In nitriding, hard stable nitrides of iron and chromium are formed on the surface. A regulated furnace atmosphere is maintained when carburizing or nitriding is performed by gaseous media. Such furnace atmosphere maintains liberal availability of carbon in the form of CO or C_2H_2 for carburizing and nitrogen in the form of NO for nitriding, in the furnace.

Table 12.1 Salt bath compositions.

Type	Nacl	Kcl	$Bacl_2$	$NaNo_3$	$NaNo_2$	KNo_3	$cacl_2$	NaCn	Na_2Co_3	KCN	M.P °c (approx)	Heating Range °C
Low Temp					40/50	50/60					160	180-650
"				40/50		50/60					145	275-650
"	30/40		25/35					15/40	30/50		565	715-835
Med. TemP	45/55	45/55									695	750-910
"	20/30		70/80								725	770-950
"	10/20		80/90								770	835-1100
High. TemP			98+								1000	1060-1350
"	4/8		92/96								890	975-1280
C	4 max							96+	4 max		715	800-975
C									4 max	96+	715	800-975
C	15/25							45/50	20/30 $BaCO_3$		715	835-975
C	10/15							70/80	10/15		715	835-975
C	40/50							40/50	5/10		715	835-975

Note : Fuel-Fired heating only below 800°C

Maintenance of a reducing atmosphere in a furnace goes contrary to the efficient usage of fuels in the furnace. Usage of excess air is prescribed and practiced to achieve a 100% combustion of the carbon in the fuel. When excess air is used, there will always be the availability of oxygen which will be a source of decarburization and oxidation of the stock. Efficient burning, followed by scavenging of the flue gases will go a long way in minimizing the oxidation effects.

Protective Atmosphere

It is recommended to cover the surface of the steel heated to high temperatures i.e above 1350 °C with vapours of certain salts. Salts are vaporized at the furnace temperatures and mixed with the circulating products of combustion. The presence of Lithium salts anywhere in the furnace will prevent decarburization and scaling.

Many types of protective atmospheres are used. This warrants a totally sealed furnace. Sealing the furnace with the required gases is a job itself, in addition to the auxiliary equipment for the production of the required gas-mix. This is practiced while heating relatively larger stock.

Smaller jobs and special alloys are best protected by heating in molten salt baths or molten metal baths. Herein also crops up a problem. Many commonly used molten salts dissolve oxygen and pass it on to the metal. A small percentage, say 2% borax is added to the salt bath to prevent this oxygen absorption from the atmosphere. Sprinkling of a small quantity of graphite powder, sodium nitrate or ferro-silicon on the molten salt (or lead) surface also has the same effect. Some common salt bath compositions are listed in Table 12.1.

The best way to control any decarburization or scale formation is to heat the metal in an inert atmosphere using Argon. Another is, of course, using a vacuum furnace.

UNIT III

Refractories

22 Introduction and Classification

Refractories

Broadly speaking, materials which withstand high temperatures can be defined as refractories. Many materials fall into the family of refractories. Amongst these, there are naturally occurring materials as well as some synthetic blends; though a majority of them are of the former variety.

Refractory should posses the following properties:

1. Good Refractoriness, capacity to withstnad high temperatures (above 700 °C)
2. Withstand thermal shock (sudden temperature variations) under load
3. Chemically stable
4. Possess abrasive resistance
5. Possess good compressive strength
6. Have low porosity
7. Have good spalling resistance, resistance to peeling or cracking at higher temperature
8. Posses low contraction or expansion coefficients (to avoid spalling) and
9. Possess thermal conductivities as required, viz, high conductivity for use in regenerators and recuperators and low conductivity for use in melting furnaces.

Refractories can be broadly classified as:

1. Clays
2. Clay materials with alumina base
3. Silica minerals
4. Lime and magnesite

5. Chromite
6. Rare metal refractory oxides and
7. Carbon

1. Clays

It is very difficult to precisely define a clay. However, it can be defined as an earthy matter which has the capacity to absorb some water and become plastic. The clay may have an alumina base or sodium base. Various names are given to the clays depending upon their composition. E.g., Fireclay, diaspore clay, flint clay, kaolin etc.,

Clay consists of various mineral particles occurring in the size ranges of 100–0.1 microns. These particles are platy in structure. Various ions like calcium, sodium are attached to these particles so that their physical properties are affected. Some impurities like quartz, mica are also associated with the clays as well as some organic materials like lignite.

Clays are established to be the weathered products, derived from rocks which are rich in feldspar. It is suggested that the rocks lose their alkali content as soluble salts and silica as colloidal silica. Clays which occur at the same place as their parental rock are called residual clays. Sometimes, clays are found at a different place than the parental rock and these are called transported clays.

All the clays contain certain percentage of some of the following non-clay minerals in a finely divided state. These have a reasonable degree of influence on the properties of the clay. These non-clayey minerals are :

1. Quartz
2. Orthoclase and plagioclase feldspars
3. Muscovite and Biotite mica
4. Iron oxides (haematite, magnetite, limonite)
5. Titanium oxides (rutile and anatase)
6. Limestone
7. Gypsum
8. Magnesite
9. Garnet and
10. Tourmaline

Most of the above minerals act as 'fluxes' and render the clay easy-softening. Thus, its refractory properties are reduced.

Physical properties of clays

Clays consist of particles of size ranging from 0.1–100 microns. The surface area increases with the increase in the fineness of the clay. This leads to a greater capacity for water absorption. That is why, the plastic clays which consist of a large percentage of 'fines' possess a high degree of plasticity than the other types of clays.

It is established that, the finer the grain size, more is the plasticity or workability of the clay. Thus, the plasticity of most clays can be increased by fine grinding, ageing or mixing another clay of finer grain size or mixing organic matter.

Some clays will readily slake or break down in water, E.g.. Plastic clays. But some, shaly or flint types, do not break down in the water and so need fine grinding. The reason for this behavior is attributed to the ion-exchange property in the presence of water.

Fine-grained clays suffer more shrinkage. They also possess a higher value of dry strength.

The fusion point of clays varies considerably in the range of 1600 - 1800 °C. of the family of clays, the ball clay and fireclay are of imminent concern to the refractory engineer. While the former is useful as a bond material between a hard and a plastic clay, the latter is directly used as the raw material in the manufacture of the common refractory, 'firebrick'. The analyses of some clays are given in Table 22.1.

Table 22.1 Analysis of clays.

Constituent	Ball Clay	Flint Clay	Semiflint Clay
SiO_2	46.00	45.00	43.00
Al_2O_3	33.00	37.00	37.00
Fe_2O_3	2.00	0.5	1.5
CaO	0.8	0.6	0.75
MgO	–	0.2	0.5
K_2O	0.7	0.6	1.1
TiO_2	–	2.0	1.8
H_2O	17.00	13.00	12.5
Others	Bal.	Bal.	Bal.

2. Clay Minerals with Alumina base

Among this family of clays are the smaller group classification

(a) Hydrated alumina

(b) Sillimanite

(c) Topaz

(d) Pyrophyllite

(e) Corundum

Clays occur with a range of chemical composition from pure diaspore to mixtures containing all kaolinite. These are used for the manufacture of what are called the 'high-alumina firebricks'. These bricks are designated with numbers starting from 50, 60, 70 and so on, the number indicating the alumina content.

Sillimanite has a chemical composition approximating to $Al_2 SiO_2$, a silica percentage of 37, and alumina 63. Large quantities of the mineral occurs in our country.

Topaz is another mineral having a composition of $Al_2 SiO_4 (FOH)_2$. Large quantities of this mineral also occur in our country.

Pyrophyllite has a formula of $Al_2 (SiO_5) 2(OH)_2$. This is more useful in the manufacture of cement and tempering of clays than as an original refractory.

Corundum is basically Al_2O_3. This has a good refractory property. This is also a good abrasive. With a suitable binder, it yields good refractory bricks.

3. Silica Minerals

Quartzite or gannister is the most commonly employed silica mineral. The mineral will be of refractory use only when pure, as in that state, it has a fusion point of over 1700 °C. Typical analysis of gannister is as follows;

Sio_2	:	97.4%
Al_2O_3	:	1.0%
CaO	:	0.1%
Fe_2O_3	:	1.0%
Mgo	:	0.2%
Na_2O, K_2O	:	0.3%

Sand is also used as a refractory material but its direct application is very limited. It is, however, employed to enrich the quartzite, in its purity.

4. Magnesite and Lime

These are two important refractories whose use in the metallurgical industry is picking up during the last 50 years. Magnesite occurs with different chemical compositions but essentially it is a carbonate mineral. The carbonate is burnt in kilns to drive off the carbon dioxide. Crystals of periclase remain after burning. The purity of the magnesia (MgO) can further be increased by magnetic concentration, if the magnesite is iron-bearing.

A double carbonate of magnesium and calcium is called dolomite. This is successfully employed in the open hearth furnaces in place of magnesite due to its cheapness. But it has a tendency to flake and not so good as magnesite in lining life.

Lime is a good refractory but its use as such is not yet exploited. It is also produced from limestone by burning in kilns.

Olivine is another refractory mineral, approximating to of Mg_2 SiO_3 composition. However, some of its magnesia (5-8%) is replaced by FeO. It has no direct use as a refractory but is used to blend magnesite. The resulting refractory bricks are called frosterite bricks.

5. Chromite

Chromite is the name of the refractory obtained from chrome ore. Chromite consists of Cr_2O_3, Al_2O_3, FeO and MgO in mutual solid solution. Sometimes the chrome ore is associated with impurities like silica, feldspars and some carbonates. The composition of the chrome ore from Zimbabwe which is the largest supplier of the ore is as follows:

Cr_2O_3	:	45.4
SiO_2	:	7.5
Al_2O_3	:	13.8
FeO	:	15.1
CaO	:	1.1
MgO	:	18.2

Nowadays Chrome ore is used for blending magnesite to manufacture what are popularly known as 'Chrome-magnesite' bricks. Chromite is also used for the manufacture of chromite bricks, of course, to a lesser extent.

6. Rare metal refractory oxides

This category can be classified Zircon (Zr SiO_4), Zirconia (Zr O_2), Titania (TiO_2), thoria, Beryllia and uranium oxide. They are mostly 'Super refractories' which are used where extraordinary high temperatures are common. Nuclear reactor technology has necessitated their development. Most of them are blended or cemented with metals for the purpose by the powder metallurgical methods. More about them can be read in the succeeding chapters.

7. Carbon

Carbon exhibits allotropy and occurs as graphite, diamond and carbon. Large deposits of graphite occur in cylon, Czek republic and Madagaskar. The main use of graphite is again in the manufacture of crucibles for which purpose it is blended with clay.

Petroleum coke is another form of carbon which is used in the manufacture of special refractories, commonly called carbon blocks. Use of carbon blocks in blast furnace for lining is gaining importance, of late. But the cost is somewhat higher.

Classification of refractories

All the refractories are mainly classified as

1. Acidic
2. Basic
3. Neutral and
4. Insulating refractories.

This classification is based on the behavior of the principal constituent of the refractory with respect to the various other metal oxides (and fluxes).

The refractories which are primarily made up of silica are readily combining with lime or magnesia in the fluxes, and vice-versa. So, the silica refractories are classified as acid and magnesite and dolomite are classified as basic refractories. Sillimanite and fireclay are broadly speaking ones neutral, in this aspect and so is carbon.

If an acid refractory is employed as the lining of a furnace in which the metallurgical processing involves the use of basic flux, the result would be – there occurs interaction between the fluxes floating and the lining near the slag rather than between the flux (slag) and the metal. Thus, the lining gets eroded in one or two heats itself due to the chemical action leading to the formation of, often, a low melting complex E.g.., CaO, SiO_2. So, it is the practice to use an acid refractory for an acid process and a basic refractory for a basic process so that no room is allowed for reactions of the aforesaid nature.

Neutral refractories resist the action of both the acid and basic slags and hence the name.

Insulating refractories are not classified on their chemical behavior but on their incapacity to conduct heat. This is very important for, if the refractory is to conduct the heat generated in the furnace towards the furnace shell, the very idea of employing a refractory itself is struck at its root. Further, cooling of the furnace shell and its protection become problems. Above all, the heat input into the furnace should be stepped up leading to greater fuel consumption.

The occurance of important refractory minerals in our country is given in Table 22.2.

Table 22.2 Refractory minerals and their occurence.

Meneral	Occurrence	Remarks
Bauxite	Ranchi and Palaman (Bihar); Saurashtra and Kutch (Gujarat); Raisi and Poonch (Kashmir); Jabalpur, Balaghat, Mandla and Bilaspur (M.P.); Salem and Nilgiris (Tamil Nadu); Klohapur and Kolaba (Maharashtra); Bababudan hills and Belgaum (Karnataka); Sambalpur (Orissa).	Mostly Saurashtra and Jabalpur deposits are employed in refractory industry. Bauxite should be low in Fe_2O_3 and TiO_2 for the manufacture of refractories.
Chromite	Jojohatu and Kittaburu (Bihar); Krishna (Andhra Pradesh); Chitradurga, Chickmagalur (Karnataka); Salem (Tamil Nadu); Ratnagiri (Maharashtra); Keonjhar and Jaipur (Orissa).	Chromite for refractory manufacture should be of the following grade : $Cr_2O_3 = 30-40$, $Cr_2O_3 + Al_2O_3 = 60$ (maximum), $SiO_2 = 10$ (maximum).
Dolomite	Birmitrapur and Sambalpur (Orissa); Hirri (M.P.); Shimoga (Karnataka); Kurnool (Andhra Pradesh); Nagpur (Maharashtra).	It should contain at least 35% $MgCO_3$, maximum 1% SiO_2 and not more than 1.5% $FeO + Al_2O_3$.
Fireclay	Hazaribagh and Jharia (Bihar); Rajkot (Gujarat); Jabalpur (M.P.); Shimoga (Karnataka); Sambalpur (Orissa); Kumardhubi (West Bengal).	
Graphite	Bolangir and Dhenkanal (Orissa); East Godavari (Andhra Pradesh); Trivandrum (Kerala);	
Silica	Hyderabad (Andhra Pradesh); Dhanbad, Gaya and Hazaribagh (Bihar); Ratnagiri (Maharashtra).	
Kyanite	Ranchi, Lapsa-Buru, Singhbhum (Bihar); Hassan (Karnataka); Jaipur (Rajasthan);	Lapsa-Buru deposit is the largest in the world.
Magnesite	Almora (U.P.); Salem (Tamil Nadu); Kadakola (Karnataka); Singhbhum (Bihar).	

23 Fire Bricks

Raw material for the manufacture of fire brick is fireclay. A great number of clays occur in nature as seen hitherto. Fire clay is found to occur generally as a secondary deposit. In our country, good quality fireclay is found to occur in Bengal, Bihar, Jharkand and Andhra Pradesh. The natural resources of Andhra Pradesh and Jharkand need to be exploited on a larger scale.

The most important property of the clay required in the manufacture of refractory is its plasticity. Further, it should not fuse below 1650 °C. If, however, a single clay is found to be wanting in plasticity, two or more clays can be mixed together to give the required plasticity. Such a clay which is plastic, naturally or by blending, is termed as the bond clay or binding clay.

Clays are generally plastic and also absorb a lot of water. This water, both mechanically mixed and hydrated, is removed during the subsequent treatments of drying and burning (firing) of the brick. This leads to the occurrence of a lot of shrinkage in the brick. Thus, fireclay as it is, cannot be used for the brick manufacture. A material called "grog" is usually mixed with the clay and a suitable refractory mixture made. Grog consists of particles of fired clay, specially added to the clay in order to make a suitable mixture for the manufacture of firebrick. The proportion of grog mixed varies upto 70% depending upon the properties of the brick required. Grog is nothing but pieces of broken firebrick. The size of the grog employed is of that of a pea. It should be very carefully selected so that no glazed particles are present in it. Further, it should be angular in its crystal shape and not rounded. Mixing of the grog to the clay and the subsequent brick manufacture somewhat reminds us of a concrete mixture – the grog being comparable to jelly in the concrete mix. Fig. 23.1 illustrates crushing of grog in a dry-edge runner mill.

Fig. 23.1 Crushing of grog.

Preparation of a Refractory Mixture

The first stage in the manufacture of refractory brick is the preparation of the refractory mixture. The chief ingredients are clay, grog and water, mixed judiciously. Mixing is important so that no segregation occurs in the mixture. Mixers are employed in mass production. In hand mixing the required quantities are weighed or measured and mixed with shovels. A simple·method is to spread the clay on the working floor to a predetermined thickness and making a layer of grog over the clay. This is done without adding water. Later, the clay and grog are turned over and mixed. Water of the required volume is added and the mixing continued in the fashion of coning and quatering. Fig. 23.2 illustrates the raw material preparation section in a mechanised refractory manufacturing shop.

Fig. 23.2 A drying chamber stacked with green refractory shapes.

The quantity of water added to the mix is very important. The mix can be studied as a three - component system, taking both clay and grog as one component water and air making up the other two in the system. A diagram of the type shown in Fig. 23.3 can be plotted using a simple apparatus in which the three components can be mixed and kneaded. The chamber has the facility to measure the volume of the mould at a particular pressure. There is also a provision for venting out of the excess water.

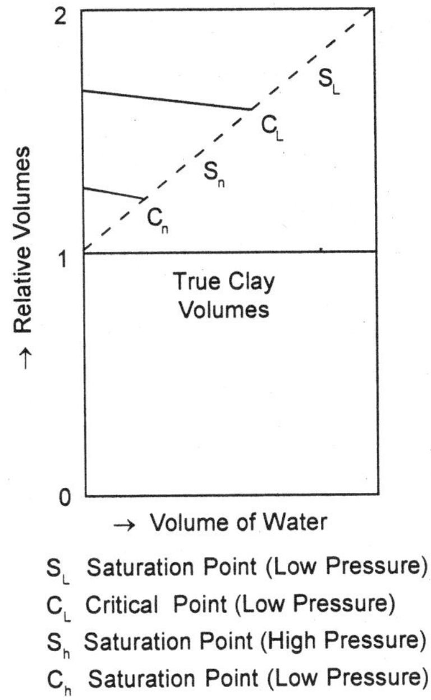

Fig. 23.3 Effect of percentage water in the clay mix on its plastic properties.

It can be seen that the volume of the clay (and air) does not alter initially when water is added. This accounts for the filling up of the pores in the clay by the water and continues upto a certain percentage of water.

At critical point, the voids in the clay are completely filled and all the air space vanishes. If the water content is further increased, water film starts to separate the clay particles. This separation continues until a certain value of the percentage of water, which is called the saturation point. These two values – the critical point and the saturation point are governed by the pressure. Any excess water, even if added to the clay, is squeezed out during the moulding process.

The critical point has great significance. In mixing (the refractory mix,) water should not be added in excess of this value, for the mould suffers shrinkage on drying.

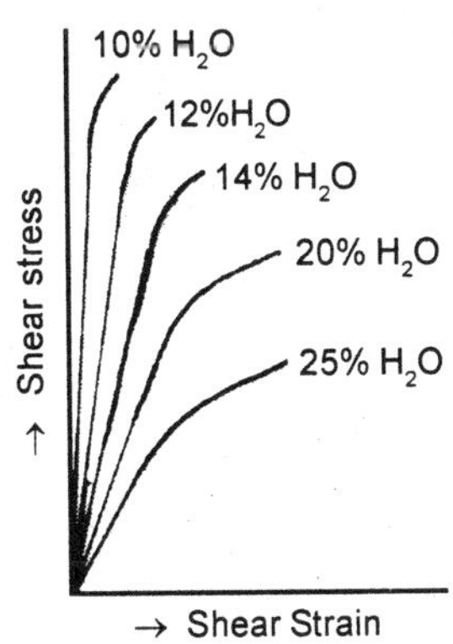

Fig. 23.4 Effect of percentage water in the clay mix on its plastic properties.

Of course, the above is a theoretical consideration. Sometimes, the volume is found to decrease (instead of remaining constant) with the addition of water. The reason for this can be understood as the lubricating nature of water when the clay particles slide and occupy more densely packed positions. See Fig. 23.4.

The above is to be scrupulously kept in view and the percentage of water to be added arrived at. Mixing is done as described above and once the three ingredients are thoroughly mixed, the material is ready for brick making.

Moulding of Bricks

Bricks can be moulded by any of the following processes:

(i) Hand moulding.

(ii) Extrusion.

(iii) Stiff plastic moulding.

(iv) Semi-dry pressing, and

(v) Slip casting.

Every method is good from the typical advantages it offers. But its applicability depends upon the type of the mix that is being moulded. Eg. A mix containing higher percentages of the grog will not be suitable for extrusion.

Hand Moulding

As the name itself suggests, the process of making the brick is performed entirely by hand. A small quantity of the mix is separated from the bulk of the mix. This quantity will be slightly more than the volume of the brick to be made. An experienced brick moulder can remove the exact quantity just like that. This lump is made roughly into the same shape of the brick by bumping it on the work table. This is the starting product for the moulding of the brick and is called 'walk'.

The mould used is either made of wood or metal. It is thoroughly oiled or dusted so that the brick can be easily removed from it. The walk is lifted high up and thrown into the mould cavity. It is then levelled in the mould and the excess is cut off with a strike bar. The mould, filled with the mix thus, is then taken away to the drying floor, inverted and tapped. The filling of the mould with the refractory mix can also be performed by using a pneumatic poker. The process, known as pneumatic tamping, can be adopted with mixes containing less water. Physical strain on the part of the moulder is saved thus.

Extrusion

The process is similar to the extrusion of rods in the metal working industry. The die opening is of the same dimensions as the breadth and height of the brick used and the refractory mix is forced through it. The material comes out of the opening just as tooth paste comes out of the tube when pressed.

Fig. 23.5 Extrusion Press.

Fig. 23.6 Repressing Press.

The lengths required are cut off the product emerging through the die, Fig. 23.5. The process is however, not suitable for the manufacture of irregular shapes.

Stiff Plastic Process

This process employs a refractory mix containing a much lower percentage of water. Mix, of the consistency of a thick paste is moulded under pressure. Many times, the product is required to be repressed in order to attain good dimensional accuracy. Fig 23.6 illustrates a repress in which metal pouring nozzles are re-pressed.

Semi-Dry Pressing

In this, the refractory mix used contains a very small percentage (2.0-5.0) of water only. The material (mix) used appears almost as a damp powder and pressing is performed at high pressures: sometimes under vacuum. Fig. 23.7 illustrates a 100 T friction screw press.

Because of the high pressures employed, there is no worry of the flow of the mix in the mould. Intricate shapes can be manufactured by this process. Excellent service characteristics are reported about the refractories made by this process.

Slip Casting

In this process, practically a slurry like refractory mix is used. It is filled in to a mould, made of plaster of Paris. The mould, by its capacity to absorb water slowly absorbs the water from the mix. Ultimately a solid brick remains in the mould which is knocked out and sent for drying. The process acquired the name slip casting because the raw material mix used to make the brick is known as slip.

Drying

After the brick is moulded, the first stage is the removal of moisture from it. This process is called drying. In our country, open drying can be performed which consists of stacking the bricks away from the direct sun. Well-ventilated rooms are enough in our country. The drying process takes about seven to twelve days. For attaining higher production rates, however, special drying chambers which are heated by flue gases are employed. These are useful in humid or cold atmospheric conditions also. Fig. 23.8 illustrates a drying chamber, with the green bricks in it.

Fig. 23.7 100 Ton. friction screw press.

Fig. 23.8 A drying chamber stacked with green refractory shapes.

Burning

During burning to following reactions occur:

1. All the water, including the water of crystallisation of the minerals present is driven off.
2. The sulphates and carbonates decompose evolving SO_2 and CO_2.
3. Chemical reactions involving the formation of complexes occur between the different oxides (Mullite is generally formed).
4. At very high temperatures, impurities like feldspars vitrify.

Vertical or horizontal kilns can be employed for burning the fire bricks. These bricks can be charged on the furnace bed or a car containing the bricks can be pushed into the furnace and the furnace door closed. The total process of burning can be sub-divided into 5 stages.

(i) Smoking.
(ii) Decomposition of the clay.
(iii) Oxidation stage.
(iv) Vitrification stage, and
(v) Annealing and cooling stage.

(i) *Smoking stage*

During this stage, the temperature of the kiln is maintained just above 100 °C. Even to this temperature, the temperature is raised very slowly. The water, added to the clay in order to make it plastic and workable, is removed. The water vapour and steam should be well-vented out. Nearly 20 kgs of water will be expelled out of every ton of dried brick (i.e. roughly 300 cubic meter of steam comes out of every metric ton of the dried brick). This stage takes about 24 hrs and the end of the stage can be ascertained by inserting a cold metallic rod into the furnace (above the brick charge) and withdrawing it. The rod should be clean and free from any mist, or vapour condensed appearance.

(ii) *Decomposition stage*

This stage commences after the smoking stage. The temperature at which the decomposition of the mineral molecules begins is about 350 °C. This lasts upto about 800 °C when the carbonates of calcium and magnesium decompose to their respective oxides. Further, the molecular (water of crystallisation) also escapes out. As the kiln is already hot and the heating being continued, this stage takes about another 24 hours.

(iii) ***Oxidation stage***

From 900 °C, the oxidation of the brick constituents occurs. Any remaining carbonates are completely decomposed and volatile constituents removed. Iron, which is an impurity and present as a carbonate, is also oxidised to ferric oxide (Fe_2O_3) giving the brownish tinge to the brick. The oxides formed, begin to fuse and sometimes the iron oxide forms iron silicate with the available silica. The atmosphere in the kiln should be maintained oxidising and the products (gases) vented out. This stage extends upto the maximum temperature of burning i.e., 1350 °C – The time taken is dependent upon:

(a) the nature of the charge,

(b) the quantity of the charge, and

(c) the properties ultimately required for the brick. However, it generally varies from 14-20 hours.

(iv) ***Incipient fusion stage***

This is a very important stage in the burning of the firebrick. This stage generally does not involve any further temperature rise than the previous stage. Sometimes, a slightly higher temperature is maintained i.e., upto 1450 °C. Some mineral grains as a glassy matter. This process is controlled both by temperature and time for, the vitreous matter fills up the pores, leading to loss of porosity of the brick. At the same time, the brick develops good hardness and resistance to slag attack. Thus, the broken molecules of clay, reorganising themselves as mullite ($3Al_2O_3SiO_2$) and develop the properties required.

(v) ***Annealing Stage***

This stage consists of cooling the burnt furnace charge. The bricks are cooled at the slowest possible rate. Theoretically, in an annealing process, the product should be cooled at equilibrium rate of cooling (that is 1 °C/min). But in actual practice, this rate of cooling is compromised to give a fairly faster rate. What is known as furnace cooling adopted in the case of metals and alloys; the same is done with refractories also. In general, the kiln is put off and the charge allowed to lose its heat by radiation. It takes about 5 to 6 days for a 250 to 300 metric ton kiln to cool to the room temperature.

Properties of Fire bricks

The refractory properties of the firebrick are controlled by many factors, like

(i) The original clay used to manufacture the brick and its properties.

(ii) The method of moulding the brick, and

(iii) The temperature of burning the brick.

Bricks whose texture is coarse (open) are more resistant to thermal shock. But, in regard to resistance to slag attack and strength, they would be inferior. Bricks fired at higher temperature or those which have closed texture have their properties vice-versa i.e., they would be strong, less porous and withstand slag attack well but would not withstand thermal shock.

Further, the constitution of the brick has a remarkable influence on its properties. The impurity part of iron, if well oxidised to iron oxide, and fluxes with silicon dioxide during the incipient fusion stage of firing, the brick will be resistant to carbon deposition and spalling. Similarly, the decomposition of the clay and formation of mullite structure also helps improve the strength (as also the refractoriness under load). In general the firebricks have the following properties.

1. They show a good refractory behaviour. They do not soften upto 1450 °C.
2. They possess a good resistance to frequent temperature changes - thermal shock.
3. They possess a good refractoriness under load property at 1300 °C.
4. The cold crushing strength of the brick is very much variable depending upon the aforesaid variables but in any case not lower then 20 Mpa.

Applications

Firebrick is the cheapest and most common refractory brick.

1. Boilers, glassmelting furnaces, chimneys, kilns of potteries etc.
2. Reheating furnaces, regenerators.
3. Ladles, metal mixers.
4. Blast furnace, cupola and blast furnace stoves.

High-Alumina fire brick

This family of refractories are known by the group name sillimanite. The chief characteristics of these refractories is their incipient fusion around 1550 °C (during the burning of the brick) to form mullite. Consequently, the brick will be very good with regard to the properties of refractoriness, shrinkage, resistance to thermal shock and slag attack.

Refractories used in the manufacture of the high-alumina brick are kyanite, andalucite, sillimanite and topaz.

Kyanite

It is a soft mineral with a specific gravity of 3.6. It transforms to mullite ($3Al_2O_32SiO_2$) and silica (SiO_2) when heated. That is why it is calcined at about 1400 °C before it is used in the refractory mix. Plenty of kyanite occurs in the Chotanagpur region of Bihar. It contains about 63% alumina (Ai_2O_3) and 34% silica (SiO_2) as its principal constituents.

Andalucite

This occurs as prismatic or granular crystals with purple, grey or red color. It has a pecific gravity of 3.15. This is more stable thermally than kyanite. It is not decomposed upto 1400 °C, but above that temperature, transforms to mullite. There are no deposits of andalucite, worth mentioning, in our country.

Sillimanite

This has a needle like structure and greenish or reddish color. Its specific gravity is 3.2. In our country large deposits occur in Rewa in MP and Khasi hills in Assam.

The chemical composition of sillimanite is as follows :

SiO_2	:	35 - 28 %
Al_2O_3	:	62.3 %
Fe_2O_3	:	1.30 %
Ti_2	:	0.22 %
MGO	:	0.15%
CaO	:	Traces
Alkatis	:	0.65 %

Sillimanite also occurs as beach sand near Travancore (Kerala). It is also proved to be suitable for use as a refractory.

Properties of sillimanite bricks

They are highly refractory is nature and soften at 1820 °C and above. They possess a vary low coefficient of thermal expansion and so are highly resistant to thermal shock. Further, they possess a good mechanical strength. They also possess good refractoriness under load characteristics (.35 Mpa at 1700 °C). But they are not resistant to metallic slags and as such not useful in the hearth linings of the metallurgical furnaces.

The method of manufacture of the sillimanite or andalucite brick or calcined kyanite brick is the same as that for the firebrick described in the previous pages. The only difference lies in the preparation of the refractory mix. Different grades are mixed with each other and a good quality of fireclay is also added to the mix before brick moulding.

Uses

Sillimanite can be successfully employed in the coke ovens, boilers, tunnel kilns, rotary kilns of the cement plant and in the glass industry. They are also used in soaking pits, open hearth and electric furnaces roofs and hot metal mixers.

Bauxite bricks

These bricks are made from bauxite, diaspore or bauxite and contain alumina (Al_2O_3) in the range of 45 - 70% depending upon the quality. Bauxite mineral is dead burnt or calcined to completely remove the water of hydration. This forms the grog in an otherwise fireclay matrix and the brick is produced by not pressing. The bricks are burnt at temperatures above 1400 °C, going upto 1500 °C.

These bricks, though neutral, behave like basic bricks. They have poor resistance to spalling but they have very high refractoriness and refractoriness under load (.35 MPa) at 1600 °C.

Bauxite bricks are employed in the gas and oil-fired furnaces and rotary kilns in the cement industry.

24 Silica Bricks

Silica is a very abundant constituent of the earth's crust. It occurs in different forms of mineral deposits. It occurs as a constituent of igneous rocks like granite and rhyolite as sedimentary rocks, as sandstone and quartizite and in the unconsolidated form as river and beach sands. In our country, besides occurring as river sand and beach sand which itself is enormous, large deposits of quartzite are found in Hyderabad in Andhra Pradesh, Dhandbad and Gaya in Bihar and Ratnagiri in Maharashtra.

Silica exhibits polymorphism and occurs in six crystallographic forms. Of these, the principal ones are silica, tridymite and cristobalite. These changes can be summarised as follows (Fig 24.1)

Quartz is stable upto 870 °C

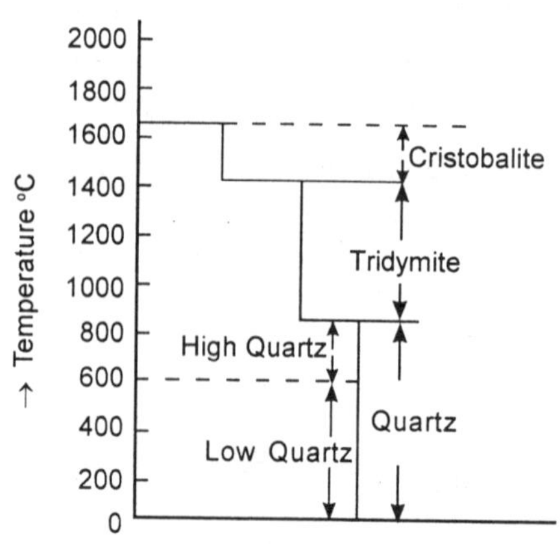

Fig. 24.1 Polymorphism of quartz.

(i) α - quartz upto 573 °C

(ii) β - quartz between 573 - 870 °C

Tri dymite is stable between 870 - 1470 °C

Cristobalite is stable between 1470 - 1728 °C

These changes are major and minor transformations do occur in the intermediary temperatures which are not of much consequence to us, from the scope of this work. However, these changes due to temperature are of concern to us from the point of view of the volume changes that occur consequently. The three forms have different specific gravities due to their differing crystalline patterns. They are as hereunder:

Quartz	-	2.65
Tridymite	-	2.23
Cristobalite	-	2.23 (α) and 2.234 (β)

The volume changes are responsible for the spalling of the silica bricks. These are graphically represented in Fig (24.2).

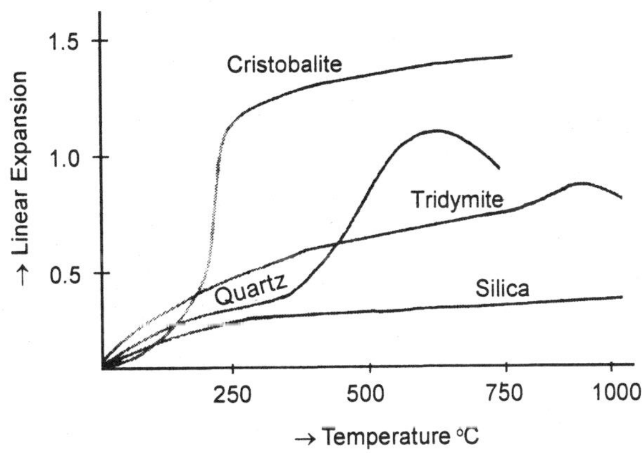

Fig. 24.2 Expansion characteristics of different forms of silica.

Due to the volume changes accompanied by the crystal structural changes, some materials called mineralisers are added to the refractory mix during the brick manufacture. The most common mineraliser is lime which serves the dual purpose of binder as well as mineraliser. It converts quartz into cristobalite and tridymite during the burning. Similar action is also reported by titanium dioxide, boric oxide and ferric chloride. However, it is necessary that addition of mineraliser should be made judiciously or else the rapid conversion may itself lead to rupture or unsoundness in the brick.

All the naturally occuring silica cannot be utilised for the brick manufacture. Quartizite and sandstone are most commonly used for the manufacture of silica bricks. Though sand is plentiful in nature and is brought by rivers every year, it is not suitable for brick manufacture as it does not consist of the binder and the grains in it are not angular. The quartzite used for brick manufacture should fulfill the following requirements :

(i) It should be pure. The total impurity content should not exceed 4.6%.

(ii) The mass, as a whole should not soften below 1720 °C.

(iii) Small amounts of alumina and lime should form part of the tolerated 4.6% impurities.

(iv) The material shall show angular grains surrounded by fine silicious cement, under the microscope.

Such silica is mixed with a suitable binder and water. Binders are added in the proportion of 1.0 - 2.0 %. Calcium oxide is a very commonly used binder but clay is also employed. Organic binders like molasses, gum, floor and even tar are used but not common.

The mixing is a very important process. Quartzite is crushed first to above 3 cm size and washed to remove the dust. The crushing and grinding are continued to produce variant sizes which are separated by proper screening. The various grades of sizes are meticulously mixed together depending upon the final quality of the brick required. Later, the requisite quantities of binder, mineraliser, and water are added so as to make a mix of the texture of semi-dry quality. The mix is tempered in a pug mill so that the various ingredients are evenly distributed.

Silica bricks are moulded by hand moulding or machine pressing. Machine pressed bricks are repressed for accurate dimensions after a few hours' drying.

Drying

Silica bricks are dried in a similar way as the fire brick, away from direct sun. A well-ventilated room is ideal for drying. These bricks dry faster than the firebricks due to the lower percentage of water in the refractory mix. About 20 hours' drying is found to be sufficient.

Burning

The total burning (cycle) time of the silica bricks is 10 days. Of this, the first three days are utilised in gradual rise of temperature and the last five days for cooling. During the intermediate 48 hours, the temperature is rised to the maximum firing level of 1500 °C.

During the burning, the initial gradual heating is carefully adhered to upto about 700 °C. This takes about 3 days. Subsequently, the rate of heating need not be so carefully controlled. The maximum temperature of burning i.e. 1450-1500 °C is maintained for about 24 hours, during which time the vitrification and cementing action of the grains occurs.

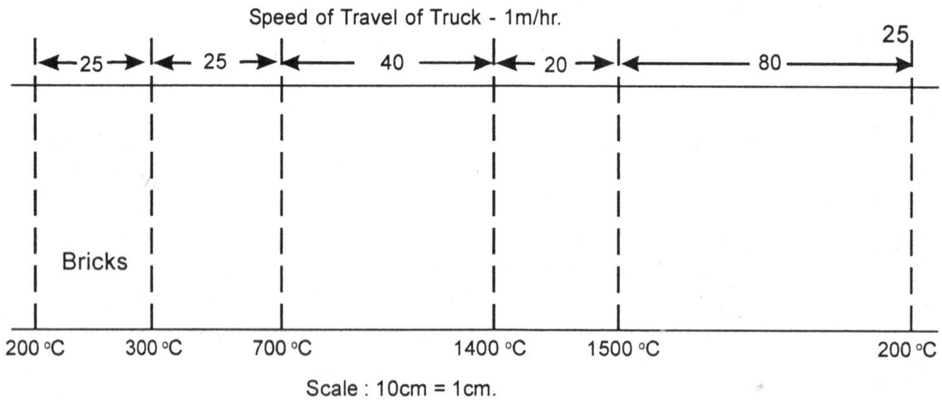

Fig. 24.3 Tunnel kiln.

Horizontal kilns through which cars charged with the bricks are passed through, are the most modern. The tunnel of the kiln divided into the different temperature zones. Depending upon the length of the temperature zones, the speed of travel of the truck is controlled. A typical horizontal kiln with the temperature distribution is illustrated in Fig. 24.3 schematically. (Fig. 24.4 & 24.5) are the photographs of a tunnel kiln. Fig. 24.6 shows a car loaded with refractories coming out of the tunnel kiln.

Fig. 24.4 A Tunnel Kiln.

Fig. 24.5 Fired refractory shapes coming out of a tunnel kiln.

Properties of silica bricks

Silica bricks are porous in texture and buffy in colour. Their specific gravity is between 2.3-2.4. Porosity is about 25%. The mechanical strength of silica bricks is more than the firebrick and ranges between 200-300 Kgf/cm^2.

These bricks, in spite of the addition of the mineraliser compounds during the brick manufacture, are found to be poor in withstanding thermal shock. Their acidic nature also inhibits their usage in basic atmospheres. Thus, their application is mainly restricted to those parts of furnaces which do not often cool and come into contact with basic slags. All furnace roofs and even hearth linings of acid steel making furnaces are lined with silica bricks. The typical analysis of a silica brick is as follows :

SiO_2	:	95.00%
Al_2O_3	:	1.4%
Fe_2O_3	:	0.5%
CaO	:	2.0%
MgO	:	0.2
Others	:	0.4 maximum
Ignition loss	:	0.5
		100.00

Recent developments in the manufacture of silica bricks have produced 'Agate brick' and 'super-duty silica brick'.

These are manufactured by using highly pure silica material and formed by pressing at very high pressures. The ultimate structure is controlled to consist of tridymite. These are claimed to possess a higher degree of resistance to thermal shock and refractoriness under load.

25 Magnesite Bricks

Magnesite occurs as magnesite, brucite and in sea water. Large deposits of magnesite occur in Austria, Greece, Canada, Czek, and Slovak republics, Russia, the U.S., and India.

In our country, deposits of magnesite are found to occur in Salem (Tamilnadu), Dodkanya (Karnataka), Idar (Gujarat), Dungarpur (Rajasthan) and Almora (U.P).

The magnesite is burnt in kilns to effect calcination when the carbon dioxide in it is completely driven out. Consequently the material shrinks – its specific gravity increasing from 3.0 to 3.6. This is a very, important stage in the production of the 'dead burnt' magnesia. If the calcination is not complete, the material obtained will have a tendency to hydrate. So, when used as a refractory, it again suffers from shrinkage and becomes useless.

On proper calcination, Mgo crystallises and in this form is known as periclase. It is found that the presence of iron accelerates periclase formation and hence the magnesite contaminated with iron oxide is preferred in the refractory industry.

Proper calcination temperature for magnesia is 1600 °C; it may be even more i.e., 1700-1800 °C in the absence of iron. The product obtained is called 'dead-burnt magnesia'. This does not absorb water.

Improper calcination, i.e., at lower temperatures (1100 °C) gives magnesia called the 'caustic magnesia'. This absorbs water from the air. This is useless as a refractory but is employed as a binder in the manufacture of magnesite bricks.

Production of magnesia from sea water is developed during the world war II. Sea water is treated with slaked dolomite (double hydroxide of calcium and magnesium). Magnesium which exists as chloride and sulphate in the sea water is released and becomes available as hydroxide, thus,

$$Mg\ SO_4\ MgCl_2 + 2\ mg\ (OH)_2 \rightarrow 4\ M\ (OH)_2\ Cacl_2\ CaSO_4$$

The magnesium hydroxide is filtered under pressure and calcined as the magnesite mineral itself. Dead burnt magnesia is obtained which can be employed for the manufacture of magnesite brick. This product is found to be equally good as the magnesia obtained from the magnesite mineral.

Magnesite bricks

The lumpy dead burnt magnesite is crushed in jaw crushers. It is sieved through a 1.5 mm. sieve and the fines are taken. The material retained on the sieve is sent back for crushing.

The crushed product is passed through a magnetic separator, to remove any iron or steel pieces that might have contaminated the material during the size reduction operations. Later, it is classified into the three grades as follows,

(i) Material in the size range of 1.5 to 0.5 mm

(ii) Material in the size range of 0.5 to 0.1 mm

(iii) Material under 0.1 mm

These three sizes are 'suitably' mixed and the binder added. Caustic magnesia is the binder used. Water is also added upto 5%. The mix is thoroughly, mixed in a pug mill or some other type of mixer.

Bricks are made using hydraulic presses and the pressures employed range upto 10 MPa. The drying of the green brick is performed similar to the way the firebrick or silica brick is dried. These bricks are very fragile and need very careful handling. The bond employed being caustic magnesia, the bricks are prone to absorb carbon dioxide from the atmosphere during the drying process. Hence, it is preferable to dry the bricks in hot rooms, so that the drying time is minimised. A 1000 Ton (10000 KN) Hydraulic Press is shown in Fig. 25.1.

Fig. 25.1 A 1000 T hydraulic press used in the manufacturing of magnesite and dolomite bricks.

Burning

The temperature cycle and other operational details of magnesite brick burning are the same as those of silica bricks. In big refractory manufacturing units, the silica and magnesite bricks are burnt together. In such cases, the arrangement of the bricks on the car would be such that the magnesite bricks are surrounded by the silica bricks. The idea behind this arrangement is to minimise the area of contact between the two types of bricks for, both are chemically of opposite nature and at the high temperatures of burning, fluxing action may not occur. Some manufacturers prefer to charge the magnesite bricks at one end of the car.

Properties

These bricks are brownish to dark brown in colour due to the presence of iron oxide in the material. The specific gravity of a well-burnt magnesite brick is about 3.5-3.6. The chemical analysis of a magnesite brick made from indigenous raw material is as follows,

Mgo	:	84.00 %
CaO	:	2.50 %
Fe_2O_3	:	7.00 %
SiO_2	:	4.80 %
Al_2O_3	:	1.00 %
Loss on ignition	:	0.2 %

Porosity of the brick is about 26% and cold crushing strength 350-500 kgf/cm^2. Their thermal stability is upto 1750 °C and refractoriness under load (of 3.5 kgf/cm^2) is 1500 °C.

Magnesite bricks have a poor resistance of shock. Further, they are good thermal conductors at lower temperatures. But the conductivity is found to decrease as the temperature increases. Their electrical conductivity is also high at elevated temperatures. Magnesite bricks are also poor in their resistance abrasion.

Magnesite bricks are very commonly used as the linings of open hearth, and electric arc furnaces. L.D converters are also lined with magnesite bricks. Copper converters and copper matte-smelting reverberatory furnaces also employ magnesite lining. Their basic nature makes them an automatic choice in metal smelting and refining furnaces involving basic slags. Besides copper, these bricks are also employed in the other non-ferrous metal extraction furnaces like nickel, lead, silver, gold and a host of other alloys.

In non-metallurgical field, the widest application of magnesite brick is found in the cement plant, lime and dolomite kilns.

Fretted Magnesite Linings

Fretting of a refractory is a process of 'in-situ' burning. The refractory is taken as a pea-size mass and a proper binder is added to it and thoroughly mixed. The lining to be laid is practically 'cast' like a concrete road and it is heated to the high temperature. The temperature recommended is as high as the temperatures of burning of the magnesite brick. The whole area laid sets and becomes a monolithic mass. This practice is common with open hearth furnace finishing, using either magnesite or dolomite refractory.

Failure of magnesite linings

Whenever a magnesite brick lining has failed, the investigation into the failure reveals, one or more of the following three causes :

(i) the chemical composition of the refractory mix,

(ii) preparation of the brick, and/or

(iii) operating temperature of the furnace.

The composition of raw magnesite is of a great importance as said above. The magnesite should contain same iron oxide which acts as a catalyst during the calcining of the magnesite and aids in the formation of periclase. Further the presence of impurities like Al_2O_3 diminishes the refractory nature by forming chemical complexes which are low melting.

During the preparation of the brick, drying should be performed as quickly as possible after the brick moulding. Perfect mixing of the various grades of the magnesia gives the optimum compactness and porosity. A close and dense structure produces a brick which is more resistance to slag attack.

Analysis of spalled brick from steel making furnaces has revealed that the brick got contaminated with iron oxide besides the usual periclase, glass and montecellite. High porosity of the brick may be the reason for such a contamination. Again, the thermal shock behavior of the magnesite brick is quite poor and it should not be employed for those parts of the furnaces which undergo frequent heating and cooling.

26 Dolomite Bricks

Dolomite is the name given to the mineral which is a double carbonate of calcium and magnesium. It contains the magnesium and calcium carbonates in the proportion 2:3. Similar to magnesite, this mineral yields a mixture of the lime and magnesia when calcined, the proportions of magnesium and calcium oxides being 7:10.

Some dolomites may contain more of calcium owing to the mixing of the mineral with calcite. Such dolomites cannot be used for refractory purposes.

There are two drawbacks in the use of dolomites as a refractory. One is the nature of the calcined dolomite. It spontaneously hydrates on exposure to air. (CaO has the tendency to hydration). This is overcome by making the CaO component of the calcined mixture inactive by converting it into a non-hydrating silicate. This compound CaO SiO_2 (mineralogically wollastonite) has a low temperature of softening 1540 °C refractory. On the other hand, if a di-calcium silicate (fusion temperature 2130 °C) or a tri-calcium silicate (fusion temperature 1900 °C) is allowed to form, the problem is solved and the material can be used as a refractory.

Yet, there is the other drawback in the use of di or tri-calcium silicate as a refractory in that the compound undergoes polymorphous changes when it is cooled from 1450 °C. These transformations are accompanied by swelling, leading to the spalling of the refractory. If this refractory is to be used, the furnace should not be allowed to cool below 1400 °C; which is too impracticable. This difficulty is overcome by the addition of chromite (Cr_2O_3) or Boron trioxide (B_2O_3) which makes the dolomite stable. Though phosphorus pentoxide (P_2O_5) is also a good stabiliser, its use is not resorted to for fear of phosphorus pick-up in steel making. The problem of volume increase due to the polymorphism and consequent damage of the dolomite as powder is referred to as 'dusting'. The process of addition of boron trioxide or chromite to overcome dusting is known as 'stabilisation' of the dolomite.

When tri-calcium silicate is formed, the stabilisation is automatically achieved. Serpentine, a mineral containing silica, is added to the powdered dolomite to the extent of 15% and the mixture is calcined at 1600 °C. Consequently, the lime in the dolomite is converted into tri-calcium-silicate which is stable.

$$6(CaCO_3\ MgCO_3) + MgO\ 2SiO_3\ 2H_2O \rightarrow$$
$$2\ (3CaO\ SiO_2) + 9MgO + 2H_2O + 12\ CO_2$$

Brick Making

The stabilised dolomite is sorted into different sizes and they are suitably mixed with each other (in the required proportions depending upon the density of packing required). A usual size classification and their relative proportions are given below:

5-10 mm size	---	60 - 75 %
1-5 mm size	---	10 - 15 %
Fines	------------	20 - 40 %

The bond employed, again depends on the requirement. Inorganic binders , magnesium chloride, magnesium silicate or milk of lime are some of the usual binding materials. Clays are never used as bonds. About 4.0 % water is also added and the mix is thoroughly mixed in pug mills.

Bricks are moulded by hydraulic or mechanical presses using pressures upto 70 MPa. The bricks are soaked at the maximum burning temperature of 1450 °C for at least 24 hours.

Properties

Though slightly inferior in refractoriness, these bricks are similar to magnesite bricks in many aspects. They are heavy, (Specific gravity 3.2) and possess an apparent porosity of about 25.0%. They are more wear-resistant than magnesite bricks. They have a cold crushing strength of the order of 40 MPa and refractoriness under load of 3500 N at 1650 °C. However, their resistance to thermal shock is doubtful, in spite of all the precautions taken to stabilise the dolomite before the brick making.

Uses

These bricks are a cheaper substitute for magnesite. Wherever the magnesite bricks are used, dolomite can replace them, though at the cost of some life of the lining but, the cost, relative availability and the thermal characteristics outweigh towards the substitution.

Monolithic Lining of Dolomite

Dolomite, which is previously calcined and stabilised, in pea size, can be mixed with tar as binder and employed for fretting the linings of flat surfaces of the furnaces. This is particularly advantageous in the preparation of the working hearth and tap hole of basic open hearth furnaces.

27 Chrome Bricks

Chromite is the mineral containing upto 45.00-50.00 % chromium trioxide. It forms the raw material for the chrome bricks. The ore also contains iron oxide varying from 15.0 to 25.0 % and some alumina. Sometimes, serpentine is also present upto 15.00% in the chromite ore.

The richness of chromite is not an important criterion for its use as a refractory. Ores with 40% Cr_2O_3 are found to be ideal. The ore should contain some Fe_2O_3 but not exceeding 18.0 %. Its silica content should not be more than 5.0% and lime 1.0%.

Good quality chromite occurs in our country in Karnataka State and Tamil Nadu, Maharashtra, Bihar and Kashmir regions also figure in the occurance list of chromite.

Chrome bricks

Powdered chromite is mixed with heated tar binder and the mixture is pressed into bricks either by mechanical or hydraulic machines. Burning is carried out in kilns as in the case of other types of bricks. The final firing temperature is low, 1400 °C.

Properties

The analysis of a typical Indian Chromite brick is as follows :

Cr_2O_3	:	44.00 %
Fe_2O_3	:	24.00 %
AL_2O_3	:	16.00 %
MgO	:	10.00 %
SiO_2	:	4.2 %

CaO	:	1.1 %
TiO_2	:	0.7 %
Loss on ignition	:	0.2 %

These bricks possess a high refractoriness. They are stable upto 1800 °C. They possess good refractoriness under load (at 3.5 kgf/cm^2 1450 °C). Their specific gravity is in the range of 3.8-4.1 and porosity 26.0%. The cold crushing strength is quite high 0.35-0.45 MPa. They withstand the action of basic slags very well and that of acid slags reasonably well. Generally, these are classified as neutral refractories.

Uses

Being chemically neutral, they find a wide application in the metallurgical industry. Copper and steel melting furnaces also employ chrome bricks . They are also employed in paper industry, high pressure boilers.

When used in iron industry, they have a tendency to chemically react with iron oxide at 1500 °C and above. This may lead to spalling of the lining. That is why, though neutral in nature, they are seldom employed for the blast furnace linings.

Chrome magnesite bricks

These bricks, as the name suggests, are made by mixing chromite and magnesite in the proportion of 70/30. Each of the material is prepared as if to manufacture that particular brick itself. At the mixing stage, the chromite and magnesite are mixed in the aforesaid proportion. Molasses or tar is used as the binder and the refractory mix is thoroughly mixed in pug mills.

Brick making is performed in machines operating hydraulically. Pressures as high as 9 kgf/cm^2 are employed in brick making.

The bricks are dried at 60-80 °C in hot air current. Burning is done in vertical or horizontal continuous kilns, the final temperature being 1500 °C.

Properties

These bricks possess a cold crushing strength upto 0.3-0.35 MPa. Their specific gravity is 3.8 and porosity 24.0-26.0 %.

These bricks withstand temperatures as high as 1700 °C. They show no expansion or contraction upto that temperature and are thus free from the danger of spalling.

Like chromite bricks, however, they are prone to the attack of iron oxide. Magnesite is absorbed by the chromite grains and this results in the grain growth leading to the 'bursting' of the lining. Once the chromite part of the brick has reacted with iron oxide, the magnesia portion also reacts forming what is called MgO Fe_2O_3. This is a low melting point complex. Thus, the chrome-magnesite brick, once comes into contact with iron oxide, the bursting occurs and the whole lining is damaged.

Uses

These bricks are used in the basic open hearth furnaces for all the portions other than the hearth. Similarly they are employed in the basic electric furnaces.

Other types of bricks using the same two constituents viz., Chromite and magnesite but in different proportions are also made for specific purposes. Proportions of chromite and magnesite such as 60/40, 50/50 and even 25/75 are also manufactured. Chemical bonds are used and the bricks are made by what is known as electro-casting process. Each variety has its own specific advantages but the degree of advantage obtained with regard to a particular property is only marginal.

Similarly, chrome alumina bricks are also made, employing a 50/50 mixture of chromite and alumina. It is claimed that these bricks possess a good mechanical strength, and refractoriness under load and resistance to spalling. But their refractoriness itself is low.

28 Special Refractories

The development of technology and science has led to the necessity for faster rates of combustion and higher temperatures. This has led to the exploration of material for high temperature service. Side by side, high temperature refractories have also become necessary. The refractory materials developed for high temperature service can be divided into the following broad groups,

1. Refractory metals
2. Refractory oxides
3. Refractory compounds
4. Refractory porcelains

1. *Refractory metals*

Amongst the refractory metals, platinum is outstanding. It is a noble metal with complete inertness towards gases and slags. Being very ductile, it can be easily shaped. The only drawback is its high cost and 'lower' melting point. Yet, it is being successfully employed for the tanks of small capacities in the fibre glass manufacture. Other metals include tungsten, tantalum, molybdenum, thorium, titanium, zirconium. Of these, most widely used metals are tungsten, tantalum and molybdenum. Of the three, the first one is very brittle while tantalum and molybdenum can be easily fabricated. Anyway, all of them can be fabricated by powder metallurgical methods. They have low vapour pressures and hence particularly suitable for high temperature work.

Metal	Vapour pressure in mm of Hg at			
	1600 °C	1800 °C	2000 °C	2200 °C
Platinum	10^{-5}	$10^{-3.5}$	$10^{-2.5}$	$10^{-1.5}$
Molybdenum	$10^{-7.5}$	10^{-6}	$10^{-4.5}$	$10^{-3.23}$
Tungsten	not known	not known	10^{-8}	10^{-7}

2. ***Refractory oxides***

Alumina, Beryllia and Zirconia are the most common refractory oxides. Alumina is obtained by the purification of bauxite by the Bayer's process. This contains impurities to the extent of 0.5%. The impurities consist of CaO, Fe_2O_3, and MgO. For use as a super refractory, even these impurities should be removed. This is done by digesting very finely ground alumina (60% below 5 size) with 15% hot hydrochloric acid. Long time (one to two days) digesting followed by washing with water eliminates the impurities as their respective chlorides.

The resulting pure alumina is mixed with a suitable binder (latex rubber, waxes or a synthetic resin) and formed into the required shape by slip casting into plaster moulds or hot pressing.

Beryllium oxide has a high melting point (above 2500 °C) reasonably low specific gravity (3) and high hardness (9 on Moh's scale) has attracted the attention of refractory engineers.

Most of the BeO produced is by calcining beryllium hydroxide. Highly pure BeO fuses at as low a temperature as 1500 °C and suffers a volume reduction to the extent of 50%. In this condition it is very hard.

The beryllia refractory shapes are made similar to the alumina ones. They can be slip cast in plaster moulds. The refractory mix will be made up of the fused grog 65% and a fine low temperature calcined oxide 35%. The refractory mix can also be hot presse using a $BeCl_2$ binder. Very high pressures are necessary 15-20 kgf/cm^2. The dies should be made up of high chromium steel with excellent surface finish, high hardness (above Ro 63) and a slight taper to facilitate easy product with-drawal.

Berryllia refractories are very useful even at 2000 °C, due to their closed pore structure. Beryllia is also inert towards cobalt and carbon even at the highest temperature. Its hot strength is also considerable and hence is particularly suitable in jet propulsion technology.

Just like uranium compounds, Beryllia refractories are suitable in nuclear reactors also. Extreme precautions are necessary during working with BeO; the dust as well as the fumes of BeO will have caustic effects on human systems.

Thorium oxide or thoria as it is often called, is as good a refractory as Beryllia. It is blended with a 20% solution of thorium chloride and fired at 1800 °C. Thoria crucibles can be used at extremely high temperatures without any damage. This makes it particularly suitable in the melting of iron, Zirconium and Uranium. A distinct disadvantage with this material is however, its radioactive nature which warrants a very careful handling.

Other refractory oxides like titania, zirconia and magnesia also need a mention but a lot of work regrading their practical utilisation (still needs to be done).

3. ***Refractory Compounds***

Many refractory compounds are useful as special refractories. Of these, the carbides are most common. Carbides of Tungsten, Titanium, Silicon and Boron are being produced on a small scale for specialised purposes. These carbides are nowadays used as abrasives. Silicon carbide is produced in an electric arc furnace.

All the carbides can be hot pressed. They are good compact bodies with nearly zero porosity. Heavy metal carbides are all good abrasives. Silicon carbide, is a good refractory also, besides being a good abrasive. It has a good thermal conductivity and high resistance to slag attack.

Next to carbides, nitrides occupy an important place among the refractory compounds. Nitrides of titanium, Zirconium and boron are quite important. These nitrides can be slip cast from water or absolute alcohol suspensions and burned in high frequency induction furnaces. They can also be hot-pressed. The typical use of nitride refractories is in the vaccum melting techniques.

Sulphides of Cerium, Thorium and Uranium are established to be good refractories. Crucibles of these sulphides can be prepared by similar methods as those for the oxides above. These form excellent refractories for melting metals in vaccum. However the most important precaution to be taken in the use of these crucibles is that oxygen should not be present during the process.

3. *Refractory Porcellains*

A porcelain is different from a pure oxide in that it contains certain other constituents (may be oxides) also. Due to this, these possess a lower softening and vitrification temperatures. However, after burning, the final product may possess the same good properties as of pure oxide refractories.

Some patented refractory porcelains are developed, on these lines. Small quantities of MgO, CaO etc., are added to otherwise pure Al_2O_3 by some researchers and the resultant product found to be equally efficient in its properties as that of pure alumina. This field is still wide open and considerable work is in progress.

29 Carbon and its Allied Refractories

Carbon occurs in nature as both amorphous and crystalline forms; the later known as graphite. It predominantly occurs as coal which contains other constituents also. Chemically, carbon is very stable upto over 4000 °C in the absence of oxygen and resists the attack of acids and alkalis equally well. Hence the attention of refractory engineers is diverted towards this product.

Graphite is the form in which carbon is used as a refractory. It is of two types, the flaky graphite and the granular graphite. It is greyish in color and possesses a metallic lustre and very soft. It is very light Sp. Gr. 0.2.

Graphite used in the refractory industry is of the granular form. Though chemically this is inferior to the flaky variety, its capacity to be easily bonded makes it the first choice for the job.

Use of graphite as a refractory is in two ways. It is mixed with clay and the mix is used to fabricate crucibles. Secondly, it is compressed to make bricks with a suitable binder; these bricks are commonly known as carbon blocks.

The purity of graphite is of paramount consideration. It should contain a minimum of 85% carbon. Impurities like mica, iron oxide etc., should be very low. Large quantities of carbon blocks are also manufactured using high quality coke as a refractory material, in place of and sometimes mixed with granular graphite. The material is crushed and ground if necessary to 0.5-1.00 mm size. The bond employed is pitch or tar which is heated to enable easy mixing. Hand mixing is done with shovels and later pug mills are employed to ensure a thorough mixing. The pug mills has a steam jacket so that the binder does not harden during mixing.

Brick moulding

Bricks are moulded by hand tamping. A full brick is rammed in three or four installments by adding small quantities of the refractory mix and tamping with hot iron pokers. If an attempt is made to fill the brick with one charge only, a porus and loose structure results.

Burning

The bricks should not come into contact with air during burning. Special racks or cup-boards are employed in which the bricks are arranged. The space between the bricks is filled up with coke breeze. Sometimes these bricks are fired alongwith fireclay bricks are burnt in the cast iron moulds themselves. Whatever is done the ultimate idea is to avoid the brick from coming into contact with the air (oxygen) so that the carbon may not burn off. The kiln is closed and all the openings are sealed off.

The temperature of burning is 1350 °C at which the bricks are soaked for nearly 60 hours before they are cooled. Even during this stage, the furnace is not opened and the bricks are allowed to cool of their own accord. It takes nearly 10 days for the whole charge to cool down to the room temperature.

Properties

Carbon bricks possess high strength both at room temperature and at elevated temperatures. They are excellent in their resistance to spalling, corrosive slags and thermal shock.

Good quality brick which are perfectly burnt appear light grey in colour and have a specific gravity of 1.6 to 1.9. Porosity of the carbon brick is in the range of 20-25%. The ash percentage is generally less than 10% but in no case should exceed 14%. The refractoriness of the carbon bricks is of the order of 2200 °C and refractoriness under load of 3.5 kg/ cm^2 is 1710 °C.

Uses

Carbon bricks are the refractories of tomorrow. Nowadays in U.K. and some continental countries, they are gradually replacing firebrick in the blast furnace hearths. Further they are also found to be of excellent service in the furnaces employed in the extraction of Aluminium, lead, titanium and copper.

30 Insulating Bricks

Thermal insulation in pyrometallurgical operations is a must, in order to achieve a reasonable degree of fuel economy. Heat loss in the form of radiation in a metallurgical process can seldom be prevented but loss due to conduction can be minimised. Apart from fuel economy, this is also useful in prolonging the life of the furnace shell. Insulating bricks are employed for this purpose. These bricks are laid next to the furnace shell. The usual refractory brick layers start upon the insulating bricks.

Heat conduction is minimum in vacuum. This principle of vacuum flask, cannot however be made much use of, in the case of refractories. Instead of vacuum, however, the next best insulator is still air. Refractory bricks made with ample pore space so that they incorporate the still air, are the insulating bricks which are commonly used. Any material, from fireclay to dolomite can be used as the principal brick material. The essential requirement is creating a cellular structure in the final brick made.

It is established that the shape and distribution of the pore space in the brick has an important bearing upon the insulating behavior of the brick. Bricks having identical porosity differ in their insulating behavior, depending upon the nature of their pore space. A fine, cellular and well-distributed porosity is found to give an optimum insulation in a brick.

Bricks are made in the same way as ordinary brick but the composition of the refractory mix differs. Saw dust, napthalene etc., are added to the mix and lower pressures of moulding are used. Such bricks, when burnt, develop a cellular structure owing to the fact that the saw dust or napthalene burn off and leave their spaces open. The maximum burning temperature of insulating bricks does not exceed 1200 °C.

Sometimes, materials like mica, kyanite etc., are also used in the manufacture of the insulating bricks. But, their use involves higher cost and unless specially warranted, they are not employed for insulating purposes.

Properties

The insulating brick should possess the following properties.

(i) Their thermal conductivity should be less.
(ii) They should possess a fairly high crushing strength.
(iii) They should possess a high degree of porosity.
(iv) They should possess a low degree of permeability.
(v) They should possess a uniform texture.
(vi) They should be able to withstand the temperature of their use and
(vii) Their thermal expansion and contraction should be less.

31 Testing of Refractories

Testing of a material is the common word used to ascertain a particular group of properties. Material manufacturers make many claims regarding the quality of their product and the customers demand their own requirements while indenting. Both of them should be satisfied as to the product, its quality and price. Testing steps in here. Various tests are evolved depending upon the properties of the material. In fact, no test is made for a particular property and the value obtained on testing needs interpretation in relation to that property. A simple test like that, for the determination of the specific gravity, reveals not simply a figure; but the intensity of compactness of the mass in the material. Similarly, the bulk density and porosity of a refractory body give us an idea of the relative open spaces left in the refractory. This controls the degree of heat penetration, slag and other corrosive gas penetration into the body of the refractory during its actual use. Similarly, other properties are determined so as to ascertain the behavior of the refractory in its actual usage.

The following descriptions under each head give a brief resume of the property, in addition to its actual definition and the method of determining the particular property.

Specific gravity

This is too familiar a term to be specifically defined here. It is determined easily either by using a specific gravity bottle or pyknometer. Most of the readers are aware of the process of determining the specific gravity of a solid substance. Hence it is skipped.

Bulk density

Bulk density of a refractory is defined as the weight per unit volume of the refractory. This volume, includes the volume of the minute openings occuring between the different particles of the solid also.

Bulk density is determined as follows :

Let W be the weight of the dried sample,

W_1 its weight in water, after boiling in water for 2 hours, (cooling and removing the extraneous moisture), and

W_2 weight of the sample in the same condition as per W_1 but in air.

Bulk density $= \dfrac{W}{(W_2 - W_1)}$ (for details, please see porosity)

Porosity

Porosity is the actual volume of the openings existing in the refractory in relation to the total volume of the refractory. It is expressed, generally, as a percentage. Porosity is expressed in two ways – the apparent porosity and the true or actual porosity.

By measuring the volume of the open pores in a block of the refractory under test, its apparent porosity can be determined. The sample under test is dried at 105 ^{o}C to a constant weight (W). The sample is then placed in boiling water completely submerged for about two hours. Later, the sample is cooled by adding cold water to the flask. The weight of the sample suspended in water is taken (W_1). The sample is later removed from water and the extraneous surface water is wiped out with blotting papers and is weighed in air (W_2). From these three weights, the apparent porosity is calculated as follows :

Apparent porosity $\quad P = \dfrac{(W_2 - W)}{(W_2 - W_1)} \times 100$

Apparent Sp. gravity $\quad S_a = \dfrac{W}{(W - W_1)}$

True porosity is that percentage which is calculated by taking into account the total pore space in the whole of the solid. This includes pores whose volume cannot be measured as in the determination of the apparent porosity. Porosity can, however, be computed from the relationship as follows:

$$\text{Porosity} = \left(1 - \frac{S_a}{S}\right) \times 100$$

Where S = Specific gravity of the refractory

Permeability

Permeability of a refractory is a property though dependent upon its porosity to some extent, is again not totally governed by the porosity. Permeability is determined by forcing a known volume of air at a pressure of 1 cm. of water through a unit volume of the refractory and determining the time taken for its travel. In this, it is obvious that the gas can pass only through the pore space, which is continuous.

The test can be performed in a similar way to that performed on moulding sands, using a permeability meter. A cylindrical specimen of the refractory [of 2 inch (50mm) dia and 2 inch (50mm) height] is used. 1000 or 1500 ml of air is allowed to pass through the specimen and the time taken in seconds is noted using a stop watch. The permeability can be determined using the following relationship.

$$P = \frac{\text{Volume of the air} \times \text{height of the specimen}}{\text{Area} \times \text{pressure} \times \text{time}}$$

A practical difficulty experienced in the case of testing refractory is preventing seepage of the air from the curved surface of the cylinder. The cylinder is enclosed in an inflatable rubber sleeve to overcome this contingency.

Refractoriness

Refractoriness is the temperature at which the refractory softens. This temperature can be determined by heating the refractory and noting the temperature of its softening with the help of a pyrometer. But, in such a determination, difficulty arises in knowing the softening of the refractory.

As the softening of the refractory occurs due to some degree of fusion, a sort of a collapse occurs to the refractory. It is therefore more convenient to observe this collapse or deformation of the refractory during heating. A 'pyrometric cone' – in fact a pyramid with a triangular base, is employed for determining the refractoriness of the refractories. The first ceramist who conceived and put the idea into practice was a German, by name Segar. The pyrometric cones are known after him.

Segar made a series of cones by varying their compositions in such a way that they possessed softening temperatures in the range of 1150 °C-1530 °C. He designated the cone softening at 1150 °C with the number 1 and that with a softening temperature of 1530 °C with the number 20. The difference in temperature of softening of two cones with successive numbers is 20 °C.

Subsequently, Segar himself extended the cones series upwards, upto 26. Further development and research necessitated the extension of the series upto the number 42, conforming to a temperature of 2015 °C. This is the temperature of fusion of pure Al_2O_3. Segar series is extended downwards also later, to cover the lower temperatures. A ceramist by name Hecht designated the lower temperatures series with numbers starting with zero. A temperature of 585 °C is also covered and the corresponding cone designated as 022. Thus, the pyrometric cone series is a wide spectrum from 585°-2015 °C, shown in Table 31.1.

Table 31.1

Cone No.	Temperature in °C
42	2015
27	1605
26	1595
23	1580
20	1520
1	1125
01	1110
010	890
022	585

Pyrometric cones are made in two sizes. The High temperature series (1 and above) and $\frac{1}{4}''$ at the bottom (side of the triangular base) and $1\frac{1}{8}''$ in height. The low temperature cones (the 0 series) are

$\frac{1}{2}''$ at the base and $2\frac{5}{8}''$ in height. The cones are set in clay plaques in such a way that they are inclined to the horizontal at 82°. The cone number is stamped both on the plaque, and of course, on the cone itself.

The use of the cones is very simple. The refractory material whose P.C.E, (Pyrometric Cone Equivalent) is to be determined is crushed, ground and sieved to pass 200 mesh sieve. The material is kneaded with enough water and formed into the shape of a cone. The cone is dried and baked to impart rigidity.

The actual process of determination of the refractoriness consists of setting the experimental cone (specimen) alongwith some standard cones of differing numbers on a common plaque. The plaque is inserted into a muffle furnace and the temperature is increased at the stipulated rate (generally 150 °C/ hour). The cones are observed to note the fusion (deformation). The temperature at which the specimen bends so that its apex comes down to the base (plaque) level is noted. Alongwith the specimen, one of the standard cones also undergoes the same deformation. The P.C.E. is reported as the number of the standard cone which had undergone deformation to the same extent as the cone under test. The various degrees of deformation of the cones are illustrated in Fig 31.1.

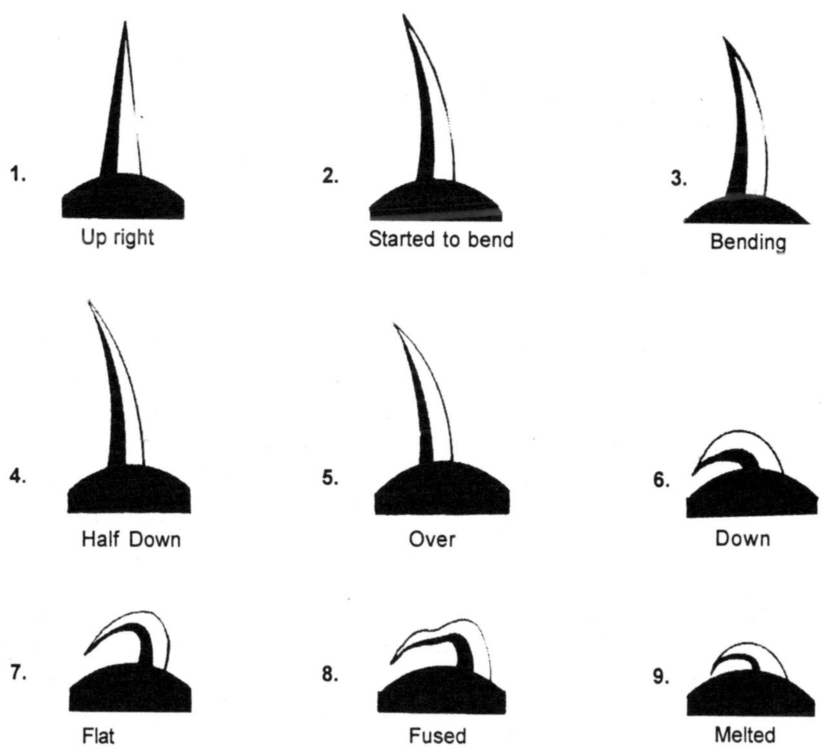

Fig. 31.1

Use of the segar cones

It should be clearly understood that in this test the pyrometric cone indicates only the fusion suffered by the clay. The degree of fusion occured depends not only on the temperature but also on the time. The effect of temperature can predominate the bending of the cone if only the rate of heating is slow, the viscous flow of the clay predominates the effect of temperature. Thus, the temperature of softening indicated by the cone is related to the rate of heating. The rate of heating and the P.C.E. are shown in Table 31.2.

Table 31.2

Cone No.	Fired 20 °C/hr.		Fired at 150 °C/hr	
	Temp °C	Bending interval °C	Temp °C	Bending interval °C
1.	1125	30	1160	45
2.	1135	30	1165	45
3.	1145	30	1170	40
4.	1165	40	1190	35
5.	1180	40	1205	50
6.	1190	40	1230	35
7.	1210	40	1250	60
8.	1225	45	1260	55
9.	1250	65	1285	115
10.	1260	40	1305	95
11.	1285	70	1325	80
12.	1310	80	1335	45
13.	1350	70	1350	55
14.	1390	100	1400	70
15.	1410	85	1435	115
16.	1450	70	1465	125
17.	1465	75	1475	125
18.	1485	90	1490	85
19.	1515	100	1520	70
20.	1520	–	1530	30

Wedgewood pyroscope

This is another method by which the refractoriness is studied. The principle of this test is not based on the softening or melting. The test is based on the principle of shrinkage.

The shrinkage suffered by a refractory during heating can be classified as follows:

(i) occuring due to the escape of the free or mechanically mixed water,

(ii) arising due to the removal of water which is remaining in the pores of the body,

(iii) arising due to the removal and escape of the hygroscopic water,

(iv) occuring due to the calcination of the clay – the removal of the water of crystallisation of the different constituents in the clay.

Fig. 31.2 Wedgewood pyroscope.

Thus the water from the clay is continuously removed during of heating. The consequent shrinkage suffered, indicates the temperature of heating the clay.

The wedgewood scale consists of Nos. 1 to 20. 1 corresponds to 022 of the segar Cone 15 to 30 and 19 to 41, respectively.

The experimental wedge is placed on the V-shaped wedgewood scale and the assembly heated. The graduation upto which the specimen descends gives its wedgewood number Fig. 31.2.

Refractoriness under load

This is a property of the refractory brick by virtue of which of withstand it both load and high temperature. Generally the refractoriness under load is determined at a constant stress (as prescribed by I.S.S.) of 2 kg per cm^2 or 3.5 kg/cm^2 and expressed in terms of temperature in °C. The conditions of heating are also stipulated. The specimen is heated at a rate of 150 °C per minute until a temperature of 1000 °C is reached and at 90 °C per minute until the failure occurs. The height of the specimen and the temperature are plotted on a curve. Failure is indicated when the curve drops by 3 mm from its peak. Complete failure is indicated when the curve drops by 20 mm.

Any type of furnace can be used for heating but an electrically heated furnace is preferrable. The deformation of the specimen can be recorded by using an extensometer.

Resistance to slag attack

The capacity of a refractory to resist a slag is particularly important during the actual service of the refractory. The particular use of the refractory, is kept in mind and the slag obtained in that process is taken and the chemical or other action of the slag on the refractory is determined. There is no set procedure for evaluating this property. Many methods are used all of which aim at the same goal; some of which are described below:

Slag penetration method

A pellet of slag is embedded in the refractory block under test. The refractory is then heated to the operating temperature and maintained at that temperature for some hours. Later, it is cooled to the room temperature. The refractory block is thereafter analysed, sectioning at different distances from the slag pellet. The degree of slag penetration can thus be evaluated. The process somewhat resembles the diffusion experiment to study the Kirkendall Effect.

Immersion method

A small piece of the refractory is immersed in the molten slag for some time and withdrawn. After cooling, it is analysed and the degree of slag contamination is studied.

Powder method

The refractory under test and the slag whose action on the refractory is in question are powdered and equal quantities are mixed thoroughly and heated in a crucible to the temperature of actual use of the refractory. After soaking for some time at the high temperature, the mixture is cooled and analysed. Whether any chemical/mineralogical complexes are formed or not is thus evaluated to enlighten us on the behavior of the two materials in contact at the elevated temperature.

Crushing strength

This is, in other words, the compression strength of the brick. When a furnace shell is lined with a refractory and is charged with a metal or metal compound for the extraction or other process, the charge exerts a compressive load on the refractory. In fact, the refractory lining is crushed by the furnace charge. Crushing strength is determined in a similar way as the compression strength of wood or cement is determined by using a 50 mm cube.

Resistance to Gas Attack

Furnace gases have a very injurious effect on the refractory linings. The extent to which furnace gases cause refractory troubles can be understood by the blast furnace irregularities like hanging and scaffolding. The regions that are affected most are the doors and roofs. Many workers have studied refractories. The experimental data can be seen from the contemporary research and some references are given in Table 31.2.

Resistance to thermal shock or spalling

This is a property of the brick by virtue of which it possesses the resistance to fluctuations of temperature. Manytimes the furnaces or ladles lined with the refractory cool after the metal is emptied and again get heated up once they are charged. The lining should not get crumbled due to these thermal changes. The expansion and contraction of the brick contribute to the damage of the brick due to the changes in temperature. However, other characteristics like the original composition of the refractory, impurities etc., also contribute to spalling to a reasonable extent.

Resistance to spalling determined as the number of quenchings a brick panel undergoes before it collapses. Indian standard specification prescribes the test to use 24 bricks in an actual panel (as a lining) which is heated to the operating temperature and quenched with water jet. The cycle is repeated and the number of cycles the bricks withstand without collapse is the number designated to the brick as a measure of the spalling resistance.

The properties of different common refractories are tabulated in Table 31.2 to be a ready reference. Their common application in the metallurgical industry is also noted in the last column.

Table 31.2 Refractory Data.

Serial No.	Name	Specific gravity	Porosity in %	Crushing strength MPa	Refractoriness °C	Ref,. in °C under a load of .35 MPa	Resistance to spalling.	Applications
1.	Fire Brick	2.6-2.7	22	15-70	1650-1725	1250-1300	20	Common refractory for all types of heating. Extensively used in regenerators, boilers, glass furnaces checkers and glass industry. Blast furnace is completely lined with fire brick only.
2.	Sillimanite	2.8	20	20	1850	1700	24	Glass melting furnaces, boilers, pyrometer sheating, low temperature coke-oven plants, oil fired furnaces, tunnel kilns, cement kilns, cupolas, blast furnaces, soaking pits and roofs of open hearth and Elec. Arc furnaces.
3.	Silica	2.3-2.4	25.4	20-30	1700-1725	1680	1	All furnace roofs in the metallurgical industry. They are also used in glass melting furnaces, sodium silicate and enamels as roofs. In acid steel making however, the complete furnace is lined with silica bricks.
4.	Magnesite	3.0-3.7	26	35-50	1785	1500	1	Basic open hearth and electric arc furnaces and hot metal mixers. Also used in the reverberatory furnaces, cooper convertors, lead extraction as well as in the cement plant kilns. Also used in the furnaces where the refining of noble metals is performed.
5.	Dolomite	3.2	22-24	32.5-40	1850	1650	9	For all the above purposes (where magnesite bricks are employed), dolomite bricks also are useful as a cheaper substitute.

Table Contd...

Serial No.	Name	Specific gravity	Porosity in %	Crushing strength MPa	Refractoriness °C	Ref,. in °C under a load of 0.35 MPa	Resistance to spalling.	Applications
6.	Chromite	3.8-4.1	26	35-50	1850	1450	2	These are neutral refractory bricks and find the widest application in the non-ferrous metal extraction and refining furnaces. Also used in the high pressure steel boilers and paper pulp plants.
7.	Chrome-Magnesite	3.8	25	12.5-24	1785	1550	4	These are replacing the silica bricks in the roof lining of open hearth and electric arc furnaces. Being stronger and bad conductors, these bricks give almost double the service of the silica bricks, besides, effecting good fuel economy.
8.	Carbon blocks	1.5-1.9	20.25	35	above 2000	1800	24	A perfect neutral refractory. Slowly being adopted as a lining of remarkable properties in the blast furnaces: especially in high top pressure designs.
9.	Zircon bricks	4.4	25	50	2000	1600	13	Another good refractory of neutral character, mostly being employed in the manufacture of crucibles and linings of furnaces used in the manufacture of special quality glasses.
10.	Insulating brick (Fire brick)	1.8-2.1	45-55	.35-30	--	--	--	Insulating bricks in all the high temperature furnaces.

References

1. Lecrivain L and Marethen - Contribution to the study of slag attack on Refractories. Trans. 9th international Ceram. Congress. P 377, 1964.
2. Brunner M. - Method for the study of slag attack on Refractories. Tran. Brit. Ceram. Soc. 62, 813, 1963.
3. Eusner G.R. and J.R. Bachman - Hydration of basic Refractories. Bulk. American Ceram. Soc. 42, 613, 1959.
4. Davies W.R., R.J. Slowson and G.R. Rigby - CO attack of firebricks : The physical state of the deposited carbon. Tran. Brit. Ceram. Soc. 56, 67, 1957.
5. Berry T.F., R.N. Ames and R.B. Snow - Deposition of Carbon from carbon monooxide . J. Amer. Ceram. Soc. 39, 308, 1956.

UNIT IV

Pyrometry

32 Introduction of Thermometry

The science of measurements of high temperature is known as pyrometry. By the word 'high', it is meant temperature over 350 °C. Ordinary thermometers are capable of measuring temperatures upto 500 °C and though instruments used for measuring temperatures upto 1000 °C also are sometimes called thermometers, the two words pyrmeters and thermometers should not be confused.

The temperature scale is continuous and in this connection a recapitulation of the word temperature and its significance is not out of place. Temperature is defined as the relative degree of hotness of a body. The various temperature scales are evolved based on the freezing and boiling points of pure water. The freeing point is taken as 0° in the Centigrade and Reamer Scales. Again, in the Centigrade scale, the boiling point of water is taken as 100 °C and in the Reamer as 80 °C. The Fahrenheit scale of temperature, which is going obsolete now, fixes the temperature of freezing of water as 32° and the boiling point as 212°. In all the three scales, the intermediate range between the freezing and boiling points is equally divided into that number of parts as per the scale. Thus a temperature of 50 °C is equal to 40 °R and 122 °F.

Mercury, which is the common thermometric liquid employed at lower temperatures, boils at 357 °C. Thus, it cannot be used for temperature measurements above 250 °C for, the vapour pressure starts to become significant and the readings become untrustworthy. Air or hydrogen thermometers are used for very precise temperature measurement at lower temperatures as well as moderately high temperatures, say, upto 800 °C.

The principle of operation of the gas thermometer is the universal gas law, which is as follows :

$$PV = RT$$

where, P = Pressure

V = Volume

R = the gas constant,

and T = Absolute temperature of the gas.,

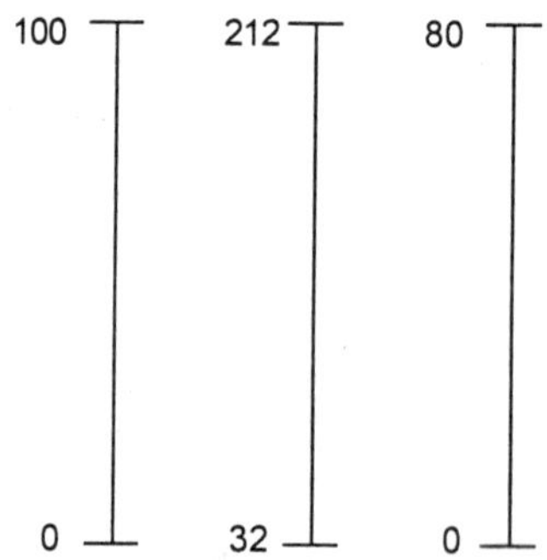

Fig. 32.1 Temperatures Scales.

The absolute temperature scale is derived depending upon the Charles' law. The absolute zero is a temperature which is 273 degree lower than the freezing point of water. The centigrade scale of temperature can thus be converted into the absolute temperature by adding 273 to its value. Thus, 25 °C will be (25 + 273) = 298 ^{0}A.

The constant volume air or gas thermometer

The instrument consists of a constant mass of a gas maintained at a constant volume, in a vessel fitted with a means for measuring its pressure. Let P_0 and P_{100} are the pressure of the gas at the freezing and boiling points of water respectively and P_t is the pressure at an unknown temperature (T °C), then the unknown temperature T can be computed from the relationship.

$$\frac{T}{100} = \frac{P_t - P_0}{P_{100} - P_0} \quad \text{or} \quad T = 100 \frac{(P_t - P_0)}{(P_{100} - P_0)} \ ^{o}C$$

The principle of the instrument is that equal changes in the pressure of the enclosed gas are brought about by equal changes in temperatures.

Jolly's constant volume air thermometer

The instrument consists of a glass bulb of about 100 ml capacity. This contains dry air. The bulb is connected by a fine glass tube and rubber pressure tubing to a movable manometer reservoir. A fixed mark X on the capillary is the constant volume mark. The vertical height of the level Y in the open limb above X is called the head h. The total pressure of the gas in the bulb is (H + h), where H is the atmospheric pressure.

In order to determine an unknown temperature, the value of H should be first ascertained by reading the barometer, later the bulb of the thermometer is maintained at the unknown temperature for about 10 minutes and the value of h is found out.

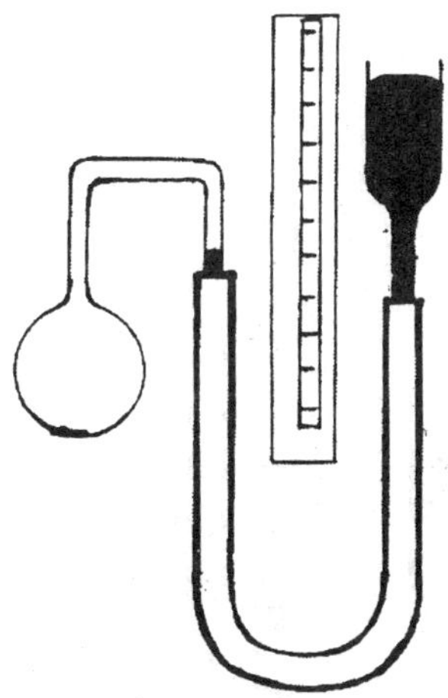

Fig. 32.2 Jolly's air thermometer.

Thus, it can be calculated (from the relation)

$$t\ ^{\circ}C = 100\ \frac{(P_t - P_0)}{(P_{100} - P_0)}$$

Where $P_t = (H + ht)$

$P_0 = (H + h_0)$

and $P_{100} = (h + h_{100})$

The experiment is rough and suffers from many drawbacks. The important drawback is that the air is not maintained at constant volume and glass bulb also expands appreciably, due to the change in temperature.

Constant Volume gas thermometer

Hydrogen is employed as the thermometric gas in this instrument. In the standard thermometer designed by Clappuis, a bulb of platinum-irridium alloy of 110cm an exact volume of 1 litre is used. The expansion of the air bulb is calculated at the temperature and allowed for. Further, the fraction of the total gas in the communicating tube is so small that the chief drawbacks of the simple air thermometer are overcome. The constant volume mark is a small pointer P_1 inside the monometer tube. The monometer incorporates a barometer, the glass tube of which is free to move. The vertically moving glass tube carries a vernier, over a scale. There is a small pointer P_2 inside the Torricellian vaccum space of the barometer. This pointer helps to coincide the level of the mercury. To measure the pressure at any measuring temperature, the reservoir P is first moved to adjust the mercury to P_1. The barometer is raised or lowered so that P_2 just touches its mercury surface. This will upset the first adjustment but a separate fine adjustment is there to make the rectification. The vertical distance between P_1 and P_2 gives the value (H + h) of the gas (Fig. 32.3).

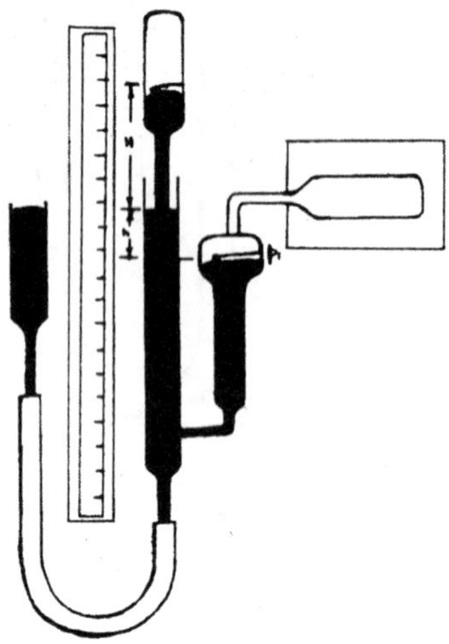

Fig. 32.3 Constant volume gas thermometer.

To measure temperatures above 500 °C, Hydrogen is not suitable and so nitrogen is employed.

Resistance thermometer

The electrical resistance of metals is found to vary with temperature. In fact, the resistance of pure metals increases with temperature. The rate of increase is also found to be uniform. Thus, to determine the temperature of a body, the resistance of a metal at that temperature is determined and the temperature computed. The metal used should be of the heighest purity and resistant to heat and oxidation. Thus, noble metals, especially Platinum, can be employed for the purpose.

Calendar has shown that the resistance of pure platinum varies with respect to its temperature (gas thermometer temperature) as per the following relation,

$$R = R_0 (1 + \propto\theta + \beta\theta^2)$$

where R_0 = Resistance of Pt at 0 °C

R = Resistance of Pt at θ °C

and $\propto$, β are constants, whose values are dependent for the particular metal specimen.

The platinum resistance scale of temperature is slightly different from that of the gas thermometer scale, but nearly equal. Equal changes in resistance of platinum denote equal changes in temperature. If the resistance of platinum at 0 °C is R_0 and that at 100 °C is R_{100}, then the resistance Rt at any temperature of t °C is related as,

$$\frac{t}{100} = \frac{(Rt - R_0)}{(R_{100} - R_0)}$$

or

$$t = \left\{\frac{100(Rt - R_0)}{(R_{100} - R_0)}\right\} \text{°C}$$

The value of t is read as the value on the platinum resistance scale.

The platinum resistance scale and the gas thermometer scale are related as,

$$(\theta - t) = \delta\left[\left(\frac{\theta}{100}\right)^2 - \left(\frac{\theta}{100}\right)\right]$$

Where δ is a constant for the particular specimen of platinum. It is suggested that the value of δ be determined by finding out the boiling point of sulphur in both the scales.

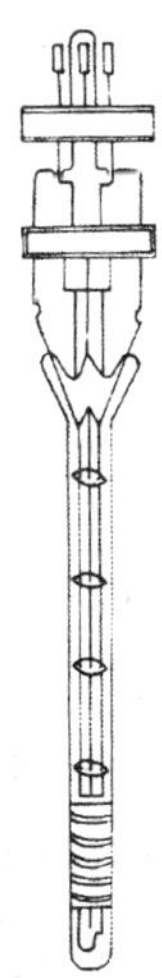

Fig. 32.4 Platinum resistance thermometer.

Construction of a Platinum Resistance Thermometer

Pure platinum wire, of a uniform cross section and generally a meter long, is doubled on itself, to avoid induction effects and is wound on a flat strip of mica. This is enclosed in a tube of hard glass or porcelain. The tube is evacuated. The leads are made of copper for lower temperature work or platinum itself for higher temperature work that is, above 700 °C. The resistance of the platinum is very accurately determined at the temperature in question (Fig. 32.4).

Resistance determination is carried out by using a precision Wheatstone bridge. In this, a series of 30 shunted coils are employed, instead of conventional bridge wires. These coils are immersed in oil which is circulated by a stirrer. Such an instrument can be successfully employed in the temperature range – 200 to 600 °C. An accuracy of 0.002 °C is attainable in this set up.

For use at temperatures above 600 °C, the conventional wheatstone bridge is itself used. The peculiarity with this bridge (Fig 32.5) known after Calendar and Griffith is that, the two ratio arms (resistances R_1 and R_2) are equal to give a direct reading pattern for the unknown resistance.

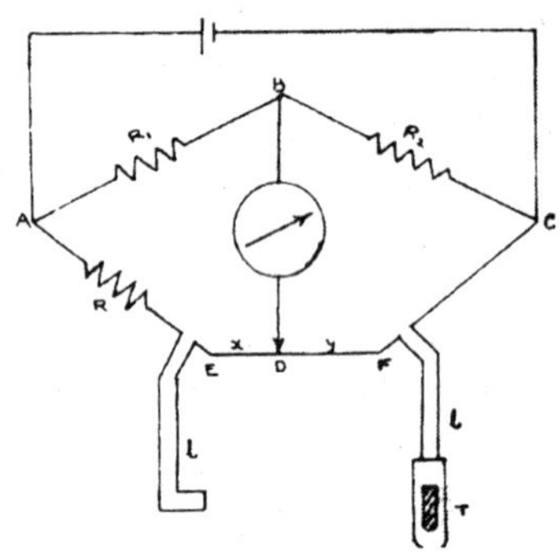

Fig. 32.5 Callendar & Griffith's Wheatstone bridge.

As,

$$R_1 = R_2$$

$$R + L + X = T + L + Y$$

$$t = R + (X - Y)$$

The resistance of the leads (L) is compensated by connecting a similar wire in the opposite arm, called compensating leads.

Platinum thermometer has a wide range of use, from – 200 °C to 1000 °C. It is extremely accurate over this range. Its chief disadvantages are however, the long time taken for it to attain the temperature of the surroundings and for making the observation. Thus, it is difficult to measure a rapidly changing temperature.

Advantages

1. It can be used over a wide range of temperature that is form 200 °C to 1000 °C.
2. It is fairly accurate, The accuracy actually depends upon the accuracy with which the resistance measurement can be effected. In general, its accuracy is of the order of 0.01 °C upto 600 °C and 0.1 °C in the range of 600 °C to 1000 °C.
3. There is no zero error.
4. Once it is standardised with the help of a gas thermometer, it can be used in turn, as a standardising equipment.
5. Very convenient to use.

Disadvantages

1. Consider able time is taken for the platinum wire to attain the actual temperature under measurement.
2. Cannot be monitored.
3. Dangers of wire contamination and hence loss of accuracy upon prolonged usage.

33 Thermocouples

If two dissimilar wires are joined together at both ends and one junction is heated, an electromotive force (e.m.f) is generated in the circuit. This discovery forms the basis of all thermocouple pyrometers. A millivoltmeter is connected in the circuit to measure the e.m.f. generated. The e.m.f generated is proportional to the temperature of the hot body. Thus, we can adopt this method to measure the temperature of a body by determining the e.m.f. developed in the thermocouple at that temperature. The thermocouple should be standardised for this purpose, by determining the e.m.f developed at different standard temperatures and plotting a curve between the temperatures and the e.m.f.

Fig. 33.1 Thermocouple.

Construction of a Thermocouple

The construction of a thermocouple is very simple. The two thermocouple wires are cleaned at the ends where the junction is to be made. An emery paper is recommended for scrapping the ends. Later, the cleaned ends are tightly twisted, one over the other, roughly making three to four rounds. Then, the twisted end is heated and dipped in a flux, either ammonium chloride or borax. Due to the heat, the flux forms a bead at the end. The next stage is to effect the weld. An oxy - acetylene flame or electric arc is used to melt the end. The junction, after the welding, develops a globular shape.

The next stage is to cover one of the two wires with insulating beads. Silica or porcelain beads are used for this purpose.

Calibration

The calibration of thermocouple is performed by measuring the e.m.fs. developed at fixed points in the temperature scale. Melting point of ice, boiling point of water and the melting point of sulphur are the common fixed temperatures taken. The setup is simple. A millivoltmeter is connected in series with the thermocouple. The cold junction is maintained in melting ice, in all the experiments (Fig. 33.2).

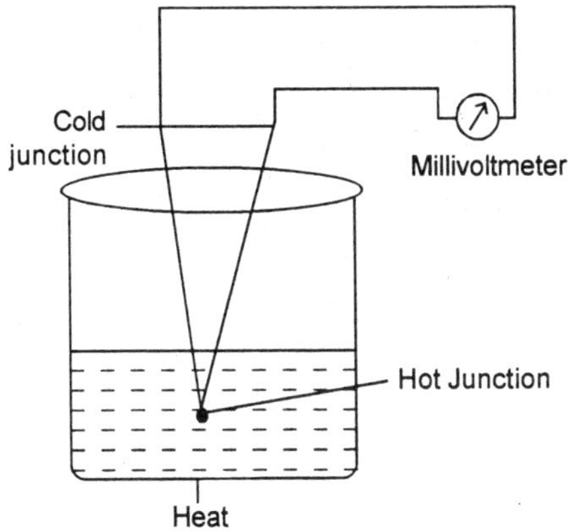

Fig. 33.2 Calibration of a thermocouple.

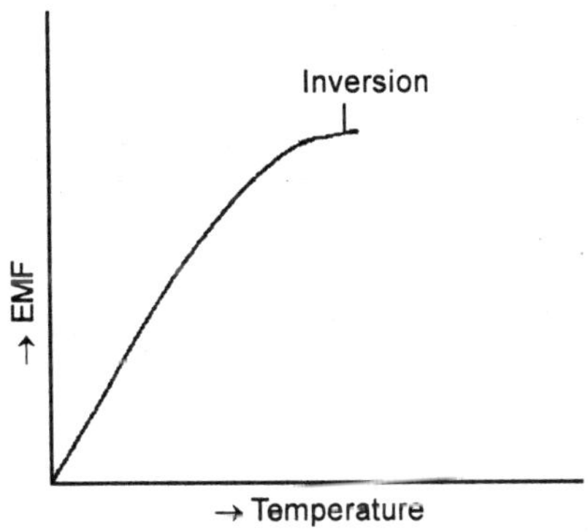

Fig. 33.3 Thermoelectric inversion.

A curve is plotted between the emf and temperature. The curve obtained is a straight line, passing through the origin (Fig 33.3) showing a slight dip at a higher temperature.

Thermoelectric Inversion

The straight line relationship between e.m.f. and temperature will prevail only over a particular range of temperature, depending upon the thermocouple materials. Later, it is found that the curve stoops and this phenomenon is called thermoeletric inversion.

The thermoelectric inversion phenomenon, in fact, governs the use of the thermocouple. The readings (temperature measurements) obtained by using the thermocouples are not reliable above the point of inflexion.

Table showing the constant with respect to various common thermocouples .

Table 33.1

Sl.No.	Thermocouple elements	Emf developed with c.j. at 0 °C and h.j. at 100 °C (in millivolts)	Practical usage of the couple in temperature measurement (maximum temperature.) °C.
1.	Copper/constantin.	4	300
2.	Chromel / Alumel	4.1	1250
3.	Iron/ constantin	5.3	1100
4.	Platinum/Platinum Rhodium	6.5	1600

Thermocouple materials

Many sets of materials are in the use as thermocouples. Constantin, an alloy of copper and nickel, is used either with copper or iron. Chromel and Alumel (both alloys) are also used. Their ranges of use, however, vary. Copper-constantin is useful upto about 500 °C, iron-constantin upto about 900 °C and chromel- alumel upto 1200 °C. These base metal thermocouples cannot be used for the measurement of temperature above 1200 °C. The thermocouples, constructed out of platinum and an ally of platinum-rhodium (10% or 13% Rh) called 'noble metal' thermocouples are used for temperature measurement above 1000 °C. They are accurate upto 1600 °C.

Protection tubes

The thermocouple materials get contaminated with the impurities during their use. Hot metal, slag or the furnace gases are found to be responsible for this contamination. A contaminated thermocouple does not develop emf as per the predicted value and thus leads to incorrect measurements. Sometimes, the thermocouple wires are found to be so much oxidised that they will collapse. In the case of base metal thermocouples, the contamination becomes so great that the thermocouple gets corroded.

Some degree of contamination of oxide formation on the surface is found to be helpful in providing greater imperviousness to the gas attack in the case of noble metal thermocouples. But, a thorough covering on the thermocouple wires by a refractory material is preferrable. Mullite (refractory) tubing is considered as the best protection upto 1500 °C, whereas for lower temperature work, silicon carbide or graphite covering can be employed.

Cold Junction correction

The thermoelectric pyrometer is calibrated for the standard condition of 0 °C temperature at its cold junction. When the actual measurement of temperature is made, the cold junction will generally, not remain at 0 °C temperature. Thus, it becomes necessary to compensate for this variation.

The emf developed in the thermocouple is due to the temperature difference between the hot and cold junctions. If the cold junction temperature is more (than that it should be, i.e., 0 °C) the temperature difference would be less and the corresponding e.m.f. also less. So, a lower temperature is recorded.

The need for the cold junction correction or compensation arises due to this effect. The procedure for correction is not complicated. The common method is to add the temperature of the cold junction to the measured temperature, i.e., if a thermocouple is employed and the temperature measured comes to 1125 °C and the cold junction is at the room temperature (say 25 °C), the actual temperature with cold junction correction is 1125 + 25 = 1150 °C.

Extension wires

It is seen above that the cold junction should be maintained always at 0 °C, or at a constant temperature. The temperature of the cold junction should not fluctuate. In order to ensure that it is advisible to locate the cold junction farther away from the furnace whose temperature is being measured. It is difficult to employ unusually long wires for the thermocouple. So, a pair of extension wires, made of the same material as the thermocouple, are employed and connected to the thermocouple at one end and the other ends to the measuring instrument.

Pairs of wires used as the extension wires can be the same wire used to make the thermocouple, as said above. This eliminates the differences in the thermo-electric characteristics. This can be done in the case of cheaper thermocouples like copper-constantin and iron-constantin. But, in the case of the noble metal thermocouples e.g., platinum, platinum-rhodium, use of the extension wires of the same materials will be costly. So, cheaper substitutes are employed which possess the same thermoelectric characteristics as the two elements of the couple. A copper wire is used to connect to the platinum-rhodium wire and a special copper-nickel ally wire is used to connect to the platinum wire. In spite of the indentical thermo-eletric properties of these extension wires, care is to be taken to avoid any temperature variation between the two points of extension connection. A zone box is used, which is an enclosure for the two extension points, so that both of them are maintained at the same temperature.

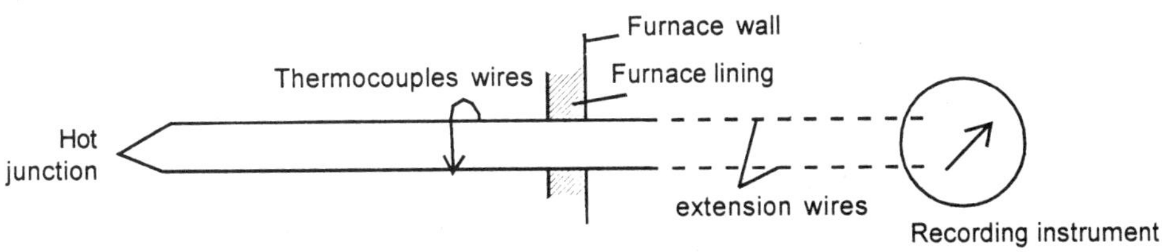

Fig. 33.4 Temperature measurement using a thermocouple.

The extension wires should be properly identified (positive and negative) by employing differently colored insulation. Also, one set of extension wires (meant for a particular thermocouple should not be used with another thermocouple.

An important point to be noted in this connection is that when the extension wires are used with a thermocouple, the cold junction is shifted to the indicating instrument itself (its terminals).

Thermopile

A thermopile is made up of more than one thermocouple of the same sets of materials, connected to each other in series. The effect should be a larger e.m.f. developed, because the total e.m.f indicated will be the sum of all the e.m.f. developed by the individual thermocouples in the thermopile.

Advantages

1. Very cheap
2. No time lag
3. Remote control is possible
4. Portable and
5. Good sensitivity

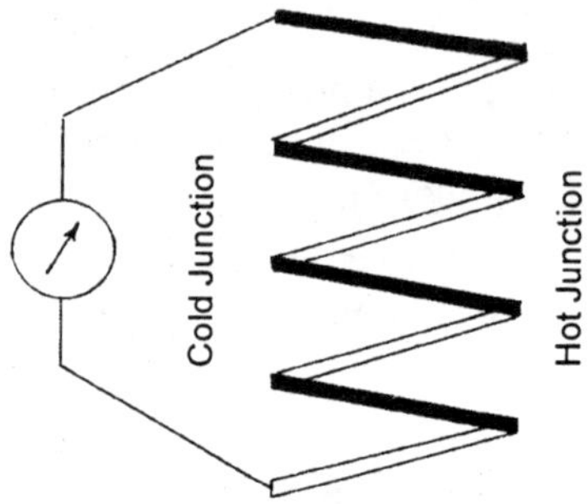

Fig. 33.5 Thermopile.

Disadvantages

1. Difficulty in maintaining the cold junction at 0 °C
2. The temperature e.m.f relationship is not well-defined and dependable and
3. Low degree of accuracy due to the leakage of currents in the circuit may give rise to error.

Measuring instruments

The electrical instruments used along with the thermocouples and radiation pyrometers can be broadly classified as :

(a) Indicators
(b) Recorders and
(c) Controllers

Sometimes, indicating controllers and recording controllers are also employed. Whatever they are called, their sensitivity is very high in comparison to the ordinary electrical instruments. They need a careful maintenance and use.

Indicators

The measuring variable in all pyrometry is the voltage. The voltage may be measured either directly or as temperature on a calibrated scale. The thermo-eletric power of the thermocouples being very small, the instrument used is millivoltmeter or potentiometer.

The milli-voltmeter, however sensitive it may be, is not reliable if the resistance of the circuit of the thermocouple varies. Pyrometric milli-voltmeters are provided with a series of resistors made of manganin (of a high resistance) in order to decrease the percentage change in the resistance of the circuit resulting from the heating up of the couple or its extension wires.

A potentiometer circuit is shown in the Fig 33.6 on its simplest form. When the sliding contact is moved on the potentiometer wire, the resistance in that arm of the bridge changes and a null point of the galvanometer is read when the voltage drops across the wire arm tapping and the e.m.fs. generated in the thermocouple are balanced. In the ordinary potentiometers, the length of the wire will be marked in centimeter or millimeters; the same can be calibrated in terms of the balancing, with voltage values or even in degrees centigrade.

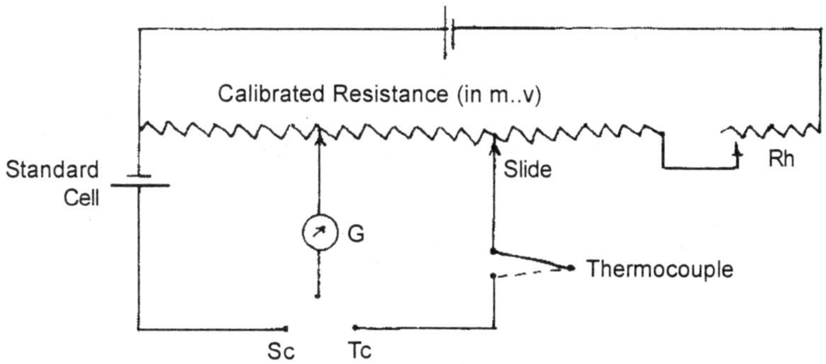

Fig. 33.6 Measurement of thermoeletric e.m.f using potentiometer.

The accuracy of the potentiometer is a function of the voltage variation of the standard cell connected in the circuit. Though this is very negligible about (0.05% per year), it is advisible to check for it frequently.

Recorders

These are instruments which function on the same principle of indicating instruments. An additional feature of recording of the indicated value is also made. An ink pen is fitted to the pointer or the pointer is substituted by an ink pen which records the readings on a strip of paper which moves on the dial portion. The strip of paper will be generally graduated in the temperature scale.

34 Radiation Pyrometers

The gas thermometer, and the resistance thermometer become useless above 1000 °C and the thermocouple pyrometers become ineffective above 1600 °C. Hence some other suitable method was to be evolved for the temperature measurement above 1600 °C. Obviously such device should preferrably be operative from a distance from the hot sources whose temperature is being measured so that

1. It need not withstand that high temperature and
2. It can measure the temperature of a source whose access is difficult.

Radiation of energy from hot source is one criterion upon which the temperature measurement is based. The instrument is called radiation pyrometer.

The total radiated energy from any temperature excited radiator is established to be proportional to the fourth power of the temperature. For this purpose (of definition of radiation) the radiator is taken as a standard radiator. A standard radiator is a 'black body'. Black body is defined as the body which absorbs all the radiation that is incident upon it. The total radiant flux or radiation from the black body W is related to its absolute temperature T as follows:

$$W = \sigma T^4$$

Where σ is a fundamental physical constant.

From the radiation spectrum, it can be further seen that the actual radiaiton is precisely calculable for a particular interval of wave length, by Wein's law, which is as follows :

$$J_{\lambda t} = C_1 \lambda^{-5} e^{-ca/\lambda (t+273)}$$

Where $J_{\lambda t}$ = intensity of the light of wave length at a temperature of t °C.

C_1 & C_2 = Constants, determinable experimentally.

From the international scale of temperature according to which the melting point of gold is 1063°C, the value of C_2 = 1.432 cm/degree

By measuring the ratio of intensities at two temperatures, the value of C1 can be eliminated and a working equation of the following type is arrived at,

$$\text{Log } e^r = \log e \frac{J\lambda t}{J\lambda_{1063}} \left[\frac{1}{(1063+273)} - \frac{1}{(t+273)}\right]$$

$$= \frac{1.432}{\lambda} \left[\frac{1}{(1063+273)} - \frac{1}{(t+273)}\right]$$

Black body

The concept of the black body should be well understood. The following experiment of Leslie's Cube (Fig 34.1) demonstrates the dependence of the heat absorption and radiation on the nature of the surface. The instrument is a cubic-metal box with a small top opening. It is capable of being rotated on the vertical axis each of its four faces is treated differentially. One is painted with dull black, another with white, the third is highly polished and the fourth left untreated. The box is filled with water and the water is boiled. A suitable heat measuring device is located near the cube. When the water is boiling and the cube rotated so as to measure the heat radiated from its surfaces, it can be seen that the surface which is painted dull black emits maximum heat energy and the least emission of heat is from the highly polished surface.

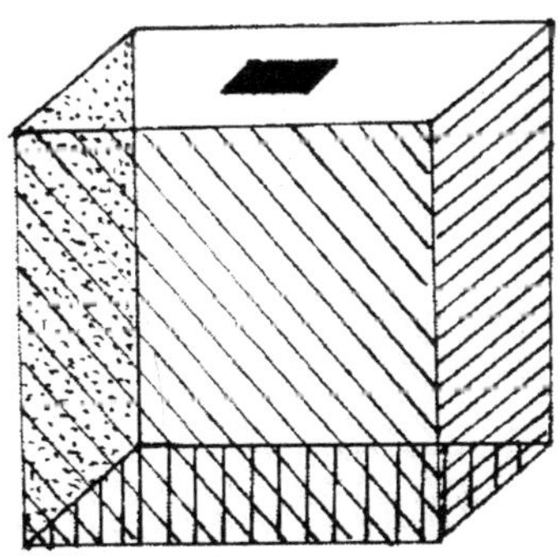

Fig. 34.1 Leslie's cube.

The reason for the black painted surface emitting the maximum energy amongst the four surfaces is that it is also capable of absorbing maximum energy from the boiling water, Thus, as it follows that a good radiator is also a good absorber.

Theoretically, a black body is defined as that body which absorbs all the radiation that is incident upon it. Not withstanding the electromagnetic radiations, the definition can be modified as hereunder.

"A body which would absorb all the visible range of radiations that are incident upon it is defined as a black body".

It is seen above that a good absorber is a good radiator. Thus when the black body is heated to a sufficiently high temperature, it emits radiations of all wavelengths; from ultraviolet to infrared full total radiation. By virtue of its being a black body, the radiation emanating from it will be more intense than the radiation from any other body maintained at the same temperature. This is called the black body radiation.

Lamp black is found absorb to about 97% of the radiation incident upon it. Platinum black is found to absorb about 98% of the radiation incident upon it. When emitting, they emit a considerable portion of the heat energy even in the ultra violet ranges; which no other natural object does. Thus, they approximate to the ideal conception for the black body.

The term 'black body' should now be clear and it should not be misunderstood. It has nothing to do with the colour of the body. Even when lamp black is heated to brilliantly white heat, its radiation is that of a black body. Similarly in this instance it is incidental that, the colour of lamp black is black when it is not heated.

Properties of thermal radiation

Thermal radiation exhibits all the properties of light. The only difference is that whereas we can see the light with our eyes, the thermal radiation can not be seen. Some of the properties of the thermal radiation which help in the understanding of pyrometrical instruments are listed below :

1. It travels through space with the same velocity as light.
2. It travels in straight lines.
3. It obeys the laws of reflection.
4. It obeys the inverse-square law.
5. It undergoes internal reflection.
6. It can be polarised like light, and
7. It exhibits the phenomena of diffraction and interference.

In addition to the above properties, heat radiation has the unique property of emission which is dependent upon various factors like nature of the surface, its size, its temperature and its surroundings. Its (emission's) quality and quantity are determinable.

Emissive power of a surface

It is found that all the conditions being the same, the radiation from a surface depends upon its nature. It is said that different surfaces possess different emissive powers. Emissive power is the rate of emission of thermal radiation per unit area of the surface at a given temperature, compared with that of a surface coated with lamp black, under identical conditions.

This, however, should not be confused with the surface emissivity which is not only temperature-dependent but also dependent upon time and atmospheric pressure. If E_s is the surface emissivity of a surface and E that of a surface coated with lamp black, the emissive power $e = E_s/E$.

For a perfect black body $e = 1$.

Absorbing power of surface

The absorbing power of a surface can also be understood in a similar way to that of the emissive power. The absorbing power of a surface is the rate of absorption of thermal energy by a unit surface compared to that of the surface coated with lamp black, under identical conditions.

If A_s is the heat absorbed by a surface and A that of a surface coated with lamp black, the absorbing power a = A_s/A. (A is the total radiation received by the surface).

Reflecting power of surface

As above, the reflecting power of a surface can also be defined. This is the ratio between the quantity of heat reflected and the quantity of heat received by the surface.

Practical black body

Kirchoff enunciated that any enclosure uniformaly heated, behaves like a black body. Basing upon this, Wein constructed an experimental black body (Fig. 34.2). This consists of a double-walled porcelain chamber at the inside of which is a platinum cylinder. The platinum cylinder is electrically heated and blackened. The inside of the platinum chamber is fitted with a series of concave diaphragms so that the radiated beam is narrowed down and emerges out from the minute opening O.

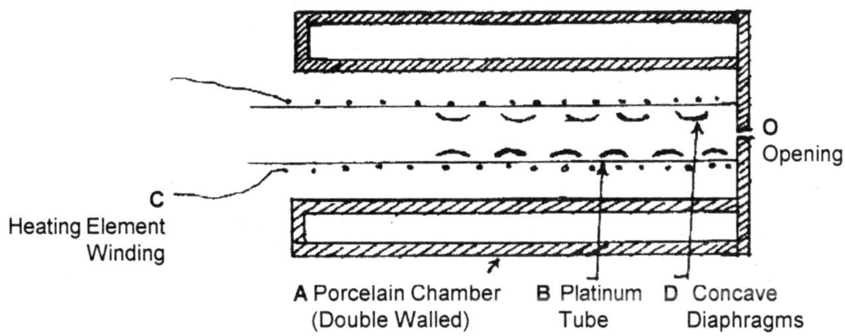

Fig. 34.2 Wein's black body.

Fery's black body

This is a simple device. It consists of a double walled metallic sphere, which is evacuated between the walls. Any radiation entering the sphere is reflected, and so on, by the internal surface of the sphere, so that 97% is absorbed by the sphere. The chance of radiation escaping out through (the small opening O) is very small compared to the total area of the internal surface (Fig 34.3).

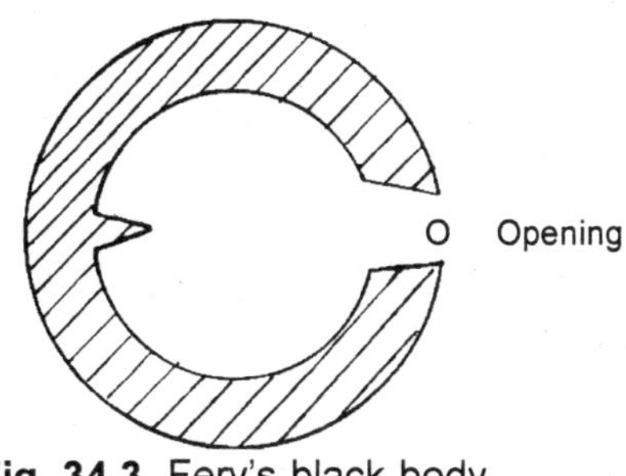

Fig. 34.3 Fery's black body.

When Fery's black body is immersed in a salt or metal bath or any hot source, the whole of it is uniformly heated. By its nature of being a black body, it starts to emit radiation commensurate with its temperature. Any temperature measuring device can be focussed at its opening O, to record the total radiation.

Radiation pyrometers

The radiation pyrometer, to be more correctly called, the total radiation pyrometer, functions basing on the following principles;

1. The radiation emanating from a body which is at a larger distance can be assumed to be parallel (the radiation travels in lines which are parallel to each other).
2. The radiator or the heat source is under black body conditions.

Fery's total radiation pyrometer

The instrument consists of a tube which is fitted with diaphragm to receive the radiation. This radiation is focussed onto the hot junction of pyrometer fitted inside the tube which heats the hot junction. The e.m.f. produced by this effect is measured on a scale, calibrated in degree centigrade. The Diaphragm opening can be adjusted as per the instructions of the manufacturers keeping in view the distance of the hot source from the pyrometer. This enables the measurer to obtain a perfect focusing of the radiation onto the thermocouple hot junction in the instrument. These instruments are very widely employed in the industry and are known as the fixed focuss type. A schematic diagram of Fery's fixed focus pyrometer is shown in Fig. 34.4.

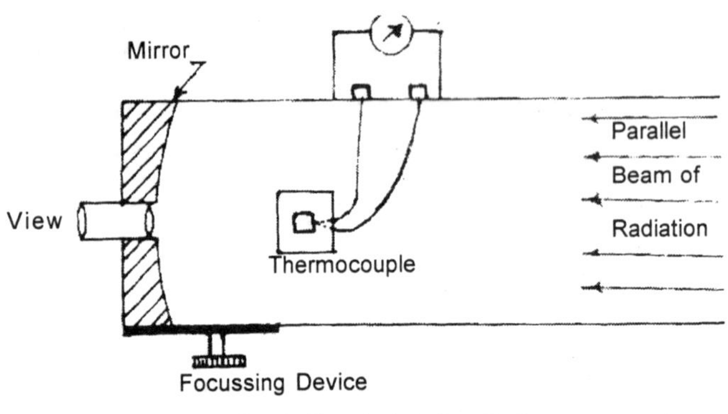

Fig. 34.4 Fery's total radiation pyrometer.

Polarising type radiation pyrometer

The radiation from the hot body enters the pyrometer through a circular opening O_1 and another beam for comparison also enters the instrument through the opening O_2. This latter beam is from a standard electric lamp. The openings O_1 and O_2 are of the same size and are situated symmetrically about the optic axis of the system and in the focal plane of the lens L_1. They are rendered parallel on passing through L_1. These parallel beams pass through the Rochon prism R. They get polarised as shown (Fig. 34.5) each in two perpendicular directions. These pass through the diaphragm S_1 and fall on the combination of an achromatic lens L_2 and biprism P. The lens L_2 focusses the ray on the diaphragm S_2 and the biprism P deviates them in such a way that the images due to O_1 and O_2 are opposed to the each other. Due to the effect of polarisation of the total of eight images (4 each from O_1 and O_2), the observer can see only two (one from O_1 and one from O_2) each at right angle to the other. They appear as two semi circular patches. They can be matched in their intensities by rotating the NICHOL prism N.

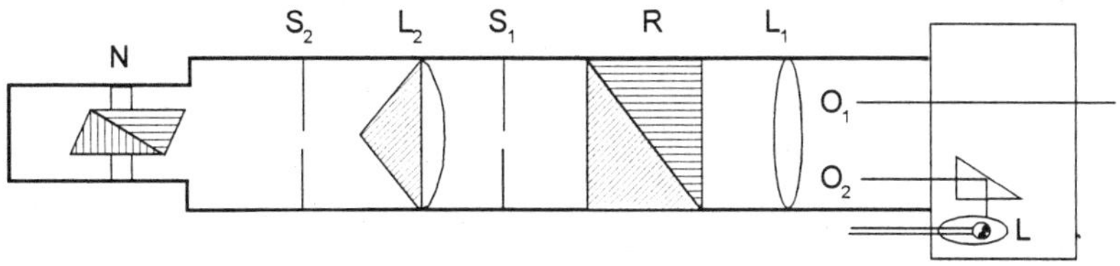

Fig. 34.5 Wanner's pyrometer.

To enable us to know that the instrument has correctly focussed, two small circular discs can be sighted, to form a perfect circle. This is illustrated in the (Fig 34.6).

Fig. 34.6 Focuss.

In addition to the above, the hot source which is under test may not behave as a perfect black body especially when the temperature measurement is performed in the open. Emissivity corrections are to be made by adding the correction value to the observed values of the temperature: depending upon the hot body sighted. Some corrections are given in the Table 34.1.

Table 34.1

Observed Tempera ture °C	Correction in °C (to be added to the observed temperature reading)				
	Platinum	Liquid iron	Liquid copper	Iron oxide	Copper oxide
500	490	--	450	15	100
750	600	360	600	20	125
1000	650	440	--	30	150
1200	--	--	--	40	--

Sources of error

1. The atmosphere, smoke etc., falling between the pyrometer and the hot body through which the radion travels, reflect away a part of the radiation.
2. The lenses fitted in the instrument absorb some radiation.
3. The hot junction of the pyrometer onto which the incident heat radiation is focussed inside the pyrometer may not be 100% black.

Optical pyrometer

This instrument operates basing on the principle of Wein's law; when the hot body emits radiation, its wavelength or colour is also dependent upon its temperature. This can be roughly seen even with the naked eye. When a rod is heated even though it gets hot, its colour does not change until about 400 °C. Above 400 °C, it starts to develop a dull red colour. This occurs around 500 °C. The colour undergoes modification as red, bright red, cherry red, white and so on, as the temperature increases gradually. A colour temperature chart is given Table 34.2, which gives approximate temperature of the body basing on its colour of radiation.

Table 34.2 Colour temperature chart

Colour	Temp. in °c
Faint red	500
Blood or dark red	550 -625
Dark cherry	635
Cherry red	700
Bright cherry red	800
Dark orange	900
Orange	950
Full yellow or lemon	950 -1000
Light yellow	1100
White	1150 &. above

The optical pyrometer is an instrument in which the temperature of a hot body is determined by matching the colour of its radiation to that of an electrical filament whose intensity of brightness can be varied independently. A schematic diagram of the instrument is shown in Fig. 34.7. The instrument is basically a telescope in which the usual cross wires are replaced by an electric filament F of a highly evacuated electric lamp. A variable resistance R is connected in series with the standard 2V battery B which feeds the lamp with the required current, so that by varying R, the intensity of the illumination of the lamp filament L can be varied. The heat radiation, coming from the body whose temperature is under determination, enters the pyrometer as a parallel beam. The objective D forms a real image of the radiation at its focus F incidentally at the place where the lamp filament L is also located. The viewer can see the 1 amp filament in the background of the coloured radiation. If the filament can be distinguished brightly from the background, it means that the filament is brighter. On the other hand, if the filament wires appear as dark coils in the bright background, the intensity of the filament brightness is less than that of the background. Both the filament and its background are matched in their brightness, by adjusting the variable resistance so that the filament sometimes 'disappears' in its background. The current flowing through the filament at that moment is measured. The instruments are made direct reading by calibrating the ammeter in degrees centigrade.

Advantages

1. The pyrometer is portable.
2. The construction of the pyrometer is simple and its readings are accurate.
3. Temperatures of small bodies can also be determined. and
4. The instrument is not affected by any deviations of the hot body from the black-body condition.

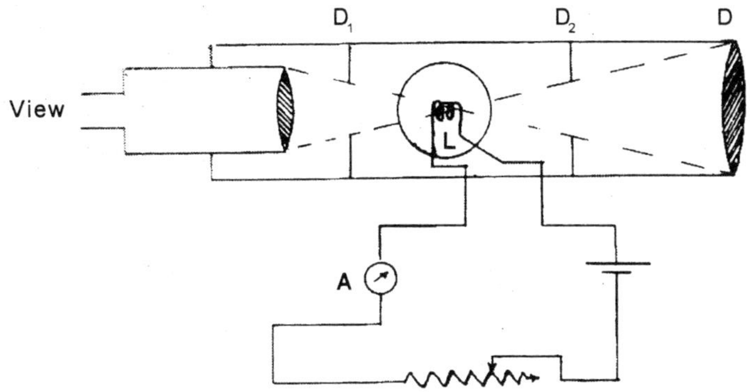

Fig. 34.7 Optical pyrometer.

Comparative study of radiation and optical pyrometers

	Radiation Pyrometer	Optical Pyrometer
1.	The instrument can be used for continuous recording of the temperature	It cannot be used for continuous recording of the temperature
2.	Though some error may creep in, temperatures as low as 350 °C can be measured	Only temperature above 650 °C can be measured
3.	Errors due to the deviation of the hot body from the ideal black body condition, are considerable.	The readings are affected to a smaller extent
4.	Cannot be used to determine the temperatures of small bodies	Can be used to determine the temperature of even very small objects
5.	Temperature at a particular region of the body cannot be measured	Temperature of any portion of a hot body can be measured
6.	Not easily portable	Easily portable in comparision to the radiation pyrometer.

35 Low Temperature Measurement

Low Temperature Measurement

Low temperature development goes hand in hand with its methods of measurement. It will not be out of place of discuss some of the techniques employed in the process.

Many measurement processes are the same that are used for the measurement of ordinary temperatures, but with suitable modification of technique. The thermometer bulb of gas thermometer is enclosed in the required enclosure whose temperature is measured, which in turn is enclosed in a Dewar (thermos flask like chamber). In this technique, the capillary contains gas whose temperature will be different from that being measured and it is a source of error, though not serious.

Vapor Pressure Thermometers

Vapour pressures of some liquids can be employed to measure the temperature. Though the range over which measurable vapour pressures are exerted by mercury (say 50 mm to 100 mm) is quite narrow, the measurement is quite accurate. Table 35.1 gives the useful ranges of temperatures that can be measured using different fluids.

Table 35.1

Fluid	Temp. Range °k
Helium	2. 3 – 4.5
Hydrogen	13.8 – 21.2
Neon	21. 0 – 28.0
Nitrogen	63.0 – 80.0
Oxygen	74.0 – 93.0
Methane	92.0 – 116.0
Carban tetrafluoride	121.0 – 145.0
Ethylene	141.0 – 184.0

The pressure exerted by the saturated vapour over the liquid surface is a definite function of temperature and hence can be used to measure the temperature of the liquid. In fact, in the International Scale of temperature (ITS 90), the vapour pressure of ^{3}He and ^{4}He are used for defining the temperature scale between 0.65 K and 5 K. With a good pressure measuring arrangement, the vapour pressure thermometer is an excellent secondary standard, since the temperature response depends on the physical property of a pure element. The vapour pressure is expressed by semi-empirical formulae with fit coefficients. The vapour pressure equations for many common cryogenic fluids and the constants are given in Table 35.2 and Table 35.3.

Table 35.2 Vapour pressure equations for some cryogenic fluids.

Substance	Equation	Units	Scale
Oxygen	$\ln P = \sum_{n=1}^{8} A_n T^{n-1}$	P atm T K	NBS 55 NBS 48
Nitrogen	$\ln P = A_1/T - A_2 + A_3 T + A_4 (Tc - T)^{1.95} + A_5 T^3 + A_6 T^4 + A_7 T^5 + A_8 T^6 + A_9 \ln T$	P atm T K	NBS 55
Neon	$\ln P = A_1 + A_2/T + A_3 + A_3 T + A_4 T^2$	P torr T K	NBS 55
Hydrogen	(1) $13.803 < T < 21$ K $\ln P = A_1 + A_2 / T + A_3 T$ (2) $20.268 < T < 29$ K $\ln P = A_4 + A_5/(T + A_6) + A_7 T$ (3) $29 < T < 32.976$ K $P = P_0 + A_8(T-29)^3 + A9(T-29)^5 + A_{10}(T-29)^7$	P atm T K P atm T K P atm T K	NBS 55 NBS 55 NBS 55
Helium	$\ln P = \sum^{10} Aj\ T^{(3\ j)}$	P μm Hg T K	$T = T_{58}$ $+ 0.001$ $+ 0.002\ T_{58}$

Table 35.3 Values of the coefficients in the vapour pressure equations.

Coeff	Oxygen	Nitrogen	Neon	Hydrogen	Helium
A_1	-62.5967185	0.8394409444×10^4	7.46116	1.772454	-3.9394635287
A_2	2.47450429	$-0.1990045259 \times 10^4$	-106.090	-4.436888×10	1.4127497598×10^3
A_3	$-4.665973315 \times 10^{-2}$	$-0.7252229165 \times 10^5$	-3.56616×10^{-2}	2.055468×10^{-1}	$-1.6407741565 \times 10^3$
A_4	$5.48202337 \times 10^{-4}$	0.1022850966×10^5	4.11092×10^{-4}	2.000520	1.1974557102×10^4
A_5	$-4.09349868 \times 10^{-6}$	$0.5560632825 \times 10^{-3}$		-5.009708×10	$-5.5283309818 \times 10^4$
A_6	$1.91471914 \times 10^{-8}$	$-0.5944544662 \times 10^{-5}$		1.0044	1.6621956504×10^4
A_7	$-5.13113688\ 0 \times 10^{-12}$	$0.2715433932 \times 10^{-10}$		1.7848495×10^2	-3.25212828×10^4
A_8	$6.02656934 \times 10^{-14}$	$-0.4879535904 \times 10^{-10}$		1.317×10^{-7}	3.9884322750×10^4
A_9		0.509536824×10^3		-5.926×10^{-3}	$-2.7771806992 \times 10^4$
A_{10}				3.913×10^{-4}	8.3395204183×10^4

The different fixed points of common vapour pressure thermometers are given in Table 35.4.

Table 35.4 Fixed points of common vapour pressure thermometer fluids

Fluid	Triple Point (K)	Normal Boiling Point (K)	Critical Point (K)
Oxygen	54.351	90.18	145.576
Nitrogen	63.148	77.347	126.20
Neon	25.54	27.09	44.40
Hydrogen	13.803	20.268	32.976
Helium – 4	2.177	4.224	5.2014

The vapour pressure thermometer is useful for temperature measurement in the range from triple point to the critical point of the liquid. One of the important advantages of vapour pressure thermometer is the extreme sensitivity in the range over which they can be used. The disadvantage is that it is useful in a limited temperature range. These thermometers are most accurate in the range of normal boiling point of the liquid chosen. The constants for the vapour pressure equations are given in Tables 35.2 and 35.4.

The apparatus for vapour pressure determination is quite simple. There are many variations of vapour pressure thermometers, but the one described by Scott is shown in Figure 35.1. The copper bulb having the liquid is connected to an accurate mercury manometer through a thin walled vacuum jacketed stainless steel tube and a coiled copper tubing. It should be obvious that the tubing between the bulb and the manometer should nowhere colder than the bulb since this can cause refluxing and pressure readings will be low.

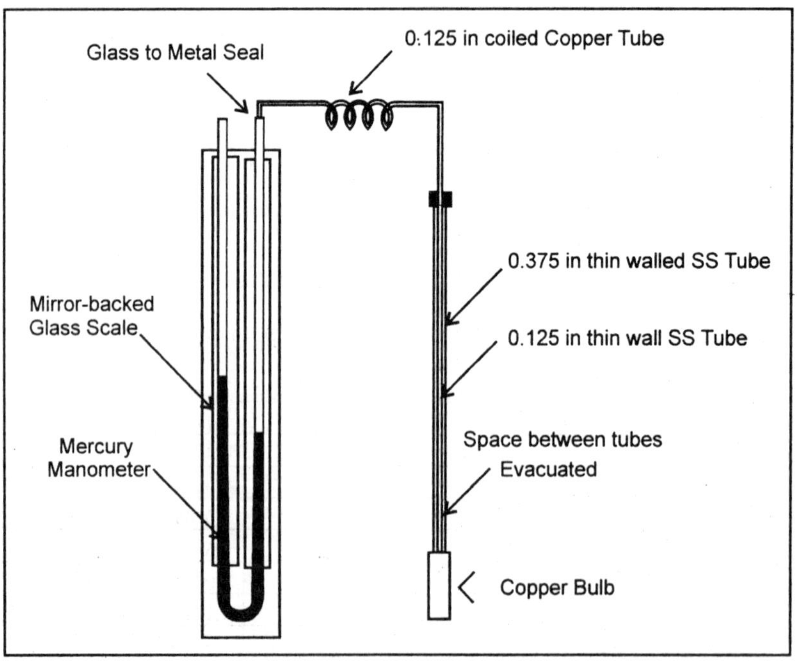

Fig. 35.1 A set-up for vapour pressure thermometry (after Scott).

Also, the gas purity is quite important. With Hydrogen, the ortho/para ratio is an important parameter due to the strong dependence of vapour pressure on this composition. In the case of helium, hydrogen is the possible source of impurity, since all the other impurities will be solidified. As mentioned earlier, the vapour pressure thermometry is quite sensitive. It also has good response and is not affected by magnetic fields and does not need calibration.

Resistance Thermometers

We have studied about making use of the property of the electrical resistance of pure metals for the measurement of temperature. The variation of resistance of pure metals is studied and measures at the temperature under determination by the use of an accurate electrical bridge. Platinum can be used for measurements up to 14 °K, the feezing point of hydrogen. Copper, instead of platinum can be employed for low temperature work upto 20 °K.

One of the most widely used techniques for measurement of temperature is resistance thermometry. In this technique the resistance of a material is measured and the temperature is deduced from the value of resistance. One can have materials with a positive temperature coefficient of resistance. In these materials the resistance increases with increase in temperature. This is usually the behaviour of metals and metallic alloys. The semi-conducting materials, on the other hand, have a negative temperature coefficient of resistance. In these materials, the resistance increases (often by a few orders of magnitude) as the sensor is cooled. In the case of positive temperature coefficient sensors one uses a constant current source to drive a constant current through the material. The voltage across the sensor is measured with a digital voltmeter. As the temperature falls the power dissipated in the sensor will decrease. With negative temperature coefficient of resistance materials, it is usual to use a constant voltage across the resistor and measure the current. The power dissipated is inversely proportional to the resistance. So, with this method of measurement, the power dissipated will decrease in negative temperature coefficient of resistance sensors as the sensor cools.

Self Heating

Why are we worried about the power dissipated in the sensor? This power will have to be conducted away to the cold object, the temperature of which is being measured. If the thermal resistance of the contact between the thermometer and the object is $\rho_{contact}$ and P is the power dissipated in the sensor during measurement, there will be a temperature difference ΔT between the thermometer and the object given by

$$\Delta T = \rho_{contact} P$$

If the object temperature is T, the temperature recorded by the thermometer will be $T+\Delta T$. This is called the self-heating effect. The contact resistance increases as the temperature falls and varies as T^{-3} below 1 K. It is therefore necessary to keep P small enough so that ΔT is a small fraction of T. The lower the temperature the smaller should be the value of P. That is the reason for using a constant current mode of measurement with positive temperature coefficient sensors and a constant voltage mode of measurement with negative temperature coefficient of resistance sensors. The power dissipated depends on the square of the current while the measuring signal will be proportional to the current. It is therefore possible to choose a current value that will give a large enough signal to measure the temperature accurately and that, at the same time, will keep the power dissipated small enough to make the error ΔT smaller than a pre-assigned value.

Two Wire and Four-Wire Measurement

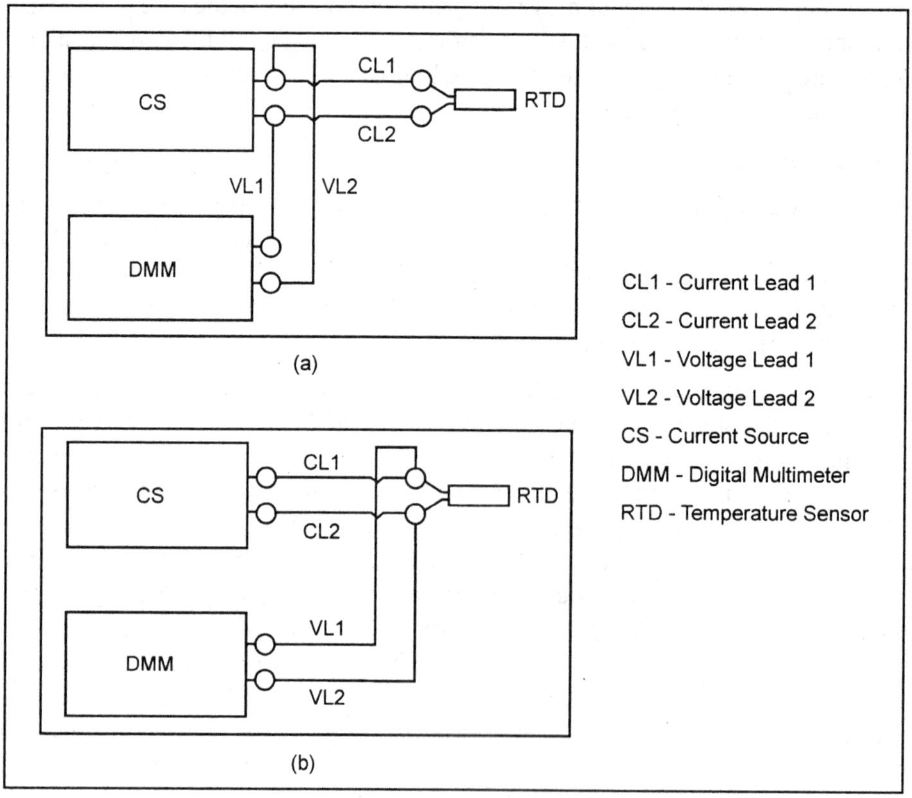

Fig. 35.2 (a) Tow wire measurement, (b) Four wire measurement.

Figure 35.2 (a) and (b) show the connections for a two-wire and a four-wire measurement of the resistance of the sensor. In the two-wire measurement the Digital Voltmeter (DVM) measures the voltage across the resistance thermometer and the current leads. So the resistance measured includes the resistance of the current leads, which will vary with temperature in a manner different from the behaviour of the resistance thermometer. Unless the resistance of the current leads is negligibly small compared to the resistance of the thermometer, the measured temperature will be in error.

In the four-wire measurement the current and voltage leads are connected to the terminals of RT. So the DVM measures only the voltage across RT and the resistance of the current leads does not enter into the measurement.

Platinum Resistance Thermometer

The platinum resistance thermometer is widely used in the temperature range 20 K to room temperature and above. The thermometer is made of a thin, high purity wire of platinum mounted strain-free and encapsulated in a ceramic tube or a glass tube. It comes with two leads. The Platinum resistance thermometer has a diameter of about 2 mm and a length varying between 5 to 20 mm. For four-wire measurement the voltage and current leads will have to be soldered to the two leads of the Platinum resistance thermometer. The resistance thermometer usually has a nominal resistance of 100 ohms at 273.15 K. For such a thermometer the sensitivity is roughly about 0.4 ohm/K from 40 K to 500 K. Below 30 K the sensitivity falls off steeply. The temperature variation of resistance is shown in Fig. 35.3.

If the thermometer is calibrated, its accuracy in measuring temperature is around 5 to 10 mK and reproducibility is also of the same magnitude. The response time of the thermometer depends on (a) its mass and (b) the temperature. The response time is a few seconds at low temperature and increases as the temperature increases. The excitation current is usually 1 mA, which will give a self-heating power of 100 microwatts at 273 K.

The platinum thermometer can be used above 50 K in magnetic fields as the magneto-resistance of platinum causes only an error of a few per cent in the measurement of temperature.

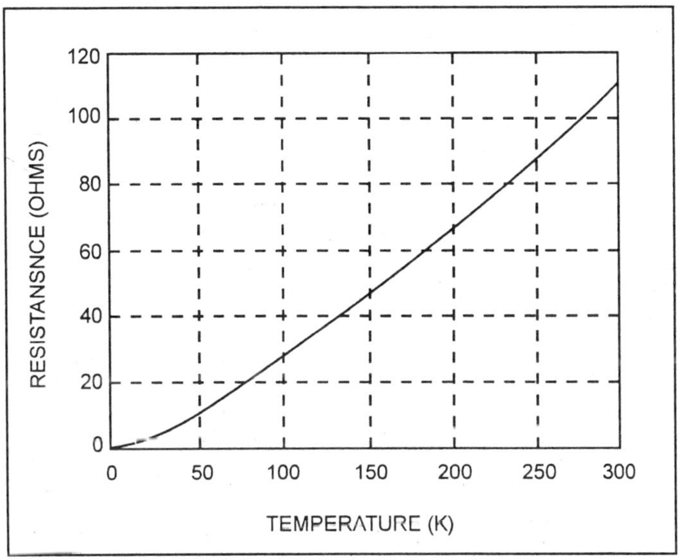

Fig. 35.3 Temperature variation of resistance of a 100 ohm Platinum resistance thermometer.

Doped Germanium Resistance Thermometer

Germanium (Ge) is a semi-conductor and appropriate doping can alter its electrical conductivity. The resistance increases sharply as the temperature is reduced. Various models are available with different suppliers, for use in the temperature range 0.05 K to 30 K. The rapid increase in sensitivity below 4.2 K makes it well suited for sub-milli Kelvin control of temperature. A typical resistance temperature curve for a Germanium Resistance Thermometer is shown in Figure 35.4.

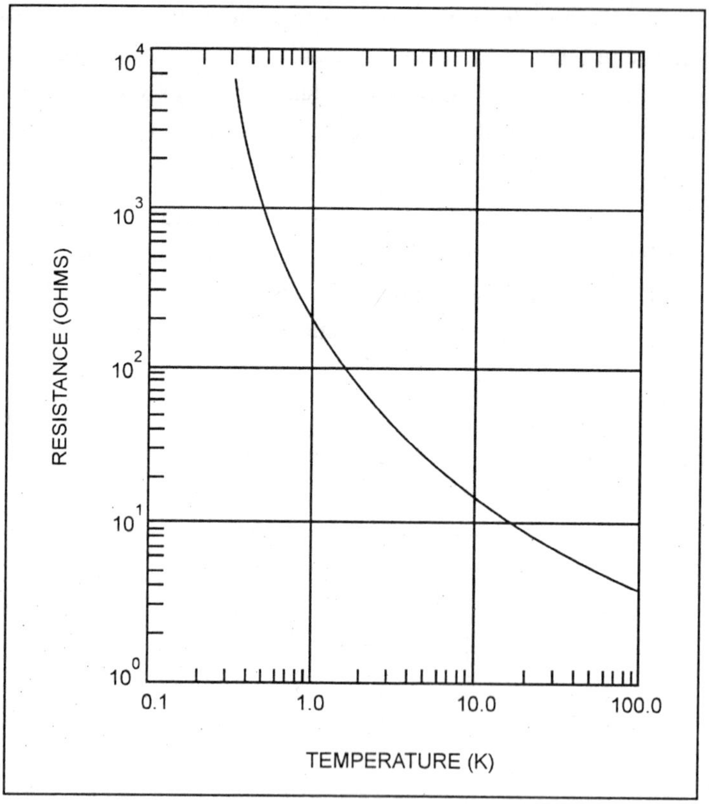

Fig. 35.4 Schematic variation of the Germanium resistance with temperature.

It is seen that above 30 K the sensitivity of the thermometer becomes poor. It has to be used with a constant voltage excitation. At 0.5 K the excitation voltage will be a few tens of microvolts and this is increased to 10 mV at 100 K. This excitation voltage is chosen so that the self-heating power at 4.2 K is about 0.1 μW and at 0.5 K is about 0.1 picó-watt. Typical thermal response time is a few hundred milliseconds at 4.2 K and a few seconds at 77 K.

Thermocouples

Thermocouples have been used often in the past for the measurement of cryogenic temperatures. They are inexpensive. When two dissimilar metals A and B joined together and the two junctions are maintained at different temperatures T_1 and T_2 an electromotive force is generated which can be measured on a digital voltmeter. The typical measurement arrangement is shown in Figure 35.5.

If T_1 is different from T_2 the Digital Voltmeter indicates an emf in millivolts. This is called the thermo-emf. The thermo-emf is a function of temperature difference $(T_1 - T_2)$ provided the junctions of leads A and A' to the terminals of the Digital Voltmeter are at the same temperature. If T_2 is a temperature of a reference bath such as melting ice then one can measure the unknown temperature T_1. Usually the reference bath is dispensed with. The open ends of A and B are connected to the Digital Voltmeter. But at the junction to the Digital Voltmeter a resistance thermometer measures the temperature and produces an appropriate voltage by a bridge circuit.

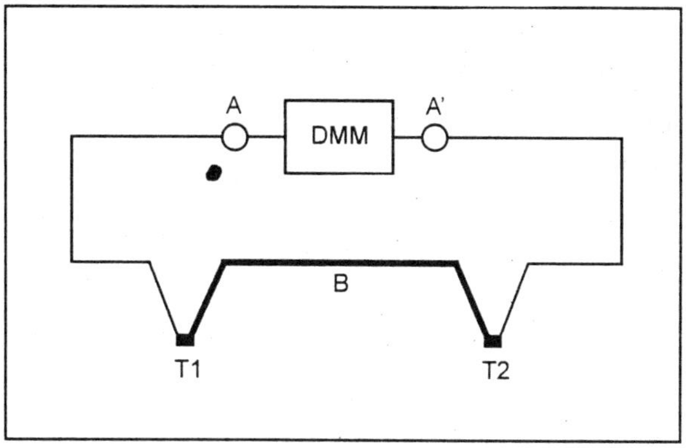

Fig. 35.5 A and B are wires of two dissimilar metals joined together to form two junctions maintained at temperatures T1 and T2. The open ends of A are conncected to the terminals of a Digital Multimeter.

There are three standard thermocouples used in the range of cryogenic temperature. These are type E (chromel-constantan), type K (chromel-alumel) and type T (copper-constantan). In Fig. 35.6 the thermoelectric emf of these standard junctions are plotted in millivolts against temperature T_1, taking the reference temperature to be that of melting ice (273.15 K). The slope of the curve gives the sensitivity.

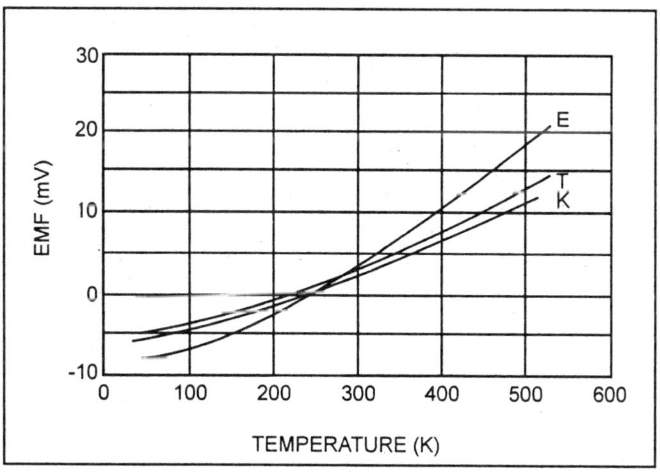

Fig. 35.6 Thermo-emf of standard thermocouples with the reference junction at 273.15 K (Source data: Lab Facility, UK).

We see that the curves flatten out at the low temperature end. The sensitivity falls at low temperature and so these thermocouples are not usable below 30 K. For example the thermoelectric power at 20 K for E, K and T type thermocouples are 8.5, 4.1 and 4.5 μV/K.

Since the wires find themselves in a region where temperature gradient exists, it is essential that the wires A and B must be homogeneous. Otherwise the temperature gradient along the length of the thermocouple wires will produce an emf of its own. The Gold- (0.7 %) Fe-Chromel thermocouple is suited for temperatures below 30 K as its thermo-electric power remains high at 15 μV/K above 10 K. One can measure the temperature to an accuracy of about 1 K. Relative changes in temperature can however be measured more accurately. The advantage of thermocouple thermometry is the low response time of the thermometer.

We have seen in the first chapter how the temperature scales are nomenclatured. The most commonly adopted temperature scale is the centigrade scale, generally called after its inventer, Celcius. In order to measure the temperature falling below the 0 °C, the kelvin scale is adopted. This is also called the absolute scale of temperature, whose zero is fixed at -273.18 °C. Thus the freezing point of water on the kelvin scale becomes 273.18 °K.

Temperature below zero degrees centigrade (Celcius) are known as sub-zero temperatures. Until the II world war, the low temperatures, their development and measurement were mostly of academic interest to the physicists. Subsequently, the low temperatures have been adopted in technological fields and their use is increasing day by day. Low temperature science, specially termed as 'cryogenics' has assumed gigantic proportions of importance.

The use of oxygen, nitrogen, helium etc., has become a matter of routine in many manufacturing processes. In bright annealing, thousands of tons of nitrogen is employed. In steel production, letting apart the L.D. and Kaldo processes which employ pure oxygen only for refining of the liquid pig iron, even the conventional open hearth process and the more recent electric arc furnace processes employ gaseous oxygen lancing to promote oxidation of the impurities. Needless to remind the readers that both these gases are separated from air after liquification of the latter by cooling to sub-zero temperatures and later by fractional distillation of the liquid air (Linde's process) .

Besides oxygen and nitrogen, liquid carbon dioxide is of immence industrial application. (It should be noted that the elemental or compound gases at room temperatures, are liquids at sub-zero temperatures. These changes in state are brought about by changes in pressure; compression liquifies the gases and release of pressure on the liquid gases again gasifies them). It is claimed that in machining, the tool tip can be made to last hundreds of times longer by cooling the tip by carbon dioxide at ice mixture, at – 60 °C. Aluminium and its alloys can be very effectively normalised and stress relieved at – 196 °C (b.p. of liquid N_2). A treatment of a few minutes is enough.

Stainless steel, when rolled at temperatures of the order of -196 °C, is claimed to possess higher yield strength, tensile strength and hardness than in the case when the same steel is worked at room temperatures. In addition, further improvement in the mechanical properties are claimed when the sub-zero rolled (zerolled) steel is reheated to about 450 °C.

A very familiar application of sub-zero temperatures in heat treatment of steels is quenching. The retained austenite is found to be only traces when the steel is quenched to temperatures of the order of – 120° to – 200 °C. At room temperature, the retained austenite may be upto 50% depending upon the alloy content. Thus, in the production of extra strength (special) alloys like super alloys, the 'sub-zero' treatment as it is called, is of vital importance.

With the satellite and rocket technology advancements, the use of special fuels has become imminent. Consequently very effective and fast coolants have become necessary and liquified or even solidified gases are handy for the purpose. Thus, the importance of low temperature development and its application can be cited in many a case.

Low temperature measurement

Low temperature development goes hand in hand with its methods of measurement. It will not be out of place to discuss some of the techniques employed in the process.

Many measurement processes are the same that are used for the measurement of ordinary temperatures, but with suitable modification of technique. The thermometer bulb of gas thermometer is enclosed in the required enclosure whose temperature is measured, which in turn is enclosed in a Dewar (thermos flask like chamber). In this technique, the capillary contains gas whose temperature will be different from that being measured and it is a source of error, though not serious.

Vapour pressure thermometers

Vapour pressures of some liquids can be employed to measure the temperature. Though the range over which measurable vapour pressures are exerted by mercury (say 50mm to 100 mm) is quite narrow, the measurement is quite accurate. The following table gives the useful ranges of temperatures that can measured using different fluids;

The measurement of the vapour pressure can be made by using a mercury manometer using a similar set up as a constant volume gas thermometer as above.

Resistance thermometers

We have studied about making use of the property of the electrical resistance of pure metals for the measurement of temperature. The variation of resistance of pure metals is studied and measured at the temperature under determination by the use of an accurate electrical bridge. Platinum can be used for measurements up to 14 °K. the freezing point of hydrogen. Copper, instead of platinum can be employed for low temperature work upto 20 °K.

A recent development is the indium resistance thermometer. Indium metal can be employed for temperature measurement upto temperatures as low as 3.4 °K. Below this temperature however, indium becomes superconductive (loses all its resistance) and cannot be used further.

Fluid	Temp. Range °k
Helium	2. 3 – 4.5
Hydrogen	13.8 – 21.2
Neon	21–0 – 28.0
Nitrogen	63.0 – 80.0
Oxygen	74.0 – 93.0
Methane	92.0 – 116.0
Carban tetrafluoride	121.0 – 145.0
Ethylene	141.0 – 184.0

Use of semiconductors

Semiconductors like germanium, silicon and carbon are found to be useful in the temperature measurement. The resistance of a semiconductor is found to vary with temperature in an exponential relationship; the temperature coefficient being negative. The increase of resistance of the semiconductors is so pronounced at sub-zero temperatures that its inordinacy presents problems of measurement, thereby limiting their usage for temperature measurement. Another practical difficulty is providing perfect electrical contacts with the semi-conductors.

Nowadays, 'doped' germanium is being tried as a semiconductor material for the determination of temperatures at the sub-zero levels (thermistor material).

Use of thermocouple

Thermocouples are an easy equipment for temperature measurement, though relatively less accurate. The thermo-electric e.m.f. developed in a thermocouple is a function of the temperature difference between the hot and cold junctions. Copper constantin thermocouples were tried for low temperature measurement down to 150 ^{o}K. The cold junction is maintained in the liquid nitrogen (-196 ^{o}C), during the process so as to reduce the voltage to be measured.

Of late, special thermocouples like that of gold-cobalt and silver-gold alloy wires are developed. However, their practical application is still under study.

References

1. Scott, R. B., "Cryogenic Engineering", D. Van Nostrand Co., Inc., Princeton, New Jersy, 1959.
2. Guy K. White, "Experimental Techniques in low temperature Physics", 3rd edition, Oxford University Press, New York, 1979.
3. Scientific Instruments, 440 West Tiffany Drive, West Plam Beach, FL 33407, USA, Product data sheets, website: http://www.scientificinstruments.com/
4. Lab Facility, Unit 3B, Outgang Lane, Dennington, Sheffield, U.K, Product data sheets. Website: http://www.labfacility.co.uk/

36 Temperature Control

Control of temperature in the industrial furnaces has become a very important feature of modern industry. Though metallurgical industry does not demand the temperature control to that precise degree as chemical and plastic industry, yet an idea into the various methods of control of temperature over which the fluctuation is allowable is to be first fixed. The required control mechanism is selected later. For any control mechanism to be successful the following basic requirements are necessary to be fulfilled.

1. The pyrometer, fixed to the furnace should be in good working condition and accurate.
2. The system selected should be clearly understood.

Temperature control mechanisms are of many types. All of these, however, fall into two categories.

1. Simple controllers.
2. Controller-cum-recorders.

It can be easily noted that the recorder type controllers perform both the operations of control and recording of the temperature.

The temperature control systems function on the following lines.

A thermoelectric or electric or electronic device is connected between the furnace and the temperature indicator. The required temperature range being known, its maximum value is fixed and a suitable mechanical device is fitted to operate by means of a lever (to be very simple) which activates the thermoelectric or other device. This device is connected to the furnace input. When the temperature increases beyond the maximum value set, the device is so activated as to feed less calories into the furnace. If, on the other hand, the furnace is of an electrically heated type, the power is cut off.

When the temperature of the furnace decreases as a result of the above, the pointer starts to move downwards on the scale. When it reaches the minimum value of the range of operation, the entire series of operations as described above take place again and then the fuel valve is opened or the electrical switch is put on. Thus the furnace starts to pick, up heat and again the temperature starts to rise. This cycle goes on, thereby maintaining the temperature of the furnace within the maximum and minimum limits. The fluctuation of temperature controlled furnace can be graphically represented as per the curve (Fig. 36.1). It should be clearly understood that, in a temperature control mechanism, there is no control of temperature or maintenance of temperature at a particular value. Only it is fluctuating about a certain mean temperature value shown by T (mean) (dotted line).

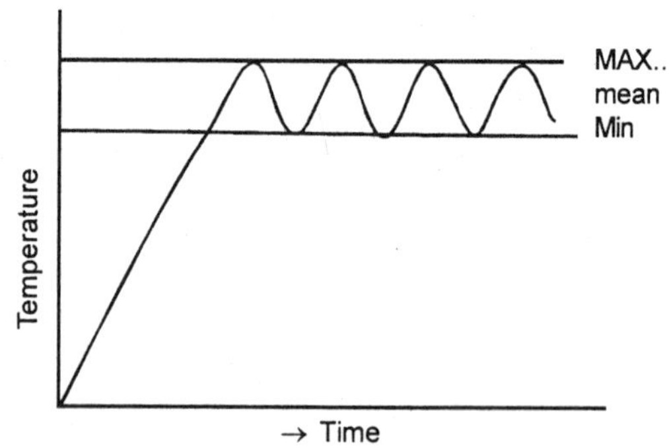

Fig. 36.1

The more sophisticated the control mechanism is, the less will be the minimum range and more the frequency of the curve. Thus, the actual-temperature is more closely followed.

Various temperature controls

Bimetallic strips **(Fig 36.2 and 36.3)**

Two metals which have dissimilar thermal expansion characteristics will be pack-rolled or clad into the form of a strip. This strip, when heated or cooled, expands or contracts respectively, in a non-uniform fashion. If one end is welded firmly at point, the other end will raise if the thermal expansion of the metal forming the top layer is less than that of the bottom one or vice versa. Thus, over a set temperature range, it can be made to make or break an electric contact in the power input circuit. The temperature variations resulting from 'on-off' control mentioned as above, are not permissible in some cases. To reduce the temperature variation, the frequency of switching on and off is to be increased. The temperature of a furnace will oscillate about its own free natural frequency, which is determined by the size and capacity of the heater. If the switching frequency of the heater B is increased, the furnace temperature cannot follow this rhythm and hence will remain constant.

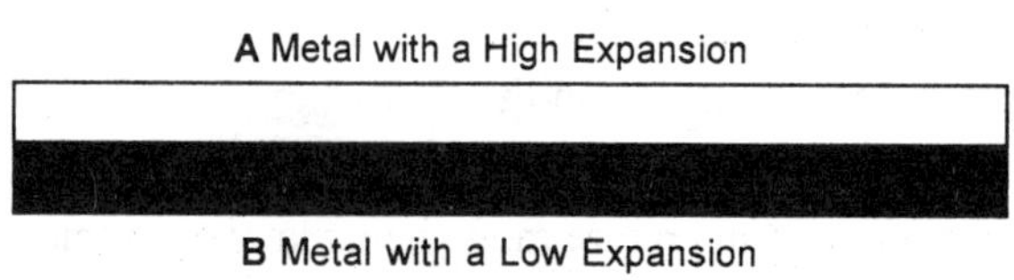

Fig. 36.2 Bimetallic strip.

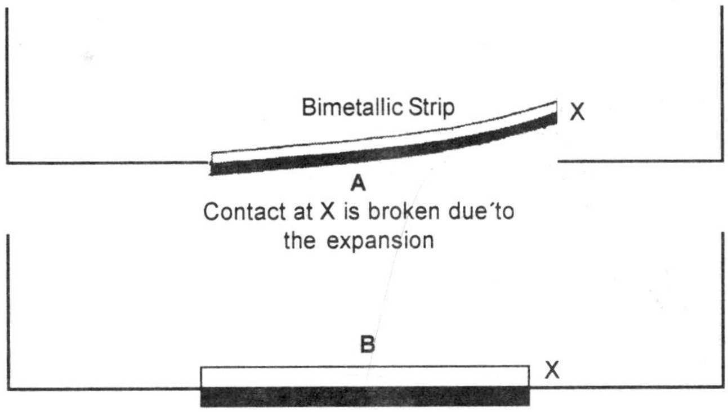

Fig. 36.3 Functioning of a bi metallic strip.

This is accomplished by using an electronic feed-back circuit Fig 36.4. Such a circuit consists of a capacitor which is charged and discharged at a particular frequency. As soon as the furnace is switched on, the output relay of the controller switches on the main heating element. The temperature of the furnace, starts to rise slowly towards the set point. The feed-back circuit is also provided with a contact so that it is also, switched on at the same time. Thus, the capacitor in the feed back starts to get voltage. The capacitor charge voltage is connected to the controller, thus adding to the e.m.f. of the thermocouple. So, the pointer in the indicator is moved further towards the higher values-the set point. After some time, when the capacitor gets fully charged, the temperature indicated is the actual recorded plus the extra due to the feed-back e.m.f (from the capacitor discharge) (Fig 36.5).

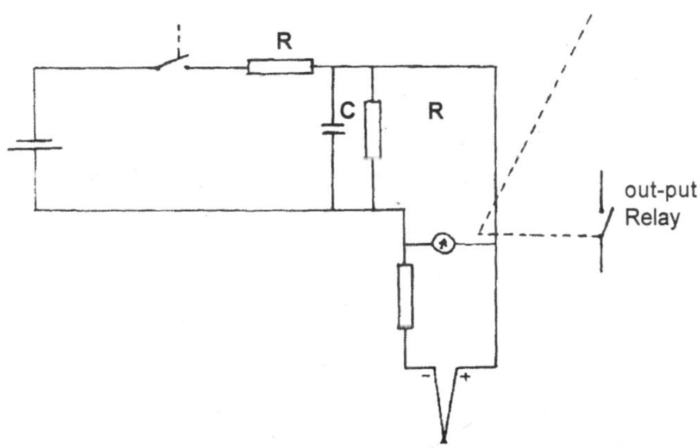

Fig. 36.4 Feedback circuit.

When the set temperature is reached and the heater is switched off by the controller mechanism, the actual temperature of the furnace has not yet reached the set point. But, there is sufficient energy stored in the heater element and the actual temperature continues to rise and tends to push up the pointer on the scale.

When the controller switches the heater off, the feed back capacitor is also switched off. In the absence of input voltage, the capacitor discharges into a parallel resistor. This tends to move the

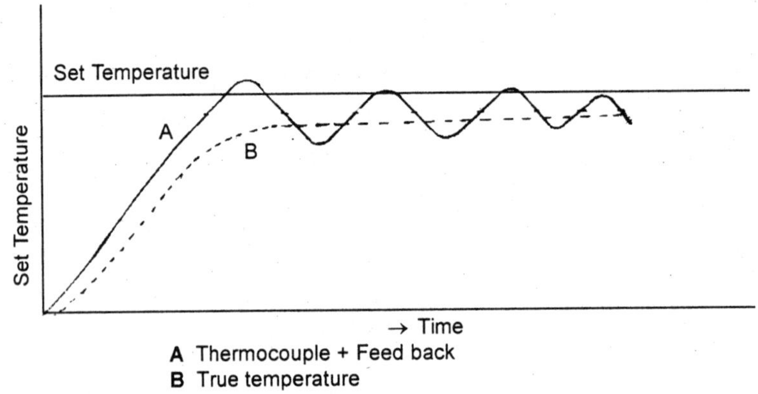

Fig. 36.5

pointer in the indicator downwards. The voltage drop due to the discharge of the feedback capacitor is faster than the rise of the thermo e.m.f. Consequently, the point moves downwards and below the set point, thereby switching on the heating element and control-relay circuits. The whole cycle commences again.

After a certain time, it can be seen that the final actual temperature will settle at a steady value. Of course, this will be slightly lower than the actually 'set' temperature. This is not much of a disadvantage. Once the steady running conditions of the furnace are known, this off-set can be adjusted in the set temperature itself. i.e., if a temperature of actual operation of 900 °C is required and the off set is 15, the set temperature itself can be fixed at 915 °C and not 900 °C (Fig. 36.6).

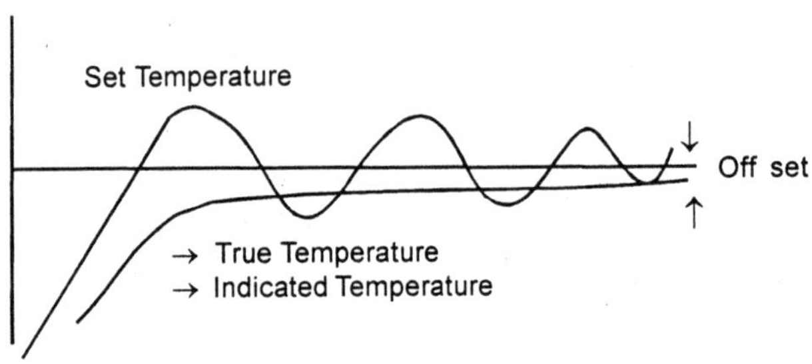

Fig. 36.6

Gas and oil fired furnaces

Gas and oil fired furnaces have the heating mechanism in the form of a burner or burners, depending upon the size of the furnace. The supply of gas and the air, either individually or mixed together and additional air inlet (secondary air) are controlled to attain the maximum thermal efficiency. There will be valves located in the gas and air intakes to regulate their supply. The temperature controls operate these valves closing them either fully or partly.

The principles of control are the same as above. Just as the electric power is put on and off by the bimetal thermostat, the air supply is restricted and released by actuation from the thermostat.

When the temperature control is necessitated to be more rigid, however, a servo-motor is made to operate the control valve. The temperature oscillations will be diminished to such a low rate that a steady temperature prevails in the furnace.

Sometimes, the control is affected by the method 'ratio control'. In this, the air or gas ratio is changed, in order to increase or decrease the temperature.

An important point to be borne in mind here is that the item controlled in gas fired furnaces is the air and in oil fired furnaces, the oil.

Nowadays, electronics has advanced to a remarkable extent. Temperature control has become more and more sophisticated and specialised systems to suit particular processes are developed and installed by reputed firms as comprehensive units. It is advisable to contact the leading firms when a new control system is to be installed, instead of piece-meal development. This saves time and labour and at the same time, gives reliable service for a long time.

TEMPERATURE CONVERSION TABLE

Formulae : $t^{o}F = 5/9\ (t - 32)C$

$t^{o}C = (1.8t + 32)^{o}F$

The column in **bold** headed 'Reading in °F or °C to be converted' refers to the temperature either in degrees Fahrenheit or Centigrade which it is desired to convert into the other scale. To convert from Fahrenheit degrees to Centigrade degrees the equivalent temperature will be found in the column on the right headed '°C'. To convert from degrees Centigrade to degrees Fahrenheit the equivalent temperature will be found in the column on the left headed '°F'. This arrangement is very similar to that of SAUVEUR and BOGLSTON, copyrighted 1920 and is published with their permission.

(The Table starts on next page)

°F	*Reading in °F or °C to be converted*	°C	°F	*Reading in °F or °C to be converted*	°C	°F	*Reading in °F or °C to be converted*	°C
–	**-458**	-272.22	–	**-338**	-205.56	-360.4	**-218**	-138.39
–	**-456**	-271.11	–	**-336**	-204.44	-356.8	**-216**	-137.78
–	**-454**	-270.00	–	**-334**	-203.33	-353.2	**-214**	-136.67
–	**-452**	-268.89	–	**-332**	-202.22	-349.6	**-212**	-135.56
–	**-450**	-267.78	–	**-330**	-201.11	-346.0	**-210**	-134.44
–	**-448**	-266.67	–	**-328**	-200.00	-342.4	**-208**	-133.33
–	**-446**	-265.56	–	**-326**	-198.89	-338.8	**-206**	-132.22
–	**-444**	-264.44	–	**-324**	-197.78	-335.2	**-204**	-131.11
–	**-442**	-263.33	–	**-322**	-196.67	-331.6	**-202**	-130.00
–	**-440**	-262.22	–	**-320**	-195.56	-328.0	**-200**	-128.89
–	**-438**	-261.11	–	**-318**	-194.44	-324.4	**-198**	-127.78
–	**-436**	-260.00	–	**-316**	-193.33	-320.8	**-196**	-126.67
–	**-434**	-258.89	–	**-314**	-192.22	-317.2	**-194**	-125.56
–	**-432**	-257.78	–	**-312**	-191.11	-313.6	**-192**	-124.44
–	**-430**	-256.67	–	**-310**	-190.00	-310.0	**-190**	-123.33
–	**-428**	-255.56	–	**-308**	-188.89	-306.4	**-188**	-122.22
–	**-426**	-254.44	–	**-306**	-187.78	-302.8	**-186**	-121.11
–	**-424**	-253.33	–	**-304**	-186.67	-299.2	**-184**	-120.00
–	**-422**	-252.22	–	**-302**	-185.56	-295.6	**-182**	-118.89
–	**-420**	-251.11	–	**-300**	-184.44	-292.0	**-180**	-117.78
–	**-418**	-250.00	–	**-298**	-183.33	-288.4	**-178**	-116.67
–	**-416**	-248.89	–	**-296**	-182.22	-284.8	**-176**	-115.56
–	**-414**	-247.78	–	**-294**	-181.11	-281.2	**-174**	-114.44
–	**-412**	-246.67	–	**-292**	-180.00	-277.6	**-172**	-113.33
–	**-410**	-245.56	–	**-290**	-178.89	-274.0	**-170**	-112.22
–	**-408**	-244.44	–	**-288**	-177.78	-270.4	**-168**	-111.11
–	**-406**	-243.33	–	**-286**	-176.67	-266.8	**-166**	-110.00
–	**-404**	-242.22	–	**-284**	-175.56	-263.2	**-164**	-108.89
–	**-402**	-241.11	–	**-282**	-174.44	-259.6	**-162**	-107.78
–	**-400**	-240.00	–	**-280**	-173.33	-256.0	**-160**	-106.67
–	**-398**	-238.89	–	**-278**	-172.22	-252.4	**-158**	-105.56
–	**-396**	-237.78	–	**-276**	-171.11	-248.8	**-156**	-104.44
–	**-394**	-236.67	–	**-274**	-170.00	-245.2	**-154**	-103.33
–	**-392**	-235.56	-457.6	**-272**	-168.89	-241.6	**-152**	-102.22
–	-390	-234.44	-454.0	**-270**	-167.78	-238.0	**-150**	-101.11
–	**-388**	-233.33	-450.4	**-268**	-166.67	-234.4	**-148**	-100.00
–	**-386**	-232.22	-446.8	**-266**	-165.56	-230.8	**-146**	- 98.89
–	**-384**	-231.11	-443.2	**-264**	-164.44	-227.2	**-144**	- 97.78
–	**-382**	-230.00	-439.6	**-262**	-163.33	-223.6	**-142**	- 96.67
–	**-380**	-228.89	-436.0	**-260**	-162.22	-220.0	**-140**	- 95.56
–	**-378**	-227.78	-432.4	**-258**	-161.11	-216.4	**-138**	- 94.44
–	**-376**	-226.67`	-428.8	**-256**	-160.00	-21.28	**-136**	- 93.33
–	**-374**	-225.56	-425.2	**-254**	-158.89	-209.2	**-134**	- 92.22
–	**-372**	-224.44	-421.6	**-252**	-157.78	-205.6	**-132**	- 91.11
–	**-370**	-223.33	-418.0	**-250**	-156.67	-202.0	**-130**	-90.00
–	**-368**	-222.22	-414.4	**-248**	-155.56	-195.4	**-128**	-88.89
–	**-366**	-221.11	-410.8	**-246**	-154.44	-194.8	**-126**	-87.78
–	**-364**	-220.00	-407.2	**-244**	-153.33	-193.2	**-124**	- 86.67
–	**-362**	-218.89	-403.6	**-242**	-152.22	-182.6	**-122**	- 85.56
–	**-360**	-217.78	-400.0	**-240**	-151.11	-181.0	**-120**	- 84.44
–	-358	-216.67	-396.5	-238	150.00	-150.4	-118	-83.33
–	-356	-215.56	-392.5	-236	-148.89	-176.8	-116	-82.22
–	-354	-214.44	-389.5	-234	-147.78	-173.2	-114	-86.11
–	-352	-213.33	-385.5	-232	-146.67	-169.6	-112	-80.00
–	-350	-212.22	-382.5	-230	-145.56	-160.0	-110	-78.89
–	**-348**	-211.11	-378.4	**-228**	-144.44	-162.4	**-108**	- 77.78
–	**-346**	-210.00	-377.8	**-226**	-143.33	-158.8	**-106**	-76.67
–	**-344**	-208.89	-376.2	**-224**	-142.22	-155.2	**-104**	-75.56
–	**-342**	-207.78	-365.6	**-222**	-141.11	-151.6	**-102**	- 74.44
–	**-340**	-206.67	-364.0	**-220**	-140.00	-148.0	**-100**	- 73.33

Temperature Conversion Table *Contd.....*

°F	Reading in °F or °C to be converted	°C	°F	Reading in °F or °C to be converted	°C	°F	Reading in °F or °C to be converted	°C
−144.4	**−98**	−72.22	+71.6	**+22**	−5.56	+206.6	**+97**	+36.11
−140.8	**−96**	−71.11	+73.4	**+23**	−5.00	+208.4	**+98**	+36.67
−137.2	**−94**	−70.00	+75.2	**+24**	−4.44	+210.2	**+99**	+37.22
−133.6	**−92**	−68.89	+77.0	**+25**	−3.89	+212.0	**+100**	+37.78
−130.0	**−90**	−67.78	+78.8	**+26**	−3.33	+213.8	**+101**	+38.33
−126.4	**−88**	−66.67	+80.6	**+27**	−2.78	+215.6	**+102**	+38.89
−122.8	**−86**	−65.56	+82.4	**+28**	−2.22	+217.4	**+103**	+39.44
−119.2	**−84**	−64.44	+84.2	**+29**	−1.67	+219.2	**+104**	+40.00
−115.6	**−82**	−63.33	+86.0	**+30**	−1.11	+221.0	**+105**	+40.56
−112.0	−80	−62.22	+87.8	**+31**	−0.56	+222.8	**+106**	+41.11
−108.4	**−78**	−61.11	+89.6	**+32**	−0.00	+224.6	**+107**	+41.67
−104.8	**−76**	−60.00	+91.4	**+33**	−0.56	+226.4	**+108**	+42.22
−101.2	**−74**	−58.89	+93.2	**+34**	−1.11	+228.2	**+109**	+42.78
−97.6	**−72**	−57.78	+95.0	**+35**	−1.67	+230.0	**+110**	+43.33
−94.0	**−70**	− 56.67	+96.8	**+36**	+2.22	+231.8	**+111**	+43.89
−90.4	**−68**	−55.56	+ 98.6	**+37**	+2.78	+233.6	**+112**	+44.44
−86.8	**−66**	−54.44	+100.4	**+38**	+3.33	+235.4	**+113**	+45.00
−83.2	**−64**	−53.33	+102.2	**+39**	+3.89	+237.2	**+114**	+45.56
−79.6	**−62**	−52.22	+104.0	**+40**	+4.44	+239.0	**+115**	+46.11
−76.0	**−60**	−51.11	+105.8	**+41**	+5.00	+240.8	**+116**	+46.67
−72.4	**−58**	−50.00	+107.6	**+42**	+5.56	+242.6	**+117**	+47.22
−68.8	**−56**	−48.89	+109.4	**+43**	+6.11	+244.4	**+118**	+47.78
−65.2	**−54**	−47.78	+111.2	**+44**	+6.67	+246.2	**+119**	+48.33
−61.6	**−52**	−46.67	+113.0	**+45**	+7.22	+248.0	**+120**	+48.89
−58.0	**−50**	−45.56	+114.8	**+46**	+7.78	+249.8	**+121**	+49.44
−54.4	**−48**	−44.44	+116.6	**+47**	+8.33	+251.6	**+122**	+50.00
−50.8	**−46**	−43.33	+118.4	**+48**	+8.89	+253.4	**+123**	+50.66
−47.2	**−44**	−42.22	+120.2	**+49**	+9.44	+255.2	**+124**	+51.11
−43.6	**−42**	−41.11	+122.0	**+50**	+10.00	+257.0	**+125**	+51.67
−40.0	**−40**	−40.00	+123.8	**+51**	+10.56	+258.8	**+126**	+52.22
−36.4	**−38**	−38.89	+125.6	**+52**	+11.11	+260.6	**+127**	+52.78
−32.8	**−36**	−37.78	+127.4	**+53**	+11.67	+262.4	**+128**	+53.33
−29.2	**−34**	−36.67	+129.2	**+54**	+12.22	+264.2	**+129**	+53.89
−25.6	**−32**	−35.56	+131.0	**+55**	+12.78	+266.0	**+130**	+54.44
−22.0	**−30**	−34.44	+132.8	**+56**	+13.33	+267.8	**+131**	+55.00
−18.4	**−28**	−33.33	+134.6	**+57**	+13.89	+269.6	**+132**	+55.56
−14.8	**−26**	−32.22	+136.4	**+58**	+14.44	+271.4	**+133**	+56.11
−11.2	**−24**	−31.11	+138.2	**+59**	+15.00	+273.2	**+134**	+56.67
−7.6	**−22**	−30.00	+140.0	**+60**	+15.56	+275.0	**+135**	+57.22
−4.0	**−20**	−28.89	+141.8	**+61**	+16.11	+276.8	**+136**	+57.78
−0.4	**−18**	−27.78	+143.6	**+62**	+16.27	+278.6	**+137**	+58.33
+3.2	**−16**	−26.67	+145.4	**+63**	+17.22	+280.4	**+138**	+58.89
+6.8	**−14**	−25.56	+147.2	**+64**	+17.78	+282.2	**+139**	+59.44
+10.4	**−12**	−24.44	+149.0	**+65**	+18.33	+284.0	**+140**	+60.00
+14.0	**−10**	−23.33	+150.8	**+66**	+18.89	+285.8	**+141**	+60.56
+17.6	**−8**	−22.22	+152.6	**+67**	+19.44	+287.6	**+142**	+61.11
+19.4	**−7**	−21.67	+154.4	**+68**	+20.00	+289.4	**+143**	+61.67
+21.2	**−6**	−21.11	+156.2	**+69**	+21.56	+291.2	**+144**	+62.22
+23.0	**−5**	−20.56	+158.0	**+70**	+21.11	+293.0	**+145**	+62.78
+24.8	**−4**	−20.00	+159.8	**+71**	+21.67	+294.8	**+146**	+63.33
+26.6	**−3**	−19.44	+161.6	**+72**	+22.22	+296.6	**+147**	+63.89
+28.4	**−2**	−18.89	+163.4	**+73**	+22.78	+298.4	**+148**	+64.44
+30.2	**−1**	−18.33	+165.2	**+74**	+23.33	+300.2	**+149**	+65.00
+32.0	**+0**	−17.78	+167.0	**+75**	+23.80	+302.0	**+150**	+65.56
+33.8	**+1**	−17.22	+168.8	**+76**	+24.44	+303.8	**+151**	+66.11
+35.6	**+2**	−16.67	+170.6	**+77**	+25.00	+305.6	**+152**	+66.67
+37.4	**+3**	−16.11	+172.4	**+78**	+25.56	+307.4	**+153**	+67.22
+39.2	**+4**	−15.56	+174.2	**+79**	+26.11	+309.2	**+154**	+67.78
+41.0	**+5**	−15.00	+176.0	**+80**	+26.67	+311.0	**+155**	+68.33
+42.8	**+6**	−14.44	+177.8	**+81**	+27.22	+312.8	**+156**	+68.89
+44.6	**+7**	−13.89	+179.6	**+82**	+27.78	+314.6	**+157**	+69.44
+46.4	**+8**	−13.33	+181.4	**+83**	+28.33	+316.4	**+158**	+70.00
+48.2	**+9**	−12.73	+183.2	**+84**	+28.89	+318.2	**+159**	+70.56
+50.0	**+10**	−12.22	+185.0	**+85**	+29.44	+320.0	**+160**	+71.11
+51.8	**+11**	−11.67	+186.8	**+86**	+30.00	+321.8	**+161**	+71.67
+53.6	**+12**	−11.11	+188.6	**+87**	+30.56	+323.6	**+162**	+72.22
+55.4	**+13**	−10.33	+190.4	**+88**	+31.11	+325.4	**+163**	+72.78
+57.2	**+14**	−10.00	+192.2	**+89**	+31.67	+327.2	**+164**	+73.33
+59.0	**+15**	− 9.44	+194.0	**+90**	+32.22	+329.0	**+165**	+73.89
+60.8	**+16**	− 8.89	+195.8	**+91**	+32.78	+330.8	**+166**	+74.44
+62.6	**+17**	− 8.33	+197.6	**+92**	+33.33	+332.6	**+167**	+75.00
+64.4	**+18**	− 7.78	+199.4	**+93**	+33.09	+334.4	**+168**	+75.56
+66.2	**+19**	− 7.72	+201.2	**+94**	+34.44	+336.2	**+169**	+70.11
+68.0	**+20**	− 6.67	+203.0	**+95**	+35.00	+338.0	**+170**	+76.67
+69.8	**+21**	− 6.11	+204.8	**+96**	+35.56	+339.8	**+171**	+77.22

Temperature Conversion Table *Contd.....*

°F	*Reading in °F or °C to be converted*	°C	°F	*Reading in °F or °C to be converted*	°C	°F	*Reading in °F or °C to be converted*	°C
+341.6	**+172**	+77.88	+525.2	**+274**	+134.44	+795.2	**+424**	+217.78
+343.4	**+173**	+78.33	+528.8	**+276**	+135.56	+798.8	**+426**	+218.89
+345.2	**+174**	+78.89	+532.4	**+278**	+136.67	+802.4	**+428**	+220.00
+347.0	**+175**	+79.44	+536.0	**+280**	+137.78	+806.0	**+430**	+221.11
+348.8	**+176**	+80.00	+539.6	**+282**	+138.89	+809.6	**+432**	+222.22
+350.6	**+177**	+80.56	+543.2	**+284**	+140.00	+813.2	**+434**	+223.33
+352.4	**+178**	+81.11	+546.8	**+286**	+141.11	+816.8	**+436**	+224.44
+354.2	**+179**	+81.67	+550.4	**+288**	+142.22	+820.4	**+438**	+225.56
+356.0	**+180**	+82.22	+554.0	**+290**	+143.33	+824.0	**+440**	+226.67
+357.8	**+181**	+82.78	+557.6	**+292**	+144.44	+827.6	**+442**	+227.78
+359.6	**+182**	+83.33	+561.2	**+294**	+145.56	+831.2	**+444**	+228.89
+361.4	**+183**	+83.89	+564.8	**+296**	+146.67	+834.8	**+446**	+230.00
+363.2	**+184**	+84.44	+568.4	**+298**	+147.78	+838.4	**+448**	+231.11
+365.0	**+185**	+85.00	+572.0	**+300**	+148.89	+842.0	**+450**	+232.22
+366.8	**+186**	+85.56	+575.6	**+302**	+150.00	+845.6	**+452**	+233.33
+368.6	**+187**	+86.11	+579.2	**+304**	+151.11	+849.2	**+454**	+234.44
+370.4	**+188**	+86.67	+582.8	**+306**	+152.22	+852.8	**+456**	+235.56
+372.2	**+189**	+87.22	+586.4	**+308**	+153.33	+856.4	**+458**	+236.67
+374.0	**+190**	+87.78	+590.0	**+310**	+154.44	+860.0	**+460**	+237.78
+375.8	**+191**	+88.33	+593.6	**+312**	+155.56	+863.6	**+462**	+238.89
+377.6	**+192**	+88.89	+597.2	**+314**	+156.67	+867.2	**+464**	+240.00
+379.4	**+193**	+89.44	+600.8	**+316**	+157.78	+870.8	**+466**	+241.11
+381.2	**+194**	+90.00	+604.4	**+318**	+158.89	+874.4	**+468**	+242.22
+383.0	**+195**	+90.56	+608.0	**+320**	+160.00	+878.0	**+470**	+243.33
+384.8	**+196**	+91.11	+611.6	**+322**	+161.11	+881.6	**+472**	+244.44
+386.6	**+197**	+91.67	+615.2	**+324**	+162.22	+885.2	**+474**	+245.56
+388.4	**+198**	+92.22	+618.8	**+326**	+163.33	+88.88	**+476**	+246.67
+390.2	**+199**	+92.78	+622.4	**+328**	+164.44	+892.4	**+478**	+247.78
+392.0	**+200**	+93.33	+626.0	**+330**	+165.56	+896.0	**+480**	+248.89
+393.8	**+201**	+93.89	+629.6	**+332**	+166.67	+899.6	**+482**	+250.00
+395.6	**+202**	+94.44	+633.2	**+334**	+167.78	+903.2	**+484**	+251.11
+397.4	**+203**	+95.00	+636.8	**+336**	+168.89	+906.8	**+486**	+252.22
+399.2	+204	+95.56	+640.4	**+338**	+170.00	+910.4	**+488**	+253.33
+401.0	+205	+96.11	+644.0	**+340**	+171.11	+914.0	**+490**	+254.44
+402.8	**+206**	+96.67	+647.6	**+342**	+172.22	+917.6	**+492**	+255.56
+404.6	**+207**	+97.22	+651.2	**+344**	+173.33	+921.2	**+494**	+256.67
+406.4	**+208**	+97.78	+654.8	**+346**	+174.44	+924.8	**+496**	+257.78
+408.2	**+209**	+98.33	+658.4	**+348**	+175.56	+928.4	**+498**	+258.89
+410.0	**+210**	+98.89	+662.0	**+350**	+176.67	+932.0	**+500**	+260.00
+411.8	**+211**	+99.44	+665.6	**+352**	+177.78	+935.6	**+502**	+261.11
+413.6	**+212**	+100.00	+669.2	**+354**	+178.89	+939.2	**+504**	+262.22
+415.4	**+213**	+100.56	+672.8	**+356**	+180.00	+942.8	**+506**	+263.33
+417.2	**+214**	+101.11	+676.4	**+358**	+181.11	+946.4	**+508**	+264.44
+419.0	**+215**	+101.67	+680.0	**+360**	+182.22	+950.0	**+510**	+265.56
+420.8	**+216**	+102.22	+683.6	**+362**	+183.33	+953.6	**+512**	+266.67
+422.6	**+217**	+102.78	+687.2	**+364**	+184.44	+957.2	**+514**	+267.78
+424.4	**+218**	+103.33	+690.8	**+366**	+185.56	+960.8	**+516**	+268.89
+426.2	**+219**	+103.89	+694.4	**+368**	+186.67	+964.4	**+518**	+270.00
+428.0	**+220**	+104.44	+698.0	**+370**	+187.78	+968.0	**+520**	+271.11
+431.6	**+222**	+105.56	+701.6	**+372**	+188.89	+971.6	**+522**	+272.22
+435.2	**+224**	+106.67	+705.2	**+374**	+190.00	+975.2	**+524**	+273.33
+438.8	**+226**	+107.78	+708.8	**+376**	+191.11	+978.8	**+526**	+274.44
+442.4	**+228**	+108.89	+712.4	**+378**	+192.22	+982.4	**+528**	+275.66
+446.0	**+230**	+110.00	+716.0	**+380**	+193.33	+986.0	**+530**	+276.67
+449.6	+232	+111.11	+719.6	+382	+194.44	+989.6	**+532**	+277.78
+453.2	**+234**	+112.22	+723.2	**+384**	+195.56	+993.2	**+534**	+278.89
+456.8	**+236**	+113.33	+726.8	**+386**	+196.67	+996.8	**+536**	+280.00
+460.4	**+238**	+114.44	+730.4	**+388**	+197.78	+1000.4	**+538**	+281.11
+464.0	**+240**	+115.56	+734.0	**+390**	+198.89	+1004.0	**+540**	+282.22
+467.6	**+242**	+116.67	+737.6	**+392**	+200.00	+1007.6	**+542**	+283.33
+471.2	**+244**	+117.78	+741.2	**+394**	+201.11	+1011.2	**+544**	+284.44
+474.8	**+246**	+118.89	+744.8	**+396**	+202.22	+1014.8	**+546**	+285.66
+478.4	**+248**	+120.00	+748.4	**+398**	+203.33	+1018.4	**+548**	+286.67
+482.0	**+250**	+121.11	+752.0	**+400**	+204.44	+1022.0	**+550**	+287.78
+485.6	**+252**	+122.22	+755.6	**+402**	+205.56	+1025.6	**+552**	+288.89
+489.2	**+254**	+123.33	+759.2	**+404**	+206.67	+1029.2	**+554**	+290.0
+492.8	**+256**	+124.44	+762.8	**+406**	+207.78	+1032.8	**+556**	+291.11
+496.4	**+258**	+125.66	+766.4	**+408**	+208.89	+1036.4	**+558**	+292.22
+500.0	**+260**	+126.67	+770.0	**+410**	+210.00	+1040.0	**+560**	+293.33
+503.6	**+262**	+127.78	+773.6	**+412**	+211.11	+1043.6	**+562**	+294.44
+507.2	**+264**	+128.89	+777.2	**+414**	+212.22	+1047.2	**+564**	+295.56
+510.8	**+266**	+130.00	+780.8	**+416**	+213.33	+1050.8	**+566**	+296.67
+514.4	**+268**	+131.11	+78.44	**+418**	+214.44	+1054.4	**+568**	+297.78
+518.0	**+270**	+132.22	+788.0	**+420**	+215.56	+1058.0	**+570**	+298.89
+521.6	**+272**	+133.33	+791.6	**+422**	+216.67	+1061.6	**+572**	+300.00

Temperature Conversion Table *Contd...*

°F	Reading in °F or °C to be converted	°C	°F	Reading in °F or °C to be converted	°C	°F	Reading in °F or °C to be converted	°C
+1065.2	**+574**	+301.11	+1335.2	**+724**	+384.44	+1605.2	**+874**	+467.78
+1068.8	**+576**	+302.22	+1338.8	**+726**	+385.56	+1608.8	**+876**	+468.89
+1072.4	**+578**	+303.33	+1342.4	**+728**	+386.67	+1612.4	**+878**	+470.00
+1076.0	**+580**	+304.44	+1346.0	**+730**	+387.78	+1616.0	**+880**	+471.11
+1079.6	**+582**	+305.56	+1349.6	**+732**	+388.89	+1619.6	**+882**	+472.22
+1083.2	**+584**	+306.67	+1353.2	**+734**	+390.00	+1623.2	**+884**	+473.33
+1086.8	**+586**	+307.78	+1356.8	**+736**	+391.11	+1626.8	**+886**	+474.44
+1090.4	**+588**	+308.89	+1360.4	**+738**	+392.22	+1630.4	**+888**	+475.55
+1094.0	**+590**	+310.00	+1364.0	**+740**	+393.33	+1634.0	**+890**	+476.67
+1097.6	**+592**	+311.11	+1367.6	**+742**	+394.44	+1637.6	**+892**	+477.78
+1101.2	**+594**	+312.22	+1371.2	**+744**	+395.56	+1641.2	**+894**	+478.89
+1104.8	**+596**	+313.33	+1374.8	**+746**	+396.67	+1644.8	**+896**	+480.00
+1108.4	**+598**	+314.44	+1378.4	**+748**	+397.78	+1648.4	**+898**	+481.11
+1112.0	**+600**	+315.56	+1382.0	**+750**	+398.89	+1652.0	**+900**	+482.22
+1115.6	**+602**	+316.67	+1385.6	**+752**	+400.00	+1655.6	**+902**	+483.33
+1119.2	**+604**	+317.78	+1389.2	**+754**	+401.11	+1659.2	**+904**	+484.44
+1122.8	**+606**	+318.89	+1392.8	**+756**	+402.22	+1662.8	**+906**	+485.56
+1126.4	**+608**	+320.00	+1396.4	**+758**	+403.33	+1666.4	**+908**	+486.67
+1130.0	**+610**	+321.11	+1400.0	**+760**	+404.44	+1670.0	**+910**	+487.78
+1133.6	**+612**	+322.22	+1403.6	**+762**	+405.56	+1673.6	**+912**	+488.89
+1137.2	**+614**	+323.33	+1407.2	**+764**	+406.67	+1677.2	**+914**	+490.00
+1140.8	**+616**	+324.44	+1401.8	**+766**	+407.78	+1680.2	**+916**	+491.11
+1144.4	**+618**	+325.56	+1414.4	**+768**	+408.89	+1684.4	**+918**	+492.22
+1148.0	**+620**	+326.67	+1418.0	**+770**	+410.00	+1688.0	**+920**	+493.33
+1151.6	**+622**	+327.78	+1421.6	**+772**	+411.11	+1691.6	**+922**	+494.44
+1155.2	**+624**	+328.89	+1425.2	**+774**	+412.22	+1695.2	**+924**	+495.56
+1158.8	**+626**	+330.00	+1428.8	**+776**	+413.33	+1698.8	**+926**	+496.67
+1162.4	**+628**	+331.11	+1432.4	**+778**	+414.44	+1702.4	**+928**	+497.78
+1166.0	**+630**	+332.22	+1436.0	**+780**	+415.56	+1706.0	**+930**	+498.89
+1169.6	**+632**	+333.33	+1439.6	**+782**	+416.67	+1709.6	**+932**	+500.00
+1173.2	**+634**	+334.44	+1443.2	**+784**	+417.78	+1713.2	**+934**	+501.11
+1176.8	**+636**	+335.56	+1446.8	**+786**	+418.89	+1716.8	**+936**	+502.22
+1180.4	**+638**	+336.67	+1450.4	**+788**	+420.00	+1720.4	**+938**	+503.33
+1184.0	**+640**	+337.78	+1454.0	**+790**	+421.11	+1724.0	**+940**	+504.44
+1187.6	**+642**	+338.89	+1457.6	**+792**	+422.22	+1727.6	**+942**	+505.56
+1191.2	**+644**	+340.00	+1461.2	**+794**	+423.33	+1731.2	**+944**	+506.67
+1194.8	**+646**	+341.11	+1464.8	**+796**	+424.44	+1734.8	**+946**	+507.78
+1198.4	**+648**	+342.22	+1468.4	**+798**	+425.56	+1738.4	**+948**	+508.89
+1202.0	**+650**	+343.33	+1472.0	**+800**	+426.67	+1742.0	**+950**	+510.00
+1205.6	**+652**	+344.44	+1475.6	**+802**	+427.78	+1745.6	**+952**	+511.11
+1209.2	**+654**	+345.56	+1479.2	**+804**	+428.89	+1749.2	**+954**	+512.22
+1212.8	**+656**	+346.67	+1482.8	**+806**	+430.00	+1752.8	**+956**	+513.33
+1216.4	**+658**	+347.78	+1486.4	**+808**	+431.11	+1756.4	**+958**	+514.44
+1220.0	**+660**	+348.89	+1490.0	**+810**	+432.22	+1760.0	**+960**	+515.56
+1223.6	**+662**	+350.00	+1493.6	**+812**	+433.33	+1763.6	**+962**	+516.67
+1227.2	**+664**	+351.11	+1497.2	**+814**	+434.44	+1767.2	**+964**	+517.78
+1230.8	**+666**	+352.22	+1500.8	**+816**	+435.56	+1770.8	**+966**	+518.89
+1234.4	**+668**	+353.33	+1504.4	**+818**	+436.67	+1774.4	**+968**	+520.00
+1238.0	**+670**	+354.44	+1508.0	**+820**	+437.78	+1778.0	**+970**	+521.11
+1241.6	**+672**	+355.56	+1511.6	**+822**	+437.89	+1718.8	**+972**	+522.22
+1245.2	**+674**	+356.67	+1515.2	**+824**	+440.00	+1785.2	**+974**	+523.33
+1240.0	**+676**	+357.78	+1518.8	**+826**	+414.11	+178.88	**+976**	+524.44
+1252.4	**+678**	+358.89	+1522.4	**+828**	+442.22	+1792.4	**+978**	+525.56
+1256.0	**+680**	+360.00	+1526.0	**+830**	+443.33	+1796.0	**+980**	+526.67
+1259.6	**+682**	+361.11	+1529.6	**+832**	+444.44	+1799.6	**+982**	+527.78
+1263.2	**+684**	+362.22	+1533	**+834**	+445.56	+1803.2	**+984**	+528.99
+1266.8	**+686**	+363.33	+1536.8	**+836**	+446.67	+1806.8	**+986**	+530.00
+1270.4	**+688**	+364.44	+1540.4	**+838**	+447.78	+1810.4	**+988**	+531.11
+1274.0	**+690**	+365.56	+1544.0	**+840**	+448.89	+1814.0	**+990**	+532.22
+1277.6	**+692**	+366.67	+1547.6	**+842**	+450.00	+1817.6	**+992**	+533.33
+1281.2	**+694**	+367.78	+1551.2	**+844**	+451.11	+1821.2	**+994**	+534.44
+1284.3	**+696**	+368.89	+1554.8	**+846**	+452.22	+1824.8	**+996**	+535.56
+1288.4	**+698**	+370.00	+1558.4	**+848**	+453.33	+1828.4	**+998**	+536.67
+1292.0	**+700**	+371.11	+1562.0	**+850**	+454.44	+1832.0	**+1000**	+537.78
+1295.6	**+702**	+372.22	+1565.6	**+852**	+455.56	+1850.0	**+1010**	+543.33
+1299.2	**+704**	+373.33	+1569.2	**+854**	+456.67	+1868.0	**+1020**	+548.89
+1302.8	**+706**	+374.44	+1572.8	**+856**	+457.78	+1886.0	**+1030**	+554.44
+1306.4	**+708**	+375.56	+1576.4	**+858**	+458.89	+1904.0	**+1040**	+560.00
+1310.0	**+710**	+376.67	+1580.0	**+860**	+460.00	+1922.0	**+1050**	+565.56
+1313.6	**+712**	+377.78	+1583.6	**+862**	+461.11	+1940.0	**+1060**	+571.11
+1317.2	**+714**	+378.89	+1587.2	**+864**	+462.22	+1958.0	**+1070**	+576.67
+1320.8	**+716**	+380.00	+1590.8	**+866**	+463.33	+1976.0	**+1080**	+582.22
+1324.4	**+718**	+381.11	+1594.4	**+868**	+464.44	+1994.0	**+1090**	+587.78
+1328.0	**+720**	+382.22	+1598.0	**+870**	+465.56	+2012.0	**+1100**	+593.33
+1331.6	**+722**	+383.33	+1601.6	**+872**	+466.67	+2050.0	**+1110**	+598.89

Temperature Conversion Table *Contd.....*

°F	*Reading in °F or °C to be converted*	°C	°F	*Reading in °F or °C to be converted*	°C	°F	*Reading in °F or °C to be converted*	°C
+2048.0	**+1120**	+604.44	+3308.0	**+1820**	+993.33	+4478.0	**+2470**	+1354.4
+2066.0	**+1130**	+610.00	+3326.0	**+1830**	+998.89	+4496.0	**+2480**	+1360.0
+2084.0	**+1140**	+615.56	+3344.0	**+1840**	+1004.4	+4514.0	**+2490**	+1365.6
+2102.0	**+1150**	+621.11	+3362.0	**+1850**	+1010.0	+4532.0	**+2500**	+1371.1
+2120.0	**+1160**	+626.67	+3380.0	**+1860**	+1015.6	+4550.0	**+2510**	+1376.7
+2138.0	**+1170**	+632.22	+3398.0	**+1870**	+1021.1	+4568.0	**+2520**	+1382.2
+2156.0	**+1180**	+637.78	+3416.0	**+1880**	+1026.7	+4586.0	**+2530**	+1387.8
+2174.0	**+1190**	+643.33	+3434.0	**+1890**	+1032.2	+4604.0	**+2540**	+1393.3
+2192.0	**+1200**	+648.89	+3452.0	**+1900**	+1037.8	+4622.0	**+2550**	+1398.9
+2210.0	**+1210**	+654.44	+3470.0	**+1910**	+1043.3	+4640.0	**+2560**	+1404.4
+2228.0	**+1220**	+660.00	+3488.0	**+1920**	+1048.9	+4658.0	**+2570**	+1410.0
+2246.0	**+1230**	+665.56	+3506.0	**+1930**	+1054.4	+4676.0	**+2580**	+1415.6
+2264.0	**+1240**	+671.11	+3524.0	**+1940**	+1060.0	+4694.0	**+2590**	+1421.1
+2282.0	**+1250**	+676.67	+3542.0	**+1950**	+1065.6	+4712.0	**+2600**	+1426.7
+2300.0	**+1260**	+682.22	+3560.0	**+1960**	+1071.1	+4730.0	**+2610**	+1432.2
+2318.0	**+1270**	+687.78	+3578.0	**+1970**	+1076.7	+4748.0	**+2620**	+1437.8
+2336.0	**+1280**	+693.33	+3596.0	**+1980**	+1082.2	+4766.0	**+2630**	+1443.3
+2354.0	**+1290**	+698.89	+3614.0	**+1990**	+1087.8	+4784.0	**+2640**	+1448.9
+2372.0	**+1300**	+704.44	+3632.0	**+2000**	+1121.1	+4802.0	**+2650**	+1454.4
+2390.0	**+1310**	+710.00	+3650.0	**+2010**	+1098.9	+4820.0	**+2660**	+1460.0
+2408.0	**+1320**	+715.56	+3668.0	**+2020**	+1104.4	+4838.0	**+2670**	+1465.6
+2426.0	**+1330**	+721.11	+3686.0	**+2030**	+1110.0	+4856.0	**+2680**	+1471.1
+2444.0	**+1340**	+726.67	+3704.0	**+2040**	+1115.6	+4874.0	**+2690**	+1476.6
+2462.0	**+1350**	+732.22	+3722.0	**+2050**	+1121.1	+4892.0	**+2700**	+1482.2
+2480.0	**+1360**	+737.78	+3740.0	**+2060**	+1126.7	+4910.0	**+2710**	+1487.8
+2498.0	**+1370**	+743.33	+3758.0	**+2070**	+1132.2	+4928.0	**+2720**	+1493.3
+2516.0	**+1380**	+748.89	+3776.0	**+2080**	+1137.8	+4946.0	**+2730**	+1498.9
+2534.0	**+1390**	+754.44	+3794.0	**+2090**	+1143.3	+4964.0	**+2740**	+1504.4
+2552.0	**+1400**	+760.00	+3812.0	**+2100**	+1148.9	+4982.0	**+2750**	+1510.0
+2570.0	**+1410**	+765.56	+383.00	**+2110**	+1154.4	+5000.0	**+2760**	+1515.6
+2588.0	**+1420**	+771.11	+3848.0	**+2120**	+1160.0	+5018.0	**+2770**	+1521.1
+2606.0	**+1430**	+776.67	+3866.0	**+2130**	+1165.6	+5036.0	**+2780**	+1526.7
+2624.0	**+1440**	+782.22	+3884.0	**+2140**	+1171.1	+5054.0	**+2790**	+1532.2
+2642.0	**+1450**	+787.78	+3902.0	**+2150**	+1176.7	+5072.0	**+2800**	+1537.8
+2660.0	**+1460**	+793.33	+3920.0	**+2160**	+1182.2	+5090.0	**+2810**	+1543.3
+2678.0	**+1470**	+798.89	+3938.0	**+2170**	+1187.8	+5108.0	**+2820**	+1548.9
+2696.0	**+1480**	+804.44	+3956.0	**+2180**	+1193.3	+5126.0	**+2830**	+1554.4
+2714.0	**+1490**	+810.00	+3974.0	**+2190**	+1198.9	+5144.0	**+2840**	+1560.0
+2732.0	**+1500**	+815.56	+3992.0	**+2200**	+1204.4	+5162.0	**+2850**	+1565.6
+2750.0	**+1510**	+821.11	+40010.0	**+2210**	+1210.0	+5180.0	**+2860**	+1571.1
+2768.0	**+1520**	+826.67	+4028.0	**+2220**	+1215.6	+5198.0	**+2870**	+1576.7
+2796.0	**+1530**	+832.22	+4046.0	**+2230**	+1221.1	+5216.0	**+2880**	+1582.2
+2804.0	**+1540**	+837.78	+4064.0	**+2240**	+1226.7	+5234.0	**+2940**	+1587.8
+2822.0	**+1550**	+843.33	+4082.0	**+2250**	+1232.2	+5252.0	**+2900**	+1593.3
+2840.0	**+1560**	+848.89	+4100.0	**+2260**	+1237.8	+5270.0	**+2910**	+1598.9
+2858.0	**+1570**	+854.44	+4118.0	**+2270**	+1243.3	+5288.0	**+2920**	+1604.4
+2876.0	**+1580**	+860.00	+4136.0	**+2280**	+1248.9	+5306.0	**+2930**	+1615.6
+2894.0	**+1590**	+865.56	+4154.0	**+2290**	+1254.4	+5234.0	**+2890**	+1587.8
+2912.0	**+1600**	+871.11	+4172.0	**+2300**	+1260.0	+5342.0	**+2950**	+1621.1
+2930.0	**+1610**	+904.44	+4190.0	**+2310**	+1265.6	+5360.0	**+2960**	+1626.7
+2948.0	**+1620**	+882.22	+4208.0	**+2320**	+1271.1	+5378.0	**+2970**	+1632.2
+2966.0	**+1630**	+887.78	+4226.0	**+2330**	+1276.1	+5396.0	**+2980**	+1637.8
+2984.0	**+1640**	+893.33	+4244.0	**+2340**	+1287.8	+5414.0	**+2990**	+1643.3
+3002.0	**+1650**	+898.89	+4262.0	**+2350**	+1287.8	+5432.0	**+3000**	+1648.9
+3020.0	**+1660**	+904.44	+4280.0	**+2360**	+1293.3	+5450.0	**+3010**	+1654.4
+3038.0	**+1670**	+910.00	+4298.0	**+2370**	+1298.9	+5468.0	**+3020**	+1660.0
+3056.0	**+1680**	+915.00	+4316.0	**+2380**	+1332.2	+5396.0	**+3030**	+1665.6
+3073.0	**+1690**	+921.11	+4334.0	**+2390**	+1310.0	+5504.0	**+3040**	+1671.1
+3092.0	**+1700**	+926.67	+4352.0	**+2400**	+1315.6	+5522.0	**+3050**	+1676.7
+3110.0	**+1710**	+932.32	+4370.0	**+2410**	+1321.1	+5540.0	**+3060**	+1682.2
+3128.0	**+1720**	+937.78	+4388.0	**+2420**	+1326.7	+5558.0	**+3070**	+1687.8
+3146.0	**+1730**	+943.33	+4406.0	**+2430**	+1332.2	+5576.0	**+3080**	+1693.3
+3164.0	**+1740**	+948.89	+4424.0	**+2440**	+1337.8	+5594.0	**+3090**	+1698.9
+3182.0	**+1750**	+954.44	+4442.0	**+2450**	+1343.3	+5612.0	**+3100**	+1704.4
+3200.0	**+1760**	+960.00	+4460.0	**+2460**	+1348.9	+5612.0	**+3100**	+1704.4
+3218.0	**+1770**	+965.56						
+3236.0	**+1780**	+971.11						
+3254.0	**+1790**	+976.67						
+3272.0	**+1800**	+982.22						
+3290.0	**+1810**	+987.78						

Index

E

F

G

H

I

K

L

M

N

O

P

R

S

T

U

V

W

Z